Group motivation

Social psychological perspectives

Group motivation
Social psychological perspectives

edited by

Michael A. Hogg

and

Dominic Abrams

HARVESTER
WHEATSHEAF

New York   London   Toronto   Sydney   Tokyo   Singapore

First published 1993 by
Harvester Wheatsheaf
Campus 400, Maylands Avenue
Hemel Hempstead
Hertfordshire, HP2 7EZ
A division of
Simon & Schuster International Group

Typeset in 10/12 Palatino
by Keyset Composition

Printed and bound in Great Britain by T.J. Press Limited,
Padstow, Cornwall

British Library Cataloguing in Publication Data

A catalogue record for this book is available from
the British Library

ISBN 0-7450-1239-6 (hbk)
ISBN 0-13-367400-2 (pbk)

2   3   4   5   97   96   95   94

Contents

vi   Contents

Contributors

Dominic Abrams, Institute of Social and Applied Psychology, University of Kent, Canterbury, Kent CT2 7LZ, UK

Bruce Blaine, Department of Psychology, State University of New York, Buffalo, NY 14260, USA

Martin J. Bourgeois, Department of Psychology, University of Toledo, Toledo, OH 43606-3390, USA

Richard Y. Bourhis, Département de psychologie, Université du Québec à Montréal, CP 8888, succursale A, Montréal, Québec H3C 3P8, Canada

Marilynn B. Brewer, Department of Psychology, Ohio State University, 1885 Neil Avenue, Columbus, OH 43210, USA

Marie A. Cini, Department of Psychology, University of Pittsburgh, Pittsburgh, PA 15260, USA

Diana I. Cordova, Department of Psychology, Stanford University, Stanford, CA 94305-2130, USA

Jennifer Crocker, Department of Psychology, State University of New York, Buffalo, NY 14260, USA

Faye J. Crosby, Department of Psychology, Smith College, Northampton, MA 01063, USA

Naomi Ellemers, Vakgroep Sociale Psychologie, Vrije Universiteit, de Boelelaan 1081, 1081 HV Amsterdam, The Netherlands

Hugh Harrington, Department of Psychology, University of Southern California, Los Angeles, CA 90089, USA

Michael A. Hogg, Department of Psychology, University of Queensland, Brisbane, QLD 4072, Australia

Karen Jaskar, Department of Psychology, Smith College, Northampton, MA 01063, USA

Steven J. Karau, Department of Psychology, University of Toledo, Toledo, OH 43606-3390, USA

John M. Levine, Department of Psychology, University of Pittsburgh, Pittsburgh, PA 15260, USA

Riia Luhtanen, Department of Psychology, State University of New York, Buffalo, NY 14260, USA

Norman Miller, Department of Psychology, University of Southern California, Los Angeles, CA 90089, USA

Richard L. Moreland, Department of Psychology, University of Pittsburgh, Pittsburgh PA 15260, USA

Itesh Sachdev, Department of Applied Linguistics, Birkbeck College, 43 Gordon Square, London WC1H 0PD, UK

Ad van Knippenberg, Department of Social Psychology, University of Nijmegen, PO Box 9104, 6500 HE Nijmegen, The Netherlands

David A. Wilder, Department of Psychology, Rutgers University, Tillett Hall, New Brunswick, NJ 08903, USA

Kipling D. Williams, Department of Psychology, University of Toledo, Toledo, OH 43606-3390, USA

Preface, introduction and acknowledgements

Michael Hogg and Dominic Abrams

This book is about the role of motivational constructs in contemporary explanations of group and intergroup phenomena. What motivational constructs, if any, are used? Are they used formally and explicitly, or are they merely part of the background of implicit assumptions? Do motivational constructs improve explanatory power? How do motivational constructs relate to cognitive processes, information-processing activities and cognitive representations? Are group motivational constructs qualitatively distinct from individual motivational constructs and, if so, how do they relate to one another? Ought they to be different? These are just some of the main issues that surface during study of this topic.

The decision to produce this book was occasioned by the conjunction of a number of factors. Over the past fifteen years or so the concepts and methods of social cognition have advanced enormously our understanding of cognitive aspects of social behaviour (cf. Fiske & Taylor, 1991) – this includes cognitive aspects of intergroup relations and group processes. However, there has been an undercurrent of concern that this social cognitive revolution may have distracted our attention from a number of other important aspects of social behaviour, such as language and communication, motivation and emotion, and group processes.

The study of group processes is an important case in point. Many of the most characteristic group phenomena involve strong feelings and emotions, powerful motivations and collective goals. For example, it is difficult to picture a satisfactory explanation of prejudice, discrimination and intergroup conflict that does not ultimately deal with emotion. Likewise, there is an entire motivational dynamic associated with the self-definitional nature of group membership, and many groups form and exist almost exclusively for the purpose of satisfying shared goals through instrumental actions (e.g. organizational groups, social pressure groups, sports teams). The study of groups is an area in which we ignore motivation at our peril.

In our own research we have encountered some of these issues, and feel that similar types of problems may exist in other areas of group research. From our work with social identity theory (e.g. Hogg & Abrams, 1988), we have become intrigued by the apparently necessary, but manifestly problematic motivational construct of self-esteem (e.g. Abrams & Hogg, 1988; Hogg & Abrams, 1990). In its broadest formulation, social identity theory explains intergroup relations and processes in terms of the interplay of the cognitive process of social categorization and the motivational process of self-esteem. The cognitive aspect has been well elaborated through self-categorization theory (e.g. Turner, 1985; Turner, Hogg, Oakes, Reicher, & Wetherell, 1987), leaving the motivational assumption, and its precise role in the theory, largely unresolved. And yet it is the motivational assumption which is the central plank for the theory's treatment of large-scale intergroup relations – which was Tajfel's initial impetus for developing the theory in the first place (cf. Tajfel, 1972a; 1974a; Tajfel & Turner, 1979). Why has this come about? Did motivation simply become unfashionable? Does the study of motivation need a motivational equivalent to the recent methodological and conceptual social cognition revolution? Is it simply a matter of time before social cognition is able to deal properly with motivation?

Another important issue concerns whether or not separate psychological processes are necessary to explain group behaviour as opposed to interpersonal or individual behaviour. Clearly if we talk about group motivation, we need to know whether we are talking about distinctly *group* as opposed to personal motivation, or whether we are talking about basic individual motivation that is mutated in some way by group membership or 'being in a group'.

Together, these currents swept us into this book. We decided to invite a wide range of prominent social psychologists to contribute a chapter on their current research into group processes. They were explicitly to highlight the motivational constructs or assumptions they used, but could choose just how they did this. Some confronted motivation directly, and others illustrated the role of motivational constructs in their research. The chapters cover a variety of group phenomena, including intergroup behaviour, stereotyping, prejudice, and small-group processes.

The purpose of this book is to focus attention on motivational constructs in the study of groups. It provides a snapshot of the explicit or implicit way in which motivation is used in contemporary research into group behaviour, and highlights some problems with existing motivational concepts. We hope the book will fuel a debate and inspire a more explicit programme of social psychological research into group motivation. We feel that the time is now ripe, and the scientific dividends potentially enormous.

The ten chapters in this book are ordered loosely so that we open with chapters focusing on intergroup relations, move on to chapters focusing on small groups, and close with chapters confronting motivation directly.

The opening chapter is by Marilynn Brewer who poses the fundamental question of why individuals should choose to define and evaluate themselves in terms of group memberships – why do people *identify* with groups, rather than remain independent? She believes that categorization alone is not the complete answer, and that the postulation of a self-enhancement motive for relatively favourable self-esteem is problematic. Optimal distinctiveness theory is introduced as a possible resolution. People are 'driven' by powerful and opposing social motives for, on the one hand, differentiation and uniqueness, and, on the other, inclusiveness and commonality. People strive for an optimal level of distinctiveness to balance these opposing motives – equilibrium is sought between being a unique idiosyncratic individual and an indistinguishable member of the group. Brewer discusses optimal distinctiveness theory and its implications for research into social identity and intergroup behaviour. In addition to reappraising some established findings, new data are presented and suggestions made for future research.

Ad van Knippenberg and Naomi Ellemers argue, in Chapter 2, that there may be only one basic motivational assumption necessary to explain behavioural strategies adopted by group members in intergroup contexts – that is, to achieve or maintain an evaluatively relatively positive social identity. Although the analysis is derived from social identity theory, the authors feel that little explanatory ground is gained by taking the further step of invoking a universal human motive for global self-esteem. Instead, in order to explain how sociostructural conditions, and people's perceptions of such conditions, affect specific strategies of intergroup behaviour, we need to know only that people in groups strive to differentiate their own group favourably from relevant outgroups. Depending on the specific intergroup context, sub-motives may come into play – for example status enhancement may prevail under certain conditions, and status protection under others. Van Knippenberg and Ellemers illustrate their argument with examples from their own recent research using experimental simulations of intergroup relations.

Intergroup relations is also the focus of Chapter 3, by Itesh Sachdev and Richard Bourhis. They address intergroup relations between large-scale social categories defined by ethnicity and language–ethnolinguistic groups. Based on social identity theory the motivational assumption is that ethnolinguistic category members strive for positive ethnolinguistic distinctiveness. How this basic motive influences the strategies adopted by ethnolinguistic group members depends on sociostructural variables to do with intergroup power and status relations. These variables determine the objective *vitality* of specific ethnolinguistic groups, but it is people's subjectively represented perception of vitality, *subjective vitality*, that is the crucial factor which channels the ethnolinguistic distinctiveness motive. Sachdev and Bourhis review recent research and theory on subjective vitality. Subjective vitality is rarely an accurate representation of objective vitality, and it would seem that the nature of the discrepancy is influenced by specific motives that arise from certain aspects of inter-group relations. Sachdev and Bourhis present a motivational explanation of the subjective distortion of vitality.

In Chapter 4 Jennifer Crocker, Bruce Blaine and Riia Luhtanen directly confront the role of self-esteem as a motivational influence on group membership and intergroup behaviour. They argue that people differ in terms of self-esteem as an enduring behavioural trait, and that although both high and low self-esteem individuals strive to improve their self-esteem, the behavioural strategies they can realistically adopt are constrained by self-referent cognitions dependent on trait self-esteem itself. For instance, low self-esteem individuals may *wish* to improve self-esteem by laying claim to personal successes, but knowledge about themselves (e.g. their self-confidence, others' reactions, the perceived plausibility of their claims) may inhibit this strategy. Crocker and colleagues distinguish between personal and group membership-based collective self-esteem, with the latter being associated with prejudice and discrimination. Although the collective self-esteem motive encourages prejudice and discrimination, the level of trait self-esteem influences whether discrimination is actually expressed. Crocker and colleagues argue, on the basis of a detailed review of relevant research, that this formulation helps account for divergent empirical findings from research on the self-esteem motive in intergroup behaviour.

Chapter 5 explores the effects of a different social motive. David Wilder proposes an anxiety-assimilation model to explain some conditions under which stereotypic outgroup perceptions are accentuated or reduced. He reviews relevant literature, describes his own programme of research, and draws implications for research into intergroup contact. Wilder believes social psychologists employ three basic motivational constructs to explain behaviour (corresponding to the general distinction between cognition, behaviour and affect): cognitive consistency; reward/outcome maximization; and positive self-image or social identity. To these, Wilder adds a fourth – to reduce stimulation, arousal and anxiety. People reduce stimulation/arousal by assimilating new information to existing repre-sentations – thus the stimulus domain is perceptually simplified. The implication is that in anxiety-provoking situations, such as intergroup encounters, group members are very likely to accentuate stereotypic perceptions of outgroups. Intergroup contact may thus work against stereotype change, unless anxiety levels can be reduced. The motivation to reduce anxiety/arousal may produce assimilation in three ways: anxiety *distracts* attention from counter-stereotypic information; anxiety *distorts* information so that it appears more stereotypic than it actually is; and anxiety causes people to *discount* counter-stereotypic information.

Chapter 6, by Faye Crosby, Diana Cordova and Karen Jaskar, concerns the phenomenon of denial of personal disadvantage. Group members may recognize disadvantage experienced by their group, at the societal level, but nevertheless deny personally experiencing such disadvantage – for example, many lesbians are cognitively aware of group disadvantage, yet deny being disadvantaged themselves. Crosby and colleagues review evidence for the robustness of this phenomenon. One explanation is a cognitive one in terms of information processing – it is simply easier to identify disadvantage on the basis of observation of the experiences of a number of people (i.e. the group as a whole) than one isolated individual (i.e. oneself). Crosby and colleagues feel, however, that the denial of personal disadvantage also has a very obvious emotional dimension. It is motivated behaviour – people are motivated to believe in a just world, to believe the best of others, and to believe that one's self is exempt from harm. Together, these motives encourage denial of personal disadvantage while recognizing that one's group is disadvantaged. However, the political seems to become personal (i.e. the implications for self of group disadvantage are recognized, and denial of personal disadvantage is reduced) as a function of degree of identification with the disadvantaged group – identification may embed self more deeply in the group.

Richard Moreland, John Levine and Marie Cini, in Chapter 7, see commitment as the process that links the individual to the group, and the group to the individual. Moreland and colleagues focus on group socialization in small groups, in their diachronic analysis of the passage of the individual through the group. Commitment, the central motivational process, may be predicated on the reward maximization motive that underpins exchange theory. Another, novel, possibility is that it is related to the self-categorization process described by self-categorization theory. In order to make the world around them more meaningful, people categorize themselves and others, with the consequence that people are judged in terms of their group prototypicality. Commitment may, in turn, depend on the relative prototypicality of self and others. A third possibility is that commitment depends on the amount of pressure from competing roles that exist in a group – if the competition is too great, commitment is inhibited. Moreland and colleagues describe new data to illustrate some of their arguments. On a more general note, they urge greater emphasis on the diachronic analysis of relatively enduring small groups in order to see more clearly how affective and non-cognitive motivational processes operate in groups.

Chapter 8 also focuses on small groups – specifically, goal-oriented groups in which people work collectively on a task. Kipling Williams, Steven Karau and Martin Bourgeois describe the phenomenon of social loafing – a non-conscious, non-strategic reduction in motivation and effort on collective tasks. Research findings are reviewed and integrated to identify factors that increase or reduce social loafing, and those that might actually produce an increase in motivation on collective tasks (called 'social compensation'). In this work, motivation is treated as an individual psychological process that energizes or drives behaviour – reduced motivation lowers the level and quality of task performance. People simply do not do as much or as well as they could. Williams and colleagues are dealing with an individual motivation that is affected by certain aspects of being in a group.

Norman Miller and Hugh Harrington go perhaps one step further. In Chapter 9 they suggest that in order to explain differences between interpersonal and group behaviour, it may be unnecessary to postulate the existence of distinctive psychological processes associated with interpersonal and group contexts. Miller and Harrington develop their argument in the context of a wide-ranging discussion which includes reductionism, social representations, information processing, inter-dependence and social identity, and go on to specify parameters for 'conclusive' research into process distinctiveness. If indeed there is no process distinctiveness, then there may be no such thing as group motivation – at least insofar as it is a separate construct from individual motivation. The motivated character of group behaviour may be entirely explicable in terms of the interplay of individual cognitive information processing and individual motivations.

The final chapter is by Michael Hogg and Dominic Abrams. In it we describe a single-process subjective uncertainty-reduction model of social motivation in groups. We briefly review common social motivational constructs invoked by social psychology, in order to show that they represent a dual-process dependency model of social motivation in which people are driven to seek social approval and positive evaluation or to seek valid knowledge about reality. We argue that this model of social motivation is reductionist because it is all about interpersonal dependence rather than group belongingness. Our contrasting model is based on, and is a development of, self-categorization theory and social identity theory. We argue that the most basic social motivation is to reduce subjective uncertainty, and that this is satisfied by group identification through self-categorization. Affect is an associated aspect but is contingent on uncertainty-reduction. The explanation of group behaviour requires articulation of the uncertainty-reduction motive with more specific group-based motives that derive from intergroup relations. The mediating construct is social identity.

As always, the production of a book involves assistance and support from many organizations and individuals. We would like to acknowledge this here. The original idea for the book came from a sabbatical stay in

1990 in the Department of Psychology at the University of California, Los Angeles – where Michael Hogg held an appointment as a visiting scholar. Funding support was provided by the University of California's Education Abroad Program. The Economic and Social Research Council helped fund Dominic Abrams for a visit to UCLA for preliminary discussions. Later that year we were able to meet, at the University of Kent, to finalize ideas for the book. This meeting was made possible by a travel grant to Michael Hogg from the British Council, through their Academic Links and Interchange Scheme. We were able to meet again in 1992, in Leuven, Belgium, for further discussions. Michael Hogg received travel support through a research grant from the Australian Research Council. The book was completed later in 1992 while Dominic Abrams was a visiting scholar on sabbatical at the University of Illinois at Urbana-Champaign.

It is not easy to edit a book when the editors live on opposite sides of the globe and the contributors come from three different continents. A special thank-you must go to Farrell Burnett, our editor at Harvester Wheatsheaf, for her enduring patience and encouragement. Finally, we would like to thank Kate Reynolds, Sarah Hawkins and Wendy Freeman, at the University of Queensland, for their assistance with the indexes and references.

Michael A. Hogg, Brisbane
Dominic Abrams, Canterbury

1 The role of distinctiveness in social identity and group behaviour

Marilynn Brewer

> . . . the soul of man is in a perpetual vacillation between two conflicting impulses: the desire to assert his individual differences, the desire for distinction, and his terror of isolation. He wants to stand out, but not too far out, and, on the contrary, he wants to merge himself with a group, with some larger body, but not altogether. Through all the things of life runs this tortuous compromise. . .
>
> H.G. Wells, *A Modern Utopia* (1905)

Social identity theory, and its extension in the form of self-categorization theory (SCT) (Turner, Hogg, Oakes, Reicher and Wetherell, 1987), has filled an important niche in social psychology by providing a link between social cognition and group behaviour. SCT makes explicit that social identity is, above all, a theory of the structure and function of the self-concept. The distinction between 'personal identity' and 'social identity' represents a fundamental transformation of the concept of self, 'a shift towards the perception of self as an interchangeable examplar of some social category and away from the perception of self as a unique person' (Turner *et al.*, 1987, p. 50). Social identity, then entails an extension of the sense of self, with associated transformations in the definition of self-interest and the bases for self-evaluation.

Twenty years of research in the social identity tradition has provided convincing evidence for the distinction between personal and social identity as levels of self-categorization. The relative salience of individual versus group identity has been demonstrated to alter significantly

Preparation of this manuscript was supported by Grant #BNS 8908681 from the National Science Foundation.
Enquiries should be addressed to Dr Marilynn B. Brewer, Department of Psychology, Ohio State University, 1885 Neil Avenue, Columbus, OH 43210.

self-perceptions (Hogg & Turner, 1987a), speech style (Giles, Bourhis & Taylor, 1977; Giles, Smith, Ford, Condor & Thakerar, 1980), belief extremity (Mackie, 1986; Ng & Wilson, 1989; Turner, Wetherell & Hogg, 1989), social attraction (Hogg & Hardie, 1991; Hogg & Turner, 1985a; 1985b), perceptions of relative deprivation (Crosby, 1982; Taylor, Wright, Moghaddam & Lalonde, 1990), and co-operative versus competitive orientation towards collective choice dilemmas (Brewer & Kramer, 1986; Insko, Schopler, Hoyle, Dardis & Graetz, 1990). But the question still remains *why* does the transformation take place? Why – particularly in highly individualistic Western societies – do persons consign their sense of self-worth to the status of the social groups to which they belong, and why do group outcomes replace individual rewards as the motivational basis for social behaviour?

Although cognitive principles of categorization clearly underlie distinctions between ingroups and outgroups, categorization *per se* is a less than compelling explanation for the affective and behavioural consequences of social identification, particularly those manifestations of group identification that defy personal self-interest, such as warfare and other forms of collective action. Category salience may dictate whether a particular entity (including the self) is classified as a member of one group versus another, but category membership is not equivalent to social identity. Membership may be voluntary or imposed, but social identities are chosen. Individuals may recognize that they belong to any number of social groups without adopting those classifications as social identities. Salient ingroup-outgroup distinctions may simply narrow the frame of reference for relevant interpersonal comparisons in defining the personal self. Why should salient intergroup distinctions entail a shift of self-concept from the personal to the social level of identity?

The motivational bases of social identity

The most prevalent explanation currently for why individuals choose group identities is the maintenance or enhancement of self-esteem. Just as self-esteem may be enhanced by positive comparisons between the personal self and other individuals, self-esteem may also be achieved through *positive distinctiveness* of the ingroup from relevant outgroups. Evidence for the role of self-esteem as a determinant of social identification is equivocal at best (Abrams & Hogg, 1988; Hogg & Abrams, 1990). If anything, research suggests that positive distinctiveness and ingroup bias are *consequences* of self-esteem and social identity rather than their cause (Brown, Collins & Schmidt, 1988; Crocker & Schwartz, 1985; Crocker, Thompson, McGraw & Ingerman, 1987). Further, positive distinctiveness motives cannot account for why members of socially disadvantaged and stigmatized minorities maintain positive self-esteem in the face of negative intergroup comparisons (Crocker & Major, 1989).

If individuals do not seek group identity in order to enhance self-esteem, what does motivate the extension of self to include collective representations? Abrams and Hogg (1988) have suggested that self-enhancement is not the only motive associated with self-esteem but that *self-integrity* is also a primary motive. The sense of coherence of the self is promoted by meaningful intergroup distinctions and inclusion of the self in differentiated social groupings. This view of the functional significance of social identity is close to my own theory of group identification as the product of a search for 'optimal distinctiveness' (Brewer, 1991).

A model of optimal distinctiveness

The concept of optimal distinctiveness represents an amalgamation of self-categorization theory (Turner *et al.*, 1987) and uniqueness theory (Snyder & Fromkin, 1980). It assumes that social identity is activated in order to meet competing needs for *differentiation* of the self from others and *inclusion* of the self into larger social collectives. Both differentiation and inclusion are powerful social motives or drives (where 'drive' is conceived not in the sense of traditional drive-reduction theories but as the activation of goal-directed behaviour). If the needs for differentiation and inclusion are opposing processes (Solomon, 1980), movement towards increased inclusion should activate the opposing drive for greater differentiation and, conversely, increased differentiation/individuation should arouse the need for inclusion.

Personal identity represents the highly individuated self, those charac-teristics that distinguish one individual from all others in a given social context. In that sense, personal identity represents maximal satisfaction of the need for differentiation. Social identities are categorizations of the self into more inclusive social units that depersonalize the self-concept and satisfy the need for inclusion. Optimal social identity can be viewed as a compromise between inclusion and differentiation, where the need for depersonalization is satisfied within ingroups, while the need for distinc-tiveness is met through intergroup comparisons.

Whether identification with a particular social group or category satisfies simultaneously both of these social needs depends on its *level of inclusiveness* – i.e., the number or variety of persons that could be classified as members of the same category. In any given social context, categories at different levels of inclusiveness can be identified, either hierarchically (e.g., in a gather of academics, subgroups are differentiated in terms of academic discipline) or orthogonally (e.g., among social psychologists, those who are sailing enthusiasts constitute a cross-cutting category membership). The higher the level of inclusiveness at which self-categorization is made, the more extended the self-concept becomes (Turner *et al.*, 1987), and the more the need for inclusion is being satisfied at the expense of the need for differentiation.

At either extreme along the inclusiveness dimension, the person's sense of security and self-integrity is threatened. Being highly individuated leaves one vulnerable to isolation and stigmatization (even excelling on positively valued dimensions creates social distance and potential rejection). On the other hand, immersion in highly inclusive groupings provides little basis for comparative appraisal or self-definition. As a consequence, individuals are uncomfortable in social situations in which they are either too distinctive (Frable, Blackstone & Scherbaum, 1990; Lord & Saenz, 1985) or too indistinctive (Fromkin, 1970; 1972).

Equilibrium, or optimal distinctiveness, is achieved through identification with categories at that level of inclusiveness where the degrees of satisfaction of the need for differentiation and of the need for inclusion are exactly equal. Association with groups that are too large or inclusive should leave residual motivation for greater differentiation of the self from that group identity, whereas too much personal distinctiveness should leave the individual seeking inclusion in a larger collective. On the other hand, social identification with groups at the optimal level of distinctiveness should leave the individual with no need to differentiate him or herself further from other members of that category. At this level, individuals should be more concerned with intergroup comparisons than with intragroup differentiation.

More formally, optimal distinctiveness theory can be represented in the form of the following assumptions:

A.1   Social identification will be strongest for social groups or categories at that level of inclusiveness which resolves the conflict between needs for differentiation of the self and inclusion with others.

A.2   The optimal level of category inclusiveness is a function of the relative strength (steepness) of the opposing drives, which is determined by cultural norms and individual socialization.

A.3   Distinctiveness of a given social identity is context-specific. It depends on the frame of reference within which possible social identities are defined, which can range from the entire human race to the participants in a specific social gathering.

A.4   Optimal distinctiveness is independent of evaluative implications of group membership although, other things being equal, individuals will prefer positive group identities to negative identities.

Empirical support for the optimality premise (A.1) is nicely illustrated by results of analyses of adolescents' music preferences conducted by

Abrams (1991). As part of a general survey of economic and political socialization of 18–21-year-olds in Britain, respondents were asked to rank-order their preferences among thirty-two different musical forms. Subsequent questions asked respondents to indicate whether they engaged in a series of activities expressive of their musical preferences (buying tapes or CDs, attending concerts, wearing clothes or hairstyles symbolic of the musical form, etc.). Composite activity scores constituted a behavioural index of commitment or social identification with a particular musical style.

The musical forms were classified into four different levels of generality or inclusiveness, based on overall popularity (frequency of selection as first-choice preferences) and category abstraction. The most general (superordinate) category level consisted of the two predominant preferences (pop/rock and disco/dance), which together accounted for 48 per cent of first-choice rankings. The next level (intermediate) consisted of the ten next most popular styles (43 per cent of total votes), which were generally subtypes within the pop/rock category (e.g. heavy metal, motown, soul, acid rock). The third level (subordinate) consisted of the next five musical styles in popularity rankings (e.g. blues, new wave), and the fourth (minority) category consisted of the least frequently selected, highly specific musical forms (e.g. gospel, mod).

Respondents who selected musical styles within each of the four categories were compared in terms of their behavioural commitment to their musical preference. Consistent with optimal distinctiveness theory, trend analyses of mean commitment scores revealed a significant quadratic component, reflecting a curvilinear (inverted-U) relationship between category inclusiveness and commitment. There was no simple linear relationship between popularity and identification with musical types. Instead, intermediate and subordinate styles were associated with significantly greater behavioural investment than either more generic musical types or highly deviant preferences. Styles that were sufficiently popular to satisfy needs for inclusion in a significant group and yet sufficiently distinctive to satisfy needs for exclusivity attained the highest commitment scores on all individual items and composite measures.

Implications of optimal distinctiveness theory for research on social identity and intergroup behaviour

The premises of optimal distinctiveness theory provide a basis for interpreting and extending several lines of research on group identification and intergroup relations. Some of the implications of the theory for specific research questions are outlined in the sections below.

Intragroup v. intergroup social comparison

One of the unresolved issues in research on social identity is the nature of the relationship between ingroup–outgroup differentiation at the group level (social identity), and self–other differentiation within the ingroup at the level of the individual (personal identity). Social identity theory is usually interpreted in terms of an assimilation-contrast model in which perceived differences between groups are exaggerated (intergroup contrast) while within-group differences are minimized (assimilation). The theory of self-categorization (Turner *et al.*, 1987) states clearly that social identity involves a reduction of perceived differentiation between self and others with the ingroup. According to this perspective, there is a 'functional antagonism' between personal and social identity such that concern for *intergroup* comparisons should reduce concern for *interpersonal* comparisons within groups. These processes can be mutually reinforcing, so that extremitization of differences between groups and conformity within groups produce polarization of attitudes and values (Mackie, 1986; Turner *et al.*, 1989).

There is a great deal of evidence from the research literature in social cognition and social identity that categorization leads to enhancement of intergroup differences (e.g. Krueger & Rothbart, 1990) and associated ingroup bias (e.g. Brewer, 1979). However, the idea that intergroup differentiation is accompanied by assimilation/perceived similarity within social categories has received less empirical support, particularly with respect to perceptions of the ingroup. Research on the so-called 'outgroup homogeneity effect' (e.g. Mullen & Hu, 1989; Park & Judd, 1990) indicates an asymmetry between ingroup and outgroup assimilation such that outgroups are perceived as relatively homogeneous but ingroups are perceived as more variable or differentiated. Contrary to self-categorization predictions, some research indicates that greater differentiation between ingroup and outgroup is associated with *higher* differentiation between self and others within the ingroup (Codol, 1984; Doise, 1988; Hinkle, Taylor, Fox-Cardamone & Cook, 1989).

Optimal distinctiveness theory provides a new perspective on conflicting evidence regarding the relationship between intergroup and intragroup differentiation (Brewer, 1993). By positing that the need for inclusion and the need for differentiation are separate, opposing drives, the theory can specify conditions under which intergroup differences will be associated with ingroup assimilation or differentiation. Which relationship predominates will depend in part on the level of inclusiveness of the self-categorization produced by particular ingroup–outgroup distinctions.

Many salient social categories, such as gender, age and race, are *superordinate* classifications that differentiate persons into large, inclusive groupings. Such groupings provide a basis for organizing social perception in terms of distinct, contrasting categories. For the individual, however, classification into such superordinate groups is likely to exceed the level of inclusiveness that is optimal for satisfying self-identity needs. Thus, the more salient such self-categorization becomes, the more the arousal of the individual's need for differentiation and the greater the concern for social comparison and interpersonal differences within the ingroup. Although individuals may not reject classification at the superordinate level, they will seek further differentiation into subgroups and will be attentive to distinctions between themselves and other category members. For large, superordinate social categories, then, optimal distinctiveness predicts that intercategory differences will be associated with intracategory differentiation of the ingroup but not the outgroup.

Identification with small, distinctive ingroups, on the other hand, should be associated with high intergroup differentiation and low intragroup differentiation. When group membership meets needs for inclusion and differentiation simultaneously, individuals should be more concerned with intergroup comparisons than with interpersonal comparisons within the ingroup.

This prediction was confirmed by results from our first experiment on group size and depersonalization effects (Brewer, Manzi & Shaw, 1992). Our primary purpose in this experiment was to determine how the preference for minority category membership is affected by loss of distinctiveness in the experimental context. At the outset of the experiment, we created conditions designed to alter subjects' placement on the continuum from individuated to inclusive group categorization. To manipulate this variable, we made use of confidentiality instructions that preceded data collection in our experimental sessions.

In the control condition, subjects received standard assurances of confidentiality and generated an ID number for use in the experiment that was unique to them but served to protect their personal identity. In the *depersonalization* condition, the subject was assigned an arbitrary ID number in the context of written instructions that emphasized membership in a large, impersonal category. The wording of the depersonalization instructions was as follows:

> Since in this study we are not interested in you as an individual but as a member of the college student population, we do not ask for any personal information. However, for statistical purposes we need to match up different questionnaires completed by the same person. In order to do this, we have assigned you an arbitrary code number that is to be used throughout this session . . . We are running this study in order to assess the attitudes and perceptions of students in general. For the purposes of this study you represent an example of

the average student no matter what your major is. We are only interested in the general category and not in individual differences. . .

After receiving these instructions, subjects were given a dot estimation task and then assigned to the category of 'underestimators' or 'overestimators'. To vary inclusiveness of the two categories, we informed all subjects that more than 80 per cent of college students fell into the underestimator category, and less than 20 per cent tested as overestimators. Thus, assignment to one of the categories meant inclusion in either a majority or minority category respectively.

Following assignment to dot estimation categories, subjects in this experiment were given a 'test' of aesthetic preferences or perceptual abilities. While they were awaiting feedback on performance from this test, they were given the opportunity to see statistics on how other college students had performed. Subjects were asked to indicate their first four preferences from among the following available statistics:

- overall mean of college students
- mean overestimator score
- mean underestimator score
- highest overestimator score
- highest underestimator score
- lowest overestimator score
- lowest underestimator score.

Each subject's pattern of choices was coded in terms of whether it indicated a preference for *intragroup* comparison (i.e., ingroup mean, high and low scores) or *intergroup* comparison (i.e., ingroup and outgroup means).

Data on the proportion of subjects in each condition who selected intracategory versus intercategory comparison information are reported in Table 1.1. Results of log-linear analyses indicated a significant interaction between confidentiality instructions and ingroup size as determinants of social comparison preferences ($\chi^2 = 4.84$, $p < 0.03$). In the control condition, subjects generally showed a preference for intragroup comparisons, regardless of whether they were assigned to the majority or minority category. Apparently for most of these subjects, the ingroup provided the important frame of reference for self-evaluations.

Subjects in the depersonalization condition, however, showed a clear distinction in their social comparison preferences depending on whether they had been classified in a majority or minority ingroup. For those in the majority category, 74 per cent expressed a preference for intragroup comparison, indicating a high degree of interest in information about

Table 1.1 Social comparison preferences as a function of depersonalization and ingroup size (proportion of subjects choosing intragroup comparison information/proportion choosing intergroup comparison).

	Ingroup size	
	Majority	Minority
Control condition	0.62/0.38	0.69/0.31
Depersonalized condition	0.74/0.26	0.54/0.46

intragroup differentiation. The depersonalized minority condition was the only setting in which a substantial proportion of subjects showed primary interest in intergroup over intragroup comparisons.

Responding to social comparison

The relative concern for interpersonal (intragroup) or intergroup social comparison has implications for how an individual can be expected to respond to social comparison information. The similarity postulate of Festinger's original statement of social comparison theory (Festinger, 1954) can be interpreted to suggest that comparisons to ingroup members should have more impact on self-evaluations than information about outgroup members. According to Tesser's (1988) self-evaluation maintenance model (SEM), upward comparison on self-relevant abilities (i.e., learning that another individual has performed better than oneself on important dimensions) is a threat to self-esteem, and this threat is greater when the other is close or similar to the self than when the other is a distant stranger. Thus, SEM theory would predict that upward comparison involving an ingroup member should result in more negative emotional response than upward comparisons involving outgroup members.

This prediction assumes that individuals are primarily concerned with *interpersonal* comparisons in defining their self-concept. When social identities are activated, however, individuals should be more concerned with intergroup than interpersonal comparisons. In that case, successful performance by ingroup members should enhance the individual's sense of self-esteem, whereas successful performance by an outgroup member should constitute a threat to collective esteem. Thus, for optimally distinctive ingroups we would make the opposite prediction from that of SEM theory: upward comparison involving an outgroup member should result in more negative emotional response than upward comparison involving ingroup members. In fact, ingroup comparisons should result in assimilation of self-evaluations to ingroup member performance, such that positive achievements by an ingroup member should enhance self-assessments on the relevant dimension of comparison (Brown, Novick, Lord & Richards, 1992).

Self-presentation and self-verification

According to self-categorization theory (Turner *et al.*, 1987), social identity leads individual group members to behave in ways that enhance similarity between themselves and their concept of the prototypic group member. Such social identification processes are assumed to underlie many group phenomena, including conformity to group norms, attitude polarization and group cohesiveness. If this analysis is correct, then ingroup identification should also have an effect on self-verification processes (Swann, 1987). Individuals who are socially identified with a particular group or social category should present themselves to others in a manner that conforms to group stereotypes (e.g. Hogg & Turner, 1987a). Thus, self-verification motives can contribute to self-fulfilling category-based expectancies.

According to optimal distinctiveness theory, the relationship between category membership and self-presentation will be mediated by the relative importance of assimilation versus differentiation needs. Again, this will depend on the level of inclusiveness of ingroup categorization within the social context. Categorization as a member of a large, inclusive social group should activate the need for self-differentiation, in which case individual self-presentation should be directed towards establishing differences between the self and the group stereotype. On the other hand, if category membership provides a distinctive identity within the social context, the individual should present him- or herself in a manner congruent with expectations of a typical group member.

Self-presentation as a group member may also be moderated by the evaluative implications of group stereotypes. For members of stigmatized groups, self-verification of social identity may conflict with the need for self-enhancement. Hogg and Turner (1987a), for instance, found that in contexts where categorization by sex was highly salient, both male and female subjects accentuated the sex-typicality of their self-perceptions. However, for females this self-categorization resulted in lowered self-esteem, compared to conditions in which sex categorization was not salient.

To protect self-esteem, individuals may actively distance themselves from their group identity, at least with respect to those attributes that are contained in the negative group stereotype (Gibbons, 1985; Gibbons, Gerrard, Lando & McGovern, 1991). On the other hand, negative attributes may have less impact on individual self-esteem if they are perceived as *group* characteristics rather than distinctive personal traits (Coates & Winston, 1983; Crocker & Major, 1989). In that case, self-esteem may actually be enhanced by self-presentation as a typical group member since it alters the context in which negative traits or experiences are evaluated. This self-protective function of group identification is suggested by results from experiments by Turner, Hogg, Turner and Smith (1984) indicating that under conditions of high group commitment, ingroup *defeat* produces greater cohesion and ingroup preference than does success.

Group status and group consciousness

The distinctiveness of a particular social category depends in part on the clarity of the boundary that distinguishes category membership from non-membership and in part on the number of people who qualify for inclusion. Although group size and distinctiveness are not perfectly negatively correlated, categories that include a vast majority of the people in a given social context are not sufficiently differentiated to constitute meaningful social groups. In general, then, optimal distinctiveness theory predicts that mobilization of ingroup identity and loyalty will be achieved more easily for minority groups than for groups that are in the numerical majority.

Results of research on ingroup bias support the predicted relationship between group size and ingroup preference. In both real and laboratory groups, evaluative biases in favour of the ingroup tend to increase as the proportionate size of the ingroup relative to the outgroup decreases (Mullen, Brown & Smith, 1992). Further, strength of identification and importance attached to membership in experimentally created groups are greater for minority than for majority categories (Simon & Brown, 1987; Simon & Pettigrew, 1990).

The effects of relative group size are more complicated, however, when intergroup differences in status are taken into consideration (Mullen *et al.*, 1992; Ng & Cram, 1988). Because minority size is often associated with disadvantages in status or power, in many contexts group distinctiveness and positive evaluation may be negatively related. Thus, members of low-status minorities face a conflict between group identification based on optimal distinctiveness and the preference for positive social identity. On the one hand, minority individuals can dissociate themselves from their group membership and seek positive identity elsewhere. Dissociation may be achieved at the cost of loss of distinctiveness (e.g. 'passing' into the majority group) or at the cost of too much individuated distinctiveness (e.g. as a 'solo' representative of a deviant group), in either case failing to satisfy optimal distinctiveness. On the other hand, minority group members can embrace their distinctive group identity, but at the cost of rejecting or defying majority criteria for positive evaluation (Steele, 1992).

The conditions under which members of disadvantaged minorities will adopt a strong group identity and commit themselves to collective action on behalf of group interests have long been of concern to social and political psychologists (e.g. Gurin, Miller & Gurin, 1980; Tajfel & Turner, 1986; Wright, Taylor & Moghaddam, 1990). Results of recent survey research by Lau (1989) provide evidence for the role of optimal distinctiveness in mobilizing group identification.

Lau used data from the US National Election Studies of 1972 and 1976 to assess the degree of group identification of black respondents as a function of *social density* – the proportion of fellow group members in the immediate environment. Consistent with optimal distinctiveness theory, Lau predicted that there would be a *curvilinear* (inverted U-shaped) relationship between residential density and the respondents' felt closeness to blacks as a social group. In areas of the country where the number of African-Americans is relatively low, increased numbers should be associated with increased group identification, but where social density is relatively high, increased numbers of blacks in the immediate environment should be associated with *decreases* in group identification as the salience of blacks as a distinctive social category decreases.

Operationalizing social density as the proportion of black residents in the same census track as the respondent, Lau (1989) found the predicted curvilinear relationship between density and probability of feeling close to blacks. Black respondents who lived in areas where 40–70 per cent of the residents were black were significantly more likely to identify themselves as 'particularly close' to blacks as a social group than those who lived in highly segregated census tracks or ones in which there were few other black residents.

The methodology and results of Lau's research on group identification highlight the context-specificity of group distinctiveness. Although blacks constitute a distinctive minority in the US population as a whole, it was their representation in the immediate social environment that affected identification with blacks as a social category. When members of statistical minority groups are surrounded by others in the same category, that categorization becomes subjectively highly inclusive and insufficiently differentiated from the social context in general. Under those conditions we would expect ingroup rivalries and conflict to dominate over social identification with the category as a whole, as the need for differentiation drives the search for optimal distinctiveness.

Results of our own experiments with laboratory-created social categories also confirm the importance of context in resolving conflict between status and distinctiveness as bases of group identification (Brewer *et al.*, 1992). The depersonalization manipulation described earlier in this chapter is, in effect, a contextual manipulation of the subjective inclusiveness of 'college student' as a social category. Our subjects – all members of that category – were then assigned to a subgroup that was representative of either the category as a whole (majority) or a distinctive intracategory minority. Following category assignment, status differences between the two subgroups were introduced in the form of differential average performance on an ability test. The status manipulation was factorially combined with the group size manipulation so that the minority category was sometimes in the high-status and sometimes in the low-status position.

In the control condition (no depersonalization instructions), subjects responded to the status differences between groups in accord with results of previous experimental literature (Mullen *et al.*, 1992). High-status group members showed high ingroup bias in their ratings of the two groups on status-relevant ability traits, and somewhat less ingroup bias on ability-irrelevant social trait ratings (see Figure 1.1a). In fact, subjects in the high-status minority ('élite') condition showed the lowest ingroup bias on these irrelevant traits. Subjects in the depersonalized condition, however, showed a very different pattern of ingroup favouritism on social trait ratings (see Figure 1.1b). In this condition, ingroup bias was unrelated to status differentials and determined entirely by group size. Subjects assigned to the minority category felt significantly closer to the ingroup (as indicated by favourable social trait ratings) than did majority subjects who *devalued* their ingroup, regardless of status position.

What is of most interest in the results of this experiment is the impact of contextual depersonalization (inclusive categorization) as a moderator variable. The depersonalization induction was a relatively subtle experimental treatment, introduced at the very beginning of the experimental session (presumably prior to the start of the study itself). Yet it altered subjects' responsiveness to different group characteristics (status versus distinctiveness) as determinants of the value placed on ingroup membership.

Outside of the laboratory, depersonalization analogous to our experimental treatment is a background state characteristic of social immersion in large institutions, large urban centres and large, heterogeneous nation-states. The effect of overly inclusive categorization activates the need for differentiation and generates conditions in which individuals are most likely to eschew assimilation to majority, superordinate social

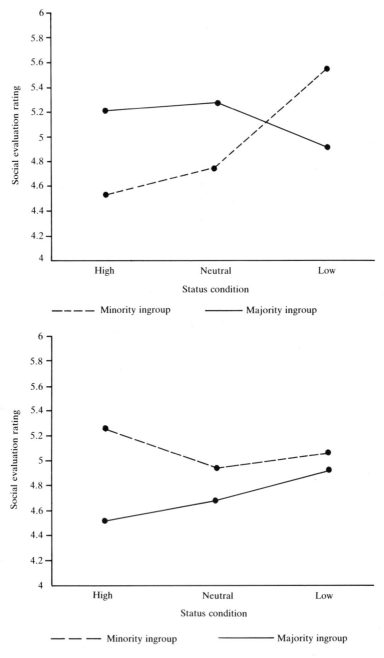

Figure 1.1 Ingroup ratings as a function of size, status and depersonalization: (a) Control condition; (b) Depersonalization condition.

categories and seek identification with distinctive subgroups, even when subgroup status is disadvantaged or devalued by the society at large. In contexts where demographic subgroups (ethnic, religious, political, etc.) constitute distinct but substantially large minorities, depersonalization will enhance group consciousness and politicization of those groups. In contexts that are demographically homogeneous, however, the search for optimal distinctiveness will lead to intracategory differentiation in the form of 'gangs', factions, sects or clans. It is these optimally distinctive subgroupings that will engage social identification of their members, to the potential detriment of the superordinate collective (Brewer & Schneider, 1990).

A dynamic equilibrium

Returning to the quote from H.G. Wells with which this chapter began, optimal distinctiveness theory provides a formal representation of the 'tortuous compromise' that characterizes group life. The competing desires for distinction and for merger can be met simultaneously, but only in the context of salient intergroup differentiation. Inclusion begets exclusion, and both are necessary components of social identity.

Although optimal distinctiveness theory is an equilibrium model of sorts, it does not dictate a static equilibrium point. Social identification with an optimally distinctive group represents a depersonalized conceptualization of self achieved through inclusion/immersion in a collective. When inclusion needs are satisfied, the need for differentiation is met only as long as there is constant awareness of the boundaries between the ingroup and outgroups – of what makes the group *exclusive* as well as inclusive. Over time, or change of context, the salience of boundary distinctions may fade, the need for differentiation become activated, and new bases for optimal distinctiveness sought in alternative or subgroup identities. Thus, optimal distinctiveness represents a dynamic equilibrium that allows for shifts in levels of social identity and the self-concept over time and place.

Further research within the optimal distinctiveness framework should be directed by this dynamic conceptualization. Thus far, our research has focused on one side of the inclusiveness dimension, demonstrating that categorization in an overly inclusive grouping enhances the need for intracategory differentiation and the value of distinctive, minority social identities. What is needed now are parallel experiments demonstrating that individuals also avoid the extremes of distinctiveness, that too much differentiation between self and others motivates a search for inclusion in larger social groupings. Suggestive evidence that this is the case comes from field studies of the effects of support groups in reducing stigmatization associated with deviant characteristics or experiences (e.g. Coates & Winston, 1983), but more systematic study of these effects is called for.

A second line of research that is suggested by this model involves studying identification with a given social category over time and over different phases of membership (e.g. from entry to exit). A promising illustration of this type of longitudinal research is provided by Brown & Wootton-Millward (1993) who monitored changes in intragroup differentiation among cohorts of student nurses across a one-year period of training. It will take this kind of systematic, longitudinal research to understand the complex interactions between motivational and contextual factors as determinants of social identity.

2 Strategies in intergroup relations

Ad van Knippenberg and Naomi Ellemers

Motivational concepts like needs, instincts and goals have played an important role in psychological theories of intergroup relations for a long time. To mention just a few examples: in Le Bon's (1896) theory of the crowd, the behaviour of people in crowds was assumed to be guided by primitive instincts. Dollard, Doob, Miller, Mowrer and Sears (1939) posited, in their frustration–aggression theory, that frustration could be understood as the blocking of goal-directed behaviour. Frustration would inevitably lead to aggression and, through the process of displacement and scapegoating, this aggression would often be directed towards members of other groups. In Sherif's (1966) realistic conflict theory of intergroup relations, psychodynamic motivational principles were abandoned in favour of a utilitarian type of motive: the incompatibility of ingroup and outgroup goals would cause prejudice, which served to justify hostile actions from the ingroup directed against the outgroup. In Tajfel's (1978a) social identity theory (although predominantly cognitive in origin and structure) 'striving for positive social identity' – which was theoretically derived from a concern for positive self-esteem – constituted the crucial motivational factor which could account for much of the dynamics in intergroup relations.

Motivational explanations tend to be viewed with suspicion. Particularly such concepts as needs and instincts, referring to inner psychological states explaining overt behaviour, may be criticized simply because of the inherent circularity of such explanations: 'One seeks power because of a need for power' (e.g. Winter, 1973). In our view, such 'correspondent inferences' should indeed be avoided in psychological theorizing.

Today, motivational explanations have lost much of their historic popularity. Students of intergroup relations tend to turn to cognitive models for the explanation of intergroup phenomena. The cognitive revolution in the past decade has substantially changed the face of social psychology and, with it, the face of the social psychology of intergroup relations. Schemata, categorization processes, heuristics, illusory correlation – to mention some of the more prominent cognitive concepts – have proved to be useful for the study of intergroup relations, particularly in the area of stereotyping processes (see, e.g., Stephan, 1985).

Yet, in our view, the avoidance of motivational assumptions may seriously impede our understanding of intergroup phenomena. It may be argued that cognitive purity may be preserved only by limiting research to a set of experimental paradigms in which the subject serves as a detached observer processing information about stimulus groups in which no personal commitment or interest is at stake. A demonstration of precisely this point was recently presented by Maass and Schaller (1991) who showed that illusory correlations were subject to ingroup biases once subjects were themselves members of one of the stimulus groups presented. The results of many minimal group experiments provide, of course, ample evidence for a motivational bias in intergroup behaviour (cf. Brewer, 1979).

In the present chapter, the focus is on strategies of identity management in intergroup relations. We aim to show how sociostructural conditions, such as intergroup status differences, permeability of intergroup boundaries and the stability and legitimacy of intergroup status differences, affect the way in which people deal with their intra- and intergroup relations. Our theoretical argument will be based largely on early formulations of social identity theory (Tajfel, 1978a; Tajfel & Turner, 1979).

Strategies serve an end, a motive or goal. The only motivational assumption we need to make at the moment is that individuals strive for a positive social identity or, for that matter, that individuals want to make positive ingroup–outgroup comparisons. Social identity theory, however, argues that these are derivatives of a deeper, more fundamental motive: the need for positive self-esteem. Therefore, before we expand on strategies, we must take a closer look at what self-esteem has to do with intergroup comparisons.

Motivation in social identity theory

In the original definition (Tajfel, 1978a), social identity is that part of the individual's self-concept which derives from the individual's membership in social groups. Assuming that individuals have a need for positive self-esteem (the core motivational assumption of social identity theory), social identity theory claims that ingroup–outgroup discrimination serves to maintain or enhance the subject's self-esteem (Turner, 1981). At first sight this would suggest a positive correlation between self-esteem and intergroup differentiation, but, on closer examination, the relationship seems to be more complicated. As Abrams and Hogg (Abrams, 1992; Abrams & Hogg, 1988; Hogg & Abrams, 1990) argue, two self-esteem predictions may be derived from social identity theory. First, ingroup–outgroup discrimination is predicted to enhance self-esteem and, second-ly, low self-esteem leads to stronger discrimination than high self-esteem. Thus self-esteem is both a (negative) cause and a (positive) effect of ingroup–outgroup discrimination. In terms of a cybernetic system, these inverse relationships constitute a negative feedback loop (as in a thermo-stat), as a result of which negative, positive and zero correlations between self-esteem and intergroup discrimination may all be obtained depending on the phase the system is in. In empirical research, positive, negative and zero correlations have indeed all been reported (see, e.g., Abrams, 1992; Hinkle & Brown, 1990; Hogg & Sunderland, 1991).

It has also been suggested that the failure to find consistent results may be due to the incompatibility of a global self-esteem measure (e.g. Rosenberg's, 1965, self-esteem scale) as an index of enduring personal self-esteem with momentary self-esteem as affected by specific intergroup comparisons (Abrams, 1992). A solution to this problem may be sought in the distinction between personal self-esteem and 'collective' self-esteem (i.e., a global evaluation of all groups one belongs to – see Crocker & Luhtanen, 1990; also see Chapter 4 this volume) but, as Abrams (1992) notes, it may be hard to assess theoretically the relationship between one particular ingroup–outgroup comparison and the global evaluation of all one's membership groups. Abrams and Hogg (1988) go one step further as they recommend, following Fishbein (1967), that the study of inter-group comparison effects should involve self-esteem measures at the appropriate level of specificity which – we would argue – would entail separate individual self-esteems for each membership group. We tend to agree with the Abrams and Hogg point of view but we emphasize that the issue is of a conceptual and theoretical rather than methodological nature.

The problem with Tajfel's conception of social identity is that it is rather static; self-concept seems to be viewed as a unitary, relatively enduring set of self-cognitions, partly determined by group memberships. As individuals are members of many groups, which may become more or less salient in particular situations at particular times, it may be more appropriate to speak of multiple social identities. Rather than a static notion of self-concept, one may therefore prefer to postulate a repertoire of self-concepts from which, in a particular situation, a specific situational identity or self-categorization may be activated (cf. Turner, 1987). There-fore, in accordance with the theoretical shift instigated by Turner, it may be more appropriate to think of social identity theory as a theory of self-conceptualization processes rather than as a theory of *the* self or of 'social identity'.

The above view on social identity theory implies a shift in emphasis with regard to the question of how intergroup comparisons affect self-esteem. Since Turner's formulation suggests that there is no such thing as *the* self-concept, it follows that self-esteem too cannot be viewed as a unitary concept: individuals have as many self-esteems as they have self-concepts. Messick and Mackie (1989) attempt to reconceptualize the issue as follows: 'groupings that contain the self are special. Not only are they easily activated, they are also positively regarded. They possess "positive distinctiveness". Ethnocentrism at the group level is analogous to self-esteem at the individual level' (p. 61). We would rather say, however, that ethnocentrism at the group level is analogous to *self-serving bias* at the individual level; both biases serve to enhance or protect *a* self-esteem.

The crucial motivational assumption in social identity theory would, then, be that people strive for positive self-esteems, i.e. for positively valued self-concepts, including positive social identities. Since the value of a social category is established through comparisons with other relevant social categories, it follows from this assumption that individuals will try to differentiate their own group from relevant comparison groups in a positively valued direction.

The general goal of achieving positive intergroup comparisons may encompass a wide range of behavioural strategies. Social identity theory provides a conceptual framework which enables us to specify how sociostructural conditions affect subjective preferences for one or the other strategy. In subsequent sections, we will, step by step, elaborate on the theoretical arguments and present empirical evidence supporting this point of view.

Group status and permeability of group boundaries

Society may be looked upon as consisting of various interlocking category systems, e.g. of categorizations in terms of professions, jobs, gender, socio-economic backgrounds or ethnic groups. These categorizations constitute status hierarchies, i.e., there exist rank orderings of social groups in terms of socially recognized value, worth or prestige. The higher a group in the status hierarchy, the more this group can contribute to the positive social identity of its members.

The status positions which groups occupy in society and the permeability of group boundaries, i.e., the extent to which individuals are free to join or leave these groups, may be considered to be key variables of social identity theory. As Tajfel (1978a) suggested, individuals will tend to seek membership in high-status groups, or maintain membership in them, because membership in such groups will contribute positively to their social identity. Membership in comparatively low-status groups will have a negative impact on one's social identity and, therefore, individuals will tend to leave such groups and join higher-status groups (social mobility), unless there are objective or emotional barriers to doing so. In the latter case, individuals will try to change the attributes of their group in a positive direction (social competition – Turner, 1975) or attempt to change evaluations of status characteristics in such a way that the favourable attributes of their ingroup (more than) compensate for the unfavourable ones (social creativity – Lemaine, 1974).

Thus, social identity theory addresses the question of how the goal of establishing positive social identity may instigate group members either to dissociate from their group (pursue individual social mobility) or to engage in collective identity management strategies (i.e., strive for positive ingroup distinctiveness by means of social competition or social creativity). Social identity theory argues that the tendency to let either individual or collective motives prevail results from the interplay of relative group status and permeability of group boundaries.

As outlined above, the interaction of group status and permeability of group boundaries determines the strategies available for the enhancement of their members' social identity. Let us briefly discuss the main characteristics of this interaction.

High-status groups contribute to their members' positive social identity, while low-status groups generally fail to do so. Research has indeed shown that membership of low-status groups has a negative effect on the self-esteem of individuals (cf. Brown & Lohr, 1987; Wagner, Lampen & Syllwasschy, 1986). Furthermore, it appears that group members tend to flaunt their affiliation with successful (high-status) groups, but are relatively reluctant to be identified as members of unsuccessful (low-status) groups.

This was illustrated in an interesting field study carried out by Cialdini, Borden, Thorne, Walker, Freeman and Sloan (1976). During the 1973 football season, Cialdini et al. recorded at different universities in the United States whether students wore clothes that identified their university affiliation. It turned out that consistently more students wore such clothes on days after their institution's football team had been victorious than after a university loss. Moreover, when asked to describe a victory of the university football team, students more often used the term 'we', whereas a university loss was described more often by saying that 'they had lost the game'.

This general pattern has also been documented under more controlled circumstances. In a laboratory experiment, Snyder, Lassegard and Ford (1986) asked groups of subjects to perform a group problem-solving task, after which they provided subjects with (bogus) feedback about their team's performance. At completion of the experiment, subjects were given the opportunity to wear a badge identifying their team affiliation. Snyder *et al.* found that subjects were quite willing to wear a team badge when their team had been successful, but that members of unsuccessful teams were relatively reluctant to be identified as such.

When group boundaries are permeable, the dominant social identity enhancement strategy of low-status group members is hypothesized to be to join higher-status groups (see Taylor & McKirnan, 1984). In an experimental study of a four-group hierarchy (Ross, 1975, cited in Tajfel and Turner, 1979), it was found that the desire to pass upwards into another group increased with decreasing group status. In research with regard to communication patterns (Cohen, 1958), evaluation of group characteristics (van Knippenberg, 1978) and group membership aspirations (Mann, 1961), there appeared to be a tendency for members of low-status groups who anticipated upward social mobility to focus their communications, evaluations and aspirations on the higher-status group instead of their own group. It is assumed that, in such situations, people identify with the higher-status group before actually passing to it.

Thus, it appears that, in situations in which a (low-status) group cannot make a satisfactory contribution to the social identity of its members, individuals will try to leave this group in order to gain membership in a higher-status group. Obviously, this identity enhancement strategy can only be used effectively by individual group members who possess whatever it takes (e.g. ability) to move upward into a higher-status group.

When group boundaries are impermeable, members of low-status groups will tend to enhance their social identity by improving the position of their present group as a whole. As outlined above, individual locomotion to a higher-status group may be the preferred way to improve one's social identity. In some situations, however, changing group membership is virtually impossible, e.g. in a strongly segregated society. In such situations, i.e. when individual mobility is not feasible, ingroup identification may be *inevitable*. Under these circumstances, members of low-status groups will have to find other ways to improve their social identity. One specific option would be to elevate the status of their group as a whole, for instance by competing with higher-status groups.

The discussion of the interaction between group status and permeability may be summarized as follows. Individuals prefer to maintain membership in high-status groups or, if they are members of a lower-status group with sufficient individual ability, they will seek membership in high-status groups. If upward mobility is not possible, one salient option is to engage in intergroup competition to improve the relative position of the ingroup as a whole.

Prospects for individual upward mobility and ingroup identification

Ellemers, van Knippenberg, de Vries and Wilke (1988) conducted two experiments to investigate the effects, hypothesized above, of group status, individual ability and permeability of group boundaries on the tendency to identify with the ingroup. In both experiments, a status hierarchy of five randomly created groups was simulated in a laboratory situation. In the first experiment, subjects were provided with false feedback about their performance on an individual problem-solving task. It was suggested that, compared to their fellow ingroup members, the subject's individual proficiency at problem-solving was either high, average or low. Furthermore, after completion of a group problem-solving task, bogus feedback about the subject's group performance was provided as well. The impression was evoked that the performance of the subject's group either put them in second place in a rank order of all five groups (high group status), or in fourth place (low group status). Finally, permeability of group boundaries was manipulated by suggesting either that, during the experiment, some subjects might be reassigned to another group (permeable group boundaries) or that the group composition would remain the same throughout the experiment (impermeable boundaries).

The main results of the first experiment were that, overall, members of high-status groups felt relatively satisfied about the performance of their group, and identified strongly with their group. This finding supports the general notion that membership in a group with high status is considered attractive, because it may contribute to positive social identity. Members of groups with low status, on the other hand, generally were less inclined to show ingroup identification. This tendency was more pronounced as group members had higher individual abilities. As predicted, the reluctance to identify with a low-status group was strongest when group members had the possibility of leaving their low-status group, i.e. when group boundaries were permeable.

This supports the theoretical argument that, if group characteristics do not contribute to a satisfactory social identity (i.e. when group status is low), group members try to evade the association with their group. The goal of establishing a more positive identity by dissociating from an unattractive membership group, is most likely to be achieved either when group members possess favourable personal characteristics that may yield a more positive identity (in this case: when they had high individual ability), or when the status structure allows for individuals to change their group affiliation (because group boundaries are permeable). Indeed, with additional satisfaction measures Ellemers *et al.* (1988) were able to show that, although all members of low-status groups were equally dissatisfied about the *performance* of their group, they only expressed dissatisfaction with their group *membership* when group boundaries were permeable. Thus, the general motivation to establish positive social identity seems to cause members of low-status groups to be dissatisfied with the *status quo*. The *focus* of their dissatisfaction, however, appears to be channelled by sociostructural conditions such as the permeability of group boundaries.

Ellemers *et al.* (1988) carried out a second experiment to explore further the effects of the extent to which individual mobility to a higher-status group may subjectively be considered a feasible prospect. In this experiment too, the position of the ingroup (high or low) in a simulated status hierarchy of five groups was manipulated by providing subjects with bogus feedback about their group's relative performance on a problem-solving task. Furthermore, subjects were told that their individual ability was either relatively high or relatively low, compared to other members of their group. The permeability manipulation in this experiment was more specific than in the first experiment. This time, possibilities for upward and downward individual mobility were manipulated separately. Furthermore, in the conditions where a reallocation of subjects to groups would be possible, it was announced that group members' individual abilities would be taken into account when decisions about a change of group membership were made.

In this experiment, there again was a general tendency for subjects to show stronger ingroup identification when they belonged to a group with high status than when they were members of a low-status group. Furthermore, when upward mobility was possible, group members with high individual ability judged it more likely that they would be eligible for membership in a higher-status group, compared to low individual ability subjects. Accordingly, ingroup identification was weakest for group members who had the structural possibility as well as the individual ability necessary to achieve membership in a higher-status group.

From these two experiments, Ellemers *et al.* (1988) conclude that the general goal of establishing positive social identity causes group members to identify with their group when it has high status. When, however, sociostructural characteristics allow low-status group members to obtain membership in a higher-status group, the tendency to identify as an ingroup member decreases; presumably, under these circumstances low-status group members are more motivated to strive for membership in a higher-status group.

Status enhancement and status protection motives

The main predictions of social identity theory are based on the assumption that 'individuals strive to *achieve or maintain* positive social identity' (Tajfel & Turner, 1979, page 40, our italics). Thus, although social identity theory tends to be more concerned with strategies group members may follow to remedy unsatisfactory social identity, it also suggests that members of groups that already have achieved positive distinctiveness from comparison groups may be actively engaged in trying to preserve the *status quo* (Tajfel, 1975).

As we have seen above, it appears that the opportunity for individual group members to achieve membership in a group with higher status renders identification with their own group less attractive by comparison. In other words, the prospect of realizing a more positive identity apparently activates status enhancement motives in group members; hence, they resist identification with their present group, in the hope that a more positive identity may be achieved. If the prospect of changing one's group affiliation indeed elicits comparisons of ingroup–outgroup attractiveness, group members may also become more keenly aware of their favourable position when they are confronted with the possibility of being demoted to a group that has lower status. In other words, the latter prospect may enhance the relative attractiveness of one's present group. Therefore, in such a situation, group members' concern with maintaining their current group membership may be activated, which may evoke increased ingroup identification. Thus, possibilities for downward individual mobility may elicit status protection motives, resulting in relatively strong identification with the ingroup.

To summarize the above argument: as we have seen, the chance of gaining membership in a group that has higher status appears to activate status enhancement motives in low-status group members (so that they are less eager to identify with the ingroup). In the same vein, it may be argued that possible demotion to a lower-status group will elicit status protection motives, resulting in relatively strong ingroup identification of higher-status group members.

A similar distinction between enhancement and protection motives has been advanced by Zuckerman (1979), who posits that differential attributions of success and failure may be seen as strategies to maintain positive self-esteem. Some experimental results suggest that the risk of losing a high-status position may indeed activate status protection strategies. Berkowitz and Macaulay (1961) observed that individuals with high-status positions were more intent on maintaining their position when there was a risk of losing it than when their position was fixed. At the group level, results of an experiment by Turner, Hogg, Turner and Smith (1984) are suggestive of similar psychological processes. In their experiment, subjects participated in a group that performed either successfully or unsuccessfully. When subjects knew they might be reassigned to another group, this resulted in low cohesiveness of unsuccessful groups (which may be attributed to group members' desire for status enhancement), whereas strong cohesion was observed in successful groups (which is likely to be motivated by status protection concerns).

In an experiment by Ellemers, Doosje, van Knippenberg and Wilke (1992) the status protection motive was investigated more explicitly. In this experiment the authors tried to create a group membership that would be considered highly attractive, by manipulating relative group size in addition to relative group status. On the basis of findings reported by McGuire and colleagues (McGuire, McGuire, Child & Fujioka, 1978; McGuire, McGuire & Winton, 1979; McGuire & Padawer-Singer, 1976), Ellemers et al. (1992) assumed that small group size would render group characteristics more salient. In this way, being a minority could be seen as enhancing the attractiveness of membership in a high-status group, because it would imply an élite position. Then, the possibility of losing membership in such an élite group should elicit the desire in group members to hold on to their present group membership, e.g. by showing enhanced ingroup identification.

Indeed, Ellemers et al. (1992) found that members of high-status minority groups considered their group highly attractive; they were most proud of their group membership, indicated their desire to maintain the group's exclusiveness, and considered a change of group membership less attractive than did members of high-status majorities or members of low-status (minority or majority) groups. With regard to ingroup identification, it turned out that it indeed made a difference whether subjects knew they might be reassigned to another group or not. When members of high-status minority groups ran the risk of losing their highly attractive group membership, they expressed significantly stronger ingroup identification than when their group membership was fixed. Thus, Ellemers et al. (1992) were able to show that, when faced with the possibility of losing a highly valuable group membership, status protection motives can be evoked, which reinforce the tendency to identify as an ingroup member.

Improving group status: only when individual mobility is not possible?

So far, we have investigated the possibilities individual group members have to express the desire either to enhance or to maintain their present status position. However, as we have already briefly mentioned before, it is also possible to pursue higher status as a group, i.e. to strive for social change instead of individual mobility. Tajfel (1978a) and Tajfel and Turner (1979) posit that the main causal factor determining whether group members opt for individual mobility or social change (or group mobility) resides in the belief systems people hold regarding properties of the status structure. More specifically, Tajfel and Turner distinguish between status structures in which individual mobility appears to be a feasible prospect on the one hand, and rigidly stratified status structures on the other hand. Furthermore, they suggest that individual mobility will always be the most preferred identity enhancement strategy; only when achievement of a change of group affiliation seems inconceivable will group members pursue status improvement collectively.

A similar argument is put forward by Taylor and McKirnan (1984). In their 'five-stage model' of intergroup relations, Taylor and McKirnan posit that there is a fixed sequential order in the employment of different status improvement strategies. Supposedly, group members always first try to alleviate an unsatisfactory status position individually, and only resort to collective strategies when the individual option turns out not to be feasible. In the empirical work we have discussed so far, status structures in which individuals could change group membership were compared to structures where groups had impermeable boundaries. From these studies it indeed appeared that group members pursuing status improvement were most inclined to identify with their group when individual upward mobility was unlikely. Similar findings are reported by Taylor, Moghaddam, Gamble and Zellerer (1987) who found that frustrated attempts at individual mobility induced subjects to undertake collective action. Similarly, Wright, Taylor and Moghaddam (1990) report that individuals who tried to gain higher status instigated a collective protest when they discovered that the high-status group did not accept any new members.

At the group level, Tajfel (1974b) distinguishes between 'secure' and 'insecure' relations between groups. Just as the permeability of group boundaries implies whether or not change of individual status (through change of group membership) is conceivable, secure intergroup relations indicate that the relative status positions of groups are fixed, whereas in an insecure relation, it is possible to imagine an alternative status order. In more recent publications, the terms 'stable' and 'unstable' status differences are used to describe this difference (e.g. Tajfel, 1978a). Thus, unstable group status implies that striving for higher group status is a feasible identity enhancement strategy, whereas the status position of a group in a stable status structure cannot be improved.

As we have seen above, opportunities for individual mobility to another group may lead group members to display decreased identification with their group, in the hope that they achieve membership in a group with higher status. In the same vein, it can be argued that unstable status differences between groups make group members aware of the possibility to achieve higher status as a group. If this is indeed the case, then the stability of group statuses may in itself constitute a motivating factor for group members to engage in collective strategies, irrespective of the (im)possibility of realizing status improvement individually.

The empirical research we have discussed so far does not allow us to test the validity of this reasoning, because it was designed to investigate whether group members would pursue individual mobility when group boundaries were permeable, and would be more concerned with collective goals when group membership was fixed. As we have argued above, however, the stability of group status also seems a plausible determinant of group members' involvement with their group's fate, which may operate independently of whether it is possible to change one's group affiliation.

To investigate whether the stability of group status does affect group members' motivation to identify as ingroup members, regardless of the permeability of group boundaries, Ellemers, van Knippenberg and Wilke (1990) designed an experiment in which the permeability of group boundaries and the stability of group status were manipulated independently. Other independent variables were the relative status position of the ingroup and group members' individual abilities.

In this experiment, members of high-status groups were more satisfied about their group's status position and about their group membership than members of low-status groups. Accordingly, ingroup identification was stronger in high-status than in low-status groups. When it was possible to obtain membership in a higher-status group, because group boundaries were permeable, group members reported less satisfaction with their group *membership* than when group boundaries were impermeable. Furthermore, permeable group boundaries caused group members to express relatively little identification with their own group; instead group members indicated they felt attracted to membership in the higher-status group, especially when they also had high individual ability.

So far, then, the results reported by Ellemers *et al.* (1990) replicate and complement the research outcomes we discussed above. With regard to the present issue it is interesting to observe that the stability of the group's status position also affected group members' responses. When group status was unstable, group members turned out to be less satisfied with their group's present *status position* and more willing to try to achieve a higher status position for their group than when group status was stable. Moreover, although overall low ingroup identification was observed in groups that had low status, members of low-status groups showed stronger ingroup identification when their group's low-status position was unstable than when it was stable.

Thus, Ellemers *et al.* (1990) demonstrated that instability of group status is in itself sufficient to raise group members' concern with group goals, and may motivate group members to pursue status improvement collectively, irrespective of whether or not it is possible for them to leave their group.

Legitimacy of existing status differences as a motivational force

Another important motivating factor, proposed in social identity theory, is the *legitimacy* of the present status relations. Tajfel (1978a) argues that illegitimacy of existing status differences between groups may function as a lever for social action. Low ingroup status may be acceptable as long as the low status position of the ingroup is considered to be the legitimate outcome of a just procedure. When the ingroup regards its low status position as illegitimate, group members may display behaviour that is usually only observed in high-status groups. Turner and Brown (1978) found, for instance, that members of groups with illegitimately low status favour the ingroup in reward allocation. In the same vein, Caddick (1982) observed evaluative and behavioural biases favouring the ingroup to be stronger when the low status position of the ingroup was illegitimate than when it was legitimate.

Furthermore, having illegitimately low status supposedly motivates group members to try to remedy this unjust situation by striving for higher ingroup status. Some empirical studies that have investigated how the legitimacy of group status affects group members' reactions seem to support this idea (cf. Commins & Lockwood, 1979a; 1979b; Taylor *et al.*, 1987). In these experiments, however, legitimacy was manipulated in such a way that the legitimate and illegitimate conditions differed with respect to the relative competence of the groups as well as with respect to the legitimacy of the status assignment procedure. The results of these studies therefore cannot be attributed unambiguously to a differential sense of legitimacy; group members could, for instance, also have had a different amount of confidence in their group's abilities.

In an attempt to disentangle the competence and procedural-justice components of the legitimacy concept, Ellemers, Wilke and van Knippenberg (1993) designed an experimental procedure in which highly competent groups were assigned to a low status position (experiment 1). The status assignment procedure was presented either as legitimate or as illegitimate. In this way, we were able to study group members' reactions to legitimate or illegitimate low group status, while keeping group competence equal in both cases. As a result of this manipulation, group members with legitimately low status were less dissatisfied about their group's low status position, and evaluated the status assignment procedure more positively than subjects whose group's low status position was illegitimate. Yet, when low group status was illegitimate, group members displayed stronger ingroup identification than did members of legitimately low-status groups.

In their second experiment, Ellemers *et al.* (1983) applied their legitimacy manipulation to the inclusion of individual group members in a low-status group. This time, equally competent individuals were assigned to a group that held low status; their allocation to this group appeared to be either legitimate or illegitimate. Similar to what Ellemers *et al.* found in their first experiment, individuals who had been assigned to a low-status group on what appeared to be legitimate grounds evaluated the status assignment procedure more positively than individuals who considered their inclusion in a low-status group to be illegitimate. The ingroup identification measure, however, showed an effect opposite to that found in the first experiment. When assignment to a low-status group took place on an individual basis (experiment 2), identification with the low-status ingroup was lower when subjects considered their membership in this group illegitimate than when it seemed legitimate.

Taken together, then, these two experiments reveal that, as could be predicted from social identity theory, having a low status position is considered more acceptable as the status assignment procedure is more legitimate. An important difference with previous research is that Ellemers *et al.* (1993) demonstrated that this effect is found even when group members in the legitimate and illegitimate conditions are equally competent. Social identity theory does not differentiate between legitimacy of group status and legitmacy of individual status. When we compare experiments 1 and 2 described above, however, we see that these manipulations do have fundamentally different effects. When having low status results from unjust treatment of one's group, this inherent collective injustice functions as a binding factor, and strengthens ingroup identification. Unjust treatment of individual group members, on the other hand, causes them to contest their belonging to a low-status group, which results in their resisting ingroup identification. If we want to predict what strategies group members will follow to improve their unsatisfactory status position, we may therefore expect that when faced with a collective injustice (experiment 1) group members are most motivated to improve the status position of their group, whereas the experience of personal injustice (experiment 2) is likely to motivate people to pursue a higher status position individually.

In order to investigate these predictions, Ellemers *et al.* (1993) also established whether group members engaged in a competition for higher status with the other group, and whether they competed with their fellow ingroup members in order to maximize their chances of being reassigned to a group with higher status. Their conclusion was that the actual behaviour group members displayed was not guided by legitimacy considerations only. In the final instance, group members' behavioural strategies were adapted to the opportunities the status structure offered (in terms of individual mobility prospects or group status improvement opportunities) instead of constituting a direct attempt to redress unjust treatment.

In experiment 1, where the group's low status position either seemed to be legitimate or appeared illegitimately low, the stability of group status mediated whether subjects tried to improve their group's position. Hence, when the ingroup's status position was illegitimately low, group members were more competitive *vis-à-vis* the other group when group statuses were unstable than when they were stable. When the group's low status position appeared to be legitimate, the stability of group status did not affect intergroup competitiveness. Moreover, in both experiments group members were more easily prepared to sacrifice their group's best interest in order to pursue individual upward mobility when group boundaries were permeable, while impermeable group boundaries induced subjects to be relatively concerned with group goals.

Thus, it turns out that, although legitimacy considerations pertaining to the present status structure may motivate group members to identify primarily as an ingroup member (experiment 1) or to resist identification with the low-status ingroup (experiment 2), the (im)possibilities of changing one's personal status position or that of one's group determine the extent to which individual or collective status improvement strategies seem relevant.

Conclusions

The experimental studies reported above constitute attempts to simulate in the laboratory some 'social context' conditions usually considered important in understanding the actions of real groups in society. Within the confines of these experiments it appears that sociostructural variables indeed shape and channel the strategies people employ for the purpose of identity management.

It was shown in several studies that permeable group boundaries, which suggest the possibility that change in group membership may be achieved, led to decreased ingroup identification of members of low-status groups. This sign of psychological dissociation was expressed by group members with (manipulated) high individual ability, at least in situations in which upward mobility was explicitly associated with high ability. Thus it appears that preference for upward mobility as an individual identity enhancement strategy is fostered by the structural possibility (permeable boundaries) as well as the individually perceived feasibility (individual ability).

Downward permeability, the possibility of demotion to a lower-status group, also affects ingroup identification, but only in very attractive high-status minorities, or élites. It seems that the prospect of losing a highly desirable group membership evokes status protection mechanisms, such as increased ingroup identification.

Stability of the status differences between groups seems to be an important sociostructural variable as well. Unstable group status, implying the possibility of changing the intergroup status ranking, elicits higher ingroup identification in low-status groups, which may be seen as indicative of a more competitive intergroup attitude: closing ranks in order to increase the chances of 'winning' as a group.

When group status is illegitimately low, subjects tend to identify more with their group (although they were less satisfied with their group's position) than when it is legitimately low. It seems that, when the group as a whole is unfairly treated, this common negative experience creates a bond among group members and between the members and their group. When, however, subjects are *individually* assigned to a low-status group, the effects of legitimacy are reversed. Subjects who find themselves unjustly allocated to a (legitimately) low-status group, show much less ingroup identification than subjects justly allocated to a low-status group.

Apart from demonstrating the pervasive impact of sociostructural conditions on identity management strategies, our experimental programme also underlies the importance of personal involvement of people participating in research on intergroup relations. It is the subject whose position is at stake, as a member of a low-status group with or without opportunities for improving his or her individual or ingroup's position, or as a member of an élite group, whose membership is threatened by possible demotion. Only in such 'high-impact' experiments (Aronson, Brewer & Carlsmith, 1985) can the rich interplay of cognitive, motivational and behavioural variables in intergroup settings be studied adequately.

3 Ethnolinguistic vitality: Some motivational and cognitive considerations

Itesh Sachdev and Richard Bourhis

Motivational and cognitive analyses of interpersonal and intergroup communication phenomena in social psychology arose partly as a reaction to the normative bias in traditional sociolinguistics (Gumperz & Hymes, 1972; Giles & Powesland, 1975). These analyses accounted for language attitudes and behaviour in terms of motivational and cognitive processes (see Giles, Mulac, Bradac & Johnson, 1987 for overview). Motivational processes have encompassed needs, wishes, values and fears involving social approval, social integration and social differentiation. Cognitive processes identified as interacting with motivational processes and central to language attitudes and behaviour have included causal attribution and categorization. In spite of the avowed importance of cognitive factors in communication phenomena, the emphasis of theorizing and research in the social psychology of language has mainly been on motivational processes (Giles *et al.*, 1987; Giles & Robinson, 1990).

Giles, Bourhis and their colleagues modelled how motivational and cognitive processes relate to attitudes and behaviour between contrasting ethnolinguistic groups (Giles, Bourhis & Taylor, 1977; Bourhis, 1979; Giles & Johnson, 1981; Sachdev & Bourhis, 1990a). Based on Tajfel and Turner's (1986) social identity theory (SIT), the primary motivational process was conceptualized as group members' need to achieve 'positive ethnolinguistic distinctiveness' (Giles *et al.*, 1977). In accordance with SIT,

We wish to thank Dominic Abrams, Nita Elmufti, Mike Hogg, Sarah Lawson and Praji Maxwell for their useful comments on earlier drafts of this chapter. Comments and suggestions concerning this chapter would be much appreciated and should be addressed to: Itesh Sachdev, Department of Applied Linguistics, Birkbeck College, 43 Gordon Square, London, England WC1H 0PD; or to Richard Y. Bourhis, Département de psychologie, Université du Québec à Montréal, CP 8888, succursale A, Montréal, Québec H3C 3P8, Canada.

the major cognitive process 'organizing' these motivations was thought to be categorization along ethnolinguistic dimensions. Significantly, Giles *et al.* (1977) also argued that cognitive and motivational processes underlying ethnolinguistic behaviour do not occur in a sociostructural vacuum (cf. Tajfel, 1972b).

Most real-life intergroup situations are characterized by social stratification based on demographic, power and status inequalities that exist between groups. Sachdev and Bourhis (1984, 1985, 1987, 1991) recently conducted a series of studies using the minimal group paradigm assessing the independent and interactive effects of group numbers, power and status on intergroup behaviour and perceptions.

In brief, the main results of their studies investigating the independent effects of power, status and group numbers showed that increases in own-group power and status led to increased discrimination against the outgroup (Sachdev & Bourhis, 1985; 1987; Finchilescu, 1986; cf. Wagner, Lampen & Syllwasschy, 1986). Dominant and high-status group members favoured members of their own groups, while subordinate and low-status group members were more egalitarian in their treatment of outgroup members (van Knippenberg, 1984). Results also showed that arbitrary numerical minority group members tended to be slightly more discriminatory than their majority counterparts (Sachdev & Bourhis, 1984; cf. Simon & Brown, 1987).

Results obtained in Sachdev and Bourhis's (1991) study of the interactive effects of sociostructural variables on intergroup behaviour showed that membership in minority groups accentuated patterns of intergroup behaviour present in majority group conditions. For example, dominant high-status group members were much more discriminatory when they were in a minority than in a majority. Similarly, subordinate low-status group members favoured outgroup members more when they were in a minority than in a majority (cf. Espinoza & Garza, 1985; Ng, 1985). Other results obtained in the Sachdev and Bourhis (1991) study showed that power and status are sociostructural variables which are clearly orthogonal in their effects on discriminatory behaviour within the intergroup structure. Results showed that low-status groups who were dominant, i.e. powerful, were more discriminatory than low-status groups who were subordinate, i.e. powerless. Thus, despite their inferior status on a salient dimension of comparison, low-status *dominant* groups used their power advantage to discriminate against high-status outgroups who were subordinate. This series of experimental studies provided the first systematic evidence for the impact of sociostructural variables on intergroup behaviour.

In their attempt to place social psychological processes mediating ethnolinguistic behaviour in their appropriate sociostructural contexts, Giles *et al.* (1977) introduced the notion of *ethnolinguistic vitality*. Essentially, the notion of ethnolinguistic vitality was introduced to assess a group's sociostructural strength in terms of its social and economic power as well as its status and demographic strength. Johnson, Giles and Bourhis (1983) pointed out that such assessments, previously ignored, are important in rigorously describing and comparing the ethnolinguistic groups one is dealing with in sociolinguistic and social psychological research.

Since its introduction, the construct of ethnolinguistic vitality has received a considerable amount of theoretical and empirical attention (see Landry & Allard, in press, a). This chapter examines some motivational and cognitive issues important in research on ethnolinguistic vitality under five headings: 1. Overview of the vitality construct; 2. Assessment of 'objective' and subjective vitality; 3. Explanations for 'objective–subjective' vitality discrepancies; 4. Vitality, identity, attitudes and behaviour; 5. Epilogue.

1 Overview of the vitality construct

Ethnolinguistic vitality was defined by Giles *et al.* (1977) as 'that which makes a group likely to behave as a distinctive and active collective entity in intergroup situations' (page 306). As can be seen in Figure 3.1, Giles *et al.* (1977) conceptualized the vitality of ethnolinguistic groups under three sets of factors: demography, institutional support/control and status.

Demographic factors relate to the sheer numbers of ethnolinguistic group members and their distribution throughout a particular urban, regional or national territory. Sachdev and Bourhis (1984, 1991, above) operationalized demographic factors as 'group numbers' factors in their laboratory studies on sociostructural variables. Demographic variables also include group rates of immigration, emigration, endogamy and birth rate. Favourable demographic factors may be used by ethnolinguistic groups as a legitimizing tool to empower them with institutional control and bolster their overall group vitality (e.g. the black majority in South Africa).

Institutional support/control factors refer to the extent to which an ethnolinguistic group enjoys representation in, and control over, the various institutions of a community, region or nation. Giles *et al.* (1977) propose that all forms of formal and informal representation in, and control over, religious, educational, political, media and cultural contexts contribute to groups' institutional support and overall vitality. To the degree that institutional control can be defined as the 'degree of control one group has over its own fate and that of outgroups' (Sachdev & Bourhis, 1985, 1991), this dimension of ethnolinguistic vitality may be considered as the degree of social power enjoyed by one ethnolinguistic group relative to outgroups (Sachdev & Bourhis, 1990b).

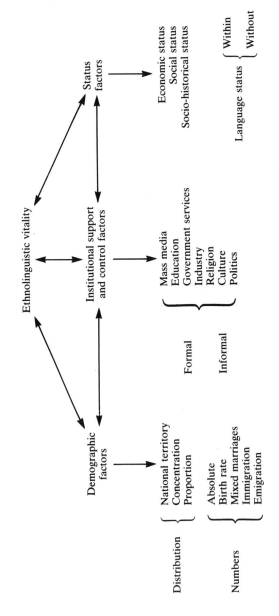

Figure 3.1 A taxonomy of the structural variables affecting ethnolinguistic vitality. Adapted from Bourhis *et al.* (1981).

Status factors, less readily quantifiable than demographic and institutional support factors, are those pertaining to an ethnolinguistic group's social prestige, its economic and socio-historical status as well as the status of its language and culture locally and internationally. Ethnolinguistic groups which have high institutional support/control and high demographic strength are likely to enjoy considerable social status relative to less dominant and minority groups in society. Results of Sachdev and Bourhis's (1984, 1985) laboratory studies manipulating group power and group numbers factors support this contention in that subjects perceived dominant and majority group members to have higher status than subordinate and minority group members.

Giles *et al.* (1977) proposed that groups' strengths and weaknesses on the above three factors could be assessed 'objectively' to provide a rough overall classification of ethnolinguistic groups as having low, medium or high vitality. It was argued that the more vitality an ethnolinguistic group has, the more likely it would be to survive as a distinctive linguistic collectivity in intergroup settings. Conversely, groups that have little or no group vitality were expected to assimilate linguistically or cease to exist as distinctive groups.

The original formulations focused on an 'objective' analysis of ethnolinguistic vitality. Data were collected from a variety of sociological, economic, demographic and historical sources. Vitality analyses of the 'objective' type tended to be largely descriptive, allowing some analytic comparison and contrasting of ethnolinguistic groups (Giles, 1978; Bourhis, 1979). In an extension of the original formulations, Bourhis, Giles and Rosenthal (1981) argued that *perceptions* of vitality can play a mediating role in accounting for group members' intergroup strategies, language attitudes, behaviours and degrees of group identification (Moscovici, 1981; Farr & Moscovici, 1984). It was argued that group members' subjective assessment of ingroup and outgroup vitality may be as important in determining sociolinguistic and interethnic behaviour as the group's 'objective' vitality.

Group members who perceive their own group vitality to be acceptably high on demography items but disproportionately low on institutional support factors may be motivated collectively to improve their own group representation and control of key institutional sectors such as the educational system, the economy and the mass media (e.g. the Québec case: Bourhis, 1984). The fruits of such efforts may have concrete beneficial effects for the 'objective' vitality of the group in institutional settings and may lead to further changes in vitality perceptions. A combination of both subjective and 'objective' vitality information was thus proposed as a more sensitive method of predicting the ethnolinguistic behaviour of group members than simply relying on 'objective' assessments of vitality (Johnson *et al.*, 1983).

The group vitality construct has been the focus of a lively theoretical and empirical debate in the last decade (Husband & Saifullah Khan, 1982; Johnson *et al.*, 1983; Edwards, 1985; Allard & Landry, 1986; Clement, 1986; Williams, 1992). However, Landry and Allard (in press, b) concluded that fifteen years of empirical research have demonstrated the construct of vitality 'to be both viable and productive'.

Studies across a wide variety of ethnolinguistic communities around the world have assessed the relationship between 'objective' and 'subjective' indices of vitality as well as the relationship between vitality and various aspects of language attitudes and behaviour (see Harwood, Giles & Bourhis, in press). Ethnolinguistic vitality has been incorporated theoretically and investigated empirically in a diverse range of models in cross-cultural communication (Bourhis, 1979; Genesee & Bourhis, 1982; 1988; Sachdev & Bourhis, 1990b), diglossia (Bourhis, 1979; Landry & Allard, in press, c), second-language acquisition (e.g. Clement, 1980; Clement & Krudenier, 1985; Giles & Byrne, 1982; Garrett, Giles & Coupland, 1989), bilingual development (Hamers & Blanc, 1989; Landry & Allard, 1984; 1987; 1990; 1991), ethnic identification (Giles & Johnson, 1987; Ytsma, Viladot & Giles, in press; Ros, Huici & Cano, in press; Sachdev & Bourhis, 1990a), language attitudes (Ryan, Giles & Sebastian, 1982; Kraemer & Olshtain, 1989; Kraemer, Olshtain & Badier, in press), social adaptation (Currie & Hogg, in press) and relations between the sexes (Kramarae, 1981). Harwood *et al.* (in press) provide the most recent critical synthesis and review of the notion of ethnolinguistic vitality.

2. Assessment of 'objective' and subjective vitality

In previous studies, 'objective' vitality has been assessed using available demographic and sociographic information from diverse sources including national censuses, language diversity surveys, historical, economic and sociological data banks. In general, such assessments can be difficult to make and remain vulnerable to inaccuracies in primary data sources (Bourhis, in press). For instance, Alladina (1985) attributed the unreliability of language diversity surveys to a variety of factors including self-reporting bias, lack of confidentiality and anonymity, evaluation apprehension, unrepresentative sampling strategies and language misclassification.

Nicholas (1988) extended these critiques further by rooting sociodemographic analyses in their ideological contexts. Thus he suggested that 'the presence and use of languages in addition to English in Britain cannot be measured as neutral, demographic, "hard facts", primarily because they exist in a hostile environment, a part of which is the monolingual English hegemony' (page 30). In France, socialist government authorities refused to include questions dealing with the knowledge of languages other than French in the 1991 census. This led members of ethnolinguistic groups such as Basques, Bretons, Occitants and Alsacians to call for a minority group boycott of the 1991 census. Refusal by the French state to acknowledge the existence of ethnolinguistic communities other than the French majority reflects a long history of intolerance towards linguistic minorities in France (Bourhis, 1982). Clearly, ideological, political and motivational considerations involved in the gathering of such data affect 'objective' assessments of ethnolinguistic vitality.

In order to assess individuals' representations of vitality mediating ethnolinguistic behaviour (Moscovici, 1981), Bourhis et al. (1981) developed the 'Subjective Vitality Questionnaire' (SVQ). Subjective vitality was proposed as a social psychological construct influenced by various affective and emotional factors. The main characteristic of the SVQ was that it asked respondents to evaluate the vitality of at least two ethnolinguistic groups on different variables specifically formulated in terms of each of the nineteen items identified in Giles et al.'s (1977) taxonomy (see Figure 3.1). Respondents were also asked to provide an overall assessment of the vitality of the ethnolinguistic groups ('how strong and active is . . .') as perceived 'today' (i.e. in the present time), in the 'past' (i.e. ten years ago) and in the 'future' (i.e. ten years hence). The original version of the SVQ was published in Bourhis et al. (1981).

The SVQ provided a great impetus for subsequent research that considered whether group members perceived their sociostructural positions along the same lines as 'objective' accounts would suggest. It is noteworthy that after fifteen years of vitality research only a few studies have assessed the factorial structure of subjective vitality. Giles, Rosenthal and Young (1985) obtained some factor-analytic support for a representation of perceived vitality along the postulated demographic, institutional support/control and status factors. However, recent results are less confirmatory and show that vitality items do not necessarily load trifactorially on their respective dimensions of demography, institutional support/control and status (e.g. Hogg, D'Agata & Abrams, 1989; Currie & Hogg, in press).

The findings of a variety of studies confirm that perceptions of majorities and minorities are often consensual and match so-called 'objective' estimates on many of the individual vitality dimensions. For instance, subjective–objective vitality concordance has been reported amongst majority Anglo-Canadian and minority Italo-Canadian teenagers (Bourhis & Sachdev, 1984), majority Anglo-Australian and minority Greek-Australian teenagers (Giles et al., 1985) and Welsh bilinguals living in Wales (Giles & Johnson, 1987). Landry and Allard's (1991; in press, c) large-scale study of francophone minorities across Canada provides perhaps the most comprehensive and systematic demonstration of the close match between subjective and 'objective' assessments of vitality.

Discrepancies between subjective and objective vitality have been found in a number of studies. Generally speaking, such discrepancies do not manifest themselves on large and obvious differentials, but rather on more marginal ingroup–outgroup contrasts. Cognitive and motivational factors that help account for discrepancies in vitality perception are discussed in the next section.

Harwood *et al.* (in press) classified discrepant vitality perceptions from previous studies into three profile types. First, *perceptual distortions in favour of ingroup vitality* were described as an accentuation of favourable ingroup differences and/or an attenuation of unfavourable ingroup differences. Exemplifying this profile were majority group members such as Anglo-Canadians (Bourhis & Sachdev, 1984) and Anglo-Australians (Giles *et al.*, 1985) as well as minority group members like Italo-Canadians and Greek-Australians. This pattern of perceptual distortion seems to reflect a need to perceive one's own group as having a vitality position which is more advantageous than may actually be the case 'objectively'.

Second, *perceptual distortions in favour of outgroup vitality* were described as the accentuation of differences favouring the outgroup and the attenuation of differences favouring the ingroup. Such patterns were found amongst German minority speakers in francophone Switzerland (Young, Bell & Giles, 1988) and Cantonese-speaking Chinese immigrants to Canada and Britain (Sachdev, Bourhis, Phang & D'Eye, 1987; Sachdev, Bourhis, D'Eye & Phang, 1990). This perceptual distortion in favour of outgroup vitality seems more prevalent amongst subordinated low-status minorities than amongst dominant high-status majorities. As was shown in recent intergroup laboratory studies (Sachdev & Bourhis, 1987; 1991), low-status subordinate minorities may sometimes be forced to acknowledge the advantaged position of high-status dominant groups on dimensions of comparison deemed most pertinent to the status differentials existing between groups.

The third type of profiles consist of *non-consensual vitality perceptions* characterized by a lack of consensus in vitality perceptions between members of contrasting ethnolinguistic groups. In such cases group members disagree not only about the degree of difference but also about the direction of difference that exists between ingroup and outgroup vitality. For instance, Pierson, Giles and Young (1987) reported that during the 1985 period of intense political and economic negotiations between the UK and mainland China about the future of Hong Kong, respondents of both Chinese and Western origin held diametrically opposed perceptions of their relative group vitalities on a number of important vitality items.

3 Explanations for 'objective–subjective' vitality discrepancies

In reviewing the results of previous empirical studies, Harwood *et al.* (in press) identified three varieties of 'situational' elements that interactively affect vitality perception: sociological, social network, and socio-psychological.

Sociological factors

The stability and/or change in objective vitality were considered important at the sociological level. For instance, it was argued that the greater the stability of a society in socio-politico-economic terms, the greater the likelihood that perceived vitality would concur with 'objective' estimates. Conversely, it was suggested that there was likely to be less cross-group consensus in 'unstable' societies characterized by rapid socio-political change, such as Hong Kong (see Pierson *et al.*, 1987). Harwood *et al.* (in press) did not articulate the relevant motivational processes underlying the relationship between sociological factors and vitality perceptions. There are at least two, not necessarily exclusive, possibilities. First, motivations may be based on an 'objective' conflict of interests over scare resources articulated within realistic conflict theory (RCT: Sherif, 1966). Second, analyses positing motivational processes based on 'competition for positive social identity' (SIT: Tajfel & Turner, 1986) may also explain some of the findings.

Social network factors

Landry and Allard (1990; in press, c) proposed the notion of individual networks of linguistic contact (INLC) as a 'bridge between the sociological and psychological levels' where the 'individual lives the totality of his ethnolinguistic experiences'. The INLC consists of all the occasions in which individuals have the opportunity to use their own languages when interacting with family members, friends, neighbours, school peers, co-workers, etc. The INLC also includes occasions to use the ingroup language when consuming services from private- and public-sector bodies including education, culture, municipal and state governments, shops, businesses, financial establishments, electronic and printed mass media. In bilingual and multilingual environments, the INLC incorporates contact with both ingroup and outgroup language users. It is proposed that the more occasions one has to use the ingroup language within one's INLC, the more likely one will perceive the ingroup ethnolinguistic community as having a strong vitality. Given that different individuals within an ethnolinguistic group each have specific INLCs, it is proposed that the INLC does mediate between a group's 'objective' vitality and individuals' vitality perceptions on the SVQ.

Findings stemming from an impressive and sustained programme of research across Canada allowed Landry and Allard (1991; in press, c) to argue that though objective vitality may affect the structure and composition of individual networks, it is the INLC which relates directly to perceptions and beliefs about vitality. Thus, based on Landry and Allard's findings, Harwood et al. (in press) proposed that an increase in the use of a particular language within the INLC will lead to perceptual distortions in favour of ingroup vitality.

Other profiles of vitality perception reported above may also be explained in terms of INLCs. However, as with the sociological factors discussed above, a cognitive-motivational analysis of the nature of the relationship between the INLC and vitality perceptions is currently unspecified. Interestingly, in discussions of the ethnolinguistic behaviour of individuals, Allard and Landry (in press) have emphasized motivational (rather than cognitive) processes based on needs to achieve satisfying social identities (Tajfel & Turner, 1986). According to Allard and Landry (in press) the development of ethnolinguistic identities and other cognitive-affective dispositions, like the development of linguistic competencies, is rooted firmly in INLCs.

Social psychological factors

Motivational processes are perhaps most directly implicated in Harwood et al.'s (in press) analyses of the socio-psychological determinants of vitality perception. Their central motivational notion – striving for positive ethnolinguistic identity (Tajfel & Turner, 1986) – may account convincingly for perceptual distortions in favour of ingroup vitality as well as non-consensual vitality perceptions reported in previous studies.

Perceptual distortions in favour of outgroup vitality are perhaps more difficult to deal with in terms of social identity needs unless the perceived legitimacy and stability of intergroup inequalities are brought to bear upon the analysis (Bourhis, 1993; Tajfel & Turner, 1986; Turner & Brown, 1978). Hinkle and Brown (1990) point out that outgroup favouring responses may also be explained in terms of other notions such as strategic responding and structural constraints (e.g. van Knippenberg, 1984; Spears & Manstead, 1989) which imply psychological mechanisms that are independent of social identity motivations. However, little attention has been paid to other motivational or cognitive explanations for distortions in vitality perceptions. Below, we propose that social cognition factors may also help account for objective–subjective vitality discrepancies.

Typically, the subjective vitality assessment procedure involves individuals making decisions not only when the information is fairly clear about ingroup and outgroup vitality, but also when it is uncertain or statistically complex. Nisbett and Ross (1980) argued that judgements under uncertainty are as likely to be influenced by cognitive informational factors as by motivational factors. However, little attention has focused on identifying sources of bias in vitality perceptions that are due to subjects' informal strategies of information processing. Tversky and Kahneman (1974) refer to such informal strategies as 'heuristics' assumed to aid cognitive simplicity. A variety of judgemental heuristics has been proposed by Tversky and Kahneman (1974). These heuristics include those of representativeness, availability, simulation, anchoring and adjustment (Fiske & Taylor, 1991). However, only the availability heuristic is considered here to illustrate how a cognitive analysis may account for some of the vitality profiles reported in previous studies.

The availability heuristic refers to the assignment of a higher subjective frequency or likelihood to objects or events which are more easily accessible from memory, or which are easier to imagine (Tversky & Kahneman, 1974). Bourhis and Sachdev (1984) suggested that English-Canadian and Italian-Canadian desires for positive ethnolinguistic identities accounted for their perceptual distortions in favour of ingroup vitality. However, such distortions may also be consistent with biased outcomes predicted by the availability heuristic. For instance, whereas both groups shared much common information about the wider social environment dominated by the Anglo-Canadian mainstream, Italian-Canadians were probably more familiar with the Italian cultural environment than were the English-Canadians whose contact with the Italian-Canadian minority remained somewhat infrequent.

Dominant majorities are often somewhat ignorant of the activities and actual characteristics of subordinate linguistic minorities. In contrast, subordinate minorities can ill afford to ignore the activities and characteristics of the dominant majority. Bourhis and Sachdev (1984) found that, overall, English-Canadian (EC) and Italian-Canadian (IC) students were consensual in perceiving that the EC majority enjoyed a stronger vitality position in Hamilton (Ontario) than did the IC minority. However, given their degree of contact and direct involvement in their own community, Italian-Canadian group members were able to generate more instances relevant to the strength of the Italian-Canadian community than could English-Canadian respondents. Therefore, at this general level the application of the availability heuristic would help explain the perceptual distortions in favour of ingroup vitality obtained with IC subjects and the perceptual distortions attenuating outgroup IC vitality reported by EC respondents.

The Bourhis and Sachdev (1984) study offers an even more detailed test of the availability heuristic explanation of the 'objective'–subjective vitality discrepancy effect. The study was in fact conducted with EC and IC senior high school students drawn from two types of school settings. The first sample of IC and EC students was drawn from two schools in which the proportion of these two groups was numerically equal (i.e. 50–50). The second sample was drawn from two majority settings: IC majority subjects were drawn from a school in which IC students constituted a 65 per cent majority relative to the outgroup EC students; EC majority subjects were drawn from a school in which they constituted an 85 per cent majority relative to the outgroup minorities including ICs. All subjects completed the SVQ with specific instructions requesting that assessments of English-Canadian and Italian-Canadian vitality be made for these two communities taken as a whole across the city of Hamilton. Note that the census data for Hamilton showed that ECs constituted 57 per cent of the population while the IC minority constituted 11 per cent of the city population.

It was noted above that EC and IC assessments of EC vitality were consistently higher than those for the IC community. However, majority IC students gave slightly higher assessments of IC vitality on a number of demographic and institutional support items than did IC students sampled in the equal-group setting. It seems that majority IC students, by virtue of their concentration in this particular setting, could retrieve more instances and cases of Italian-Canadian activities and demographic strength than could IC students sampled in the equal-group setting. 'Conversely, equal-group EC students, for whom the IC student presence was quite salient, rated IC vitality to be somewhat less weak on some demographic items than did EC majority students. Taken together, these vitality assessments seem consistent with predicted biases characteristic of availability heuristics.

The immediate school setting in which both the Italian-Canadians and English-Canadians were tested, produced patterns of vitality perceptions which seemed better explained by a cognitive heuristic than by a more global motivational process reflecting the need for maintaining as positive an image of ingroup vitality as is possible within a specific social-comparison context. However, given that linguistic groups both in this study and in many other vitality studies tend to perceive their own group to have a more favourable vitality than their rival outgroup gives them credit for, it would seem that both motivational and cognitive processes are necessary to account fully for the range of vitality perception profiles documented in the literature so far (Harwood et al., in press).

Results of other vitality studies also resist straightforward motivational explanations and may be more amenable to a cognitive analysis. For instance, Sachdev *et al*. (1987, 1990) build on a different aspect of Festinger's (1954) social comparison theory in attempting to explain why studies amongst first-generation Chinese in Canada and the UK reveal perceptual distortions in favour of outgroup vitality. They argue that the immigrants' perceptions reflect the outcome of an increase in salience of intra-personal comparisons stemming from their changed circumstances due to immigration (cf. Young *et al*., 1988).

First-generation immigrants leave a country of origin in which their own group is often the dominant high-status majority. Upon arriving in the host country, first-generation immigrants often experience a drop from majority group status to minority group status. When asked to provide a vitality assessment of their own group relative to the outgroup host community, they use anchoring comparisons of owngroup vitality which contrast unfavourably not only with the outgroup host majority but also with the majority group status of their own group in the country of origin. This doubly discrepant comparison may lead to perceptual distortions which greatly attenuate owngroup vitality and accentuate outgroup host majority vitality leading to perceptual distortions in favour of outgroup vitality. However, for second-generation immigrants, comparisons with country of origin majority owngroup have lost their relevance and are no longer available as a source of bias in owngroup vitality assessments in the host country, thus leading to fewer perceptual distortions in favour of outgroup host community vitality.

The above cognitive explanations invoke the operation of a number of judgemental heuristics which include availability, anchoring and adjustment heuristics (Fiske & Taylor, 1991). Though not discussed here, the relevance of other social cognitive notions such as 'the outgroup homogeneity effect' (Quattrone & Jones, 1980; Simon & Brown, 1987; Marques, 1990), emphasizing the joint effects of perceivers' cognitive liabilities and stimulus properties, also needs to be incorporated in theorizing and research on subjective vitality.

Perhaps the most interesting challenge to motivational explanations of perceptual distortions of vitality may stem from considering the cognitive and informational consequences of Landry and Allard's (in press, c) notion of individuals' networks of linguistic contacts (INLCs). They report findings showing that beliefs about subjective vitality are strongly related to INLC experiences (Landry & Allard, 1991) and hypothesize that 'all ethnolinguistic vitality beliefs may ultimately be influenced by ethnolinguistic contacts experienced via the INLC' (Allard & Landry, in press).

One implication of an INLC analysis is that infrequent contact with individuals from ethnolinguistic outgroups lessens the availability of information about them, as well as reducing the likelihood of encountering additional and unusual information about outgroup vitality (Higgins, Kuiper & Olson, 1981). If this results in increased automatic encoding of information (Bargh, 1984) then the likelihood of other available information being utilized for subsequent judgements of vitality may also be reduced (Hastie, 1981). This may result in decreasing the complexity of the vitality schema and beliefs associated with ethnolinguistic outgroups (Ostrom, Pryor & Simpson, 1981; Marques, 1990). This line of reasoning suggests that INLCs may provide fertile ground for examining the influence of cognitive processes in the arena of ethnolinguistic relations. Clearly, subjective vitality research needs to pay greater attention to social cognition notions like judgemental heuristics, especially as such processes are likely to interact with motivational factors related to the ingroup/ outgroup differentiation strategies already well known in the intergroup relations literature (Abrams & Hogg, 1990a; Brown, 1978; Tajfel & Turner, 1986).

4 Vitality, identity, attitudes and behaviour

A number of researchers have argued that the construct of ethnolinguistic vitality should not only serve to describe ethnolinguistic situations but should also be predictive of ethnolinguistic attitudes and behaviour (Giles *et al.*, 1977; Bourhis *et al.*, 1981; Husband & Saifullah Khan, 1982; Johnson *et al.*, 1983; Clement & Noels, 1991; Landry & Allard, 1991; in press, b, c). As noted earlier, recent laboratory studies conducted by Sachdev and Bourhis (1984, 1985, 1987, 1991) have shown that 'objective' changes in group numbers, status and power differentials have predictably independent and interactive effects on patterns of intergroup behaviour and perceptions.

In the field, Bourhis and Sachdev (1984) had reported that the 'objectively' high English-Canadian vitality in Hamilton was reflected in the findings that self-reported use of English was higher than self-reported use of Italian not only by majority ECs, but also by minority IC subjects, across all public and private domains. Recently, Landry and Allard (in press, c) who surveyed over 1,500 anglophone and francophone students across Canada, obtained impressive empirical data showing that French and English usage across a wide array of social domains increased linearly in relation to the 'objective' vitality of the respective ethnolinguistic groups. In their study 'objective' vitality accounted for over 60 per cent of the variance in patterns of language use (Landry & Allard, in press, c).

While acknowledging the predictive power of 'objective' vitality, Bourhis *et al.* (1981) argued that subjective vitality is likely to be an important mediating variable determining sociolinguistic and interethnic behaviour. Moreover, they suggested that in some cases subjective vitality may emerge as a better predictor of ethnolinguistic behaviour than only 'objective' assessments of vitality (cf. Giles, Leets & Coupland, 1990). However, until relatively recently, few attempts had been made to test directly how well perceived vitality predicts ethnolinguistic be- haviour, identifications and attitudes.

In the first such study, Bourhis and Sachdev (1984) provided some indirect, non-statistical evidence for a link between subjective vitality and self-reported language use. They reported that group members who perceived they had high vitality (English-Canadians) were likely to use their own language more frequently in a wider range of settings than group members who perceive themselves to have low vitality (Italian- Canadians).

Results of recent studies have provided some statistical evidence relating perceived vitality to ethnolinguistic identification. For instance, positive correlations between subjective vitality and identification have been obtained amongst Mexican-Americans in the USA (Gao, Schmidt & Gudykunst, 1990), Catalan speakers in Catalonia (Ytsma et al., in press) and the Acadians of New Brunswick (Landry & Allard, in press, d).

Other studies have not yielded findings confirming a positive rela- tionship between subjective vitality and ethnolinguistic attitudes and behaviour. Giles and Johnson (1987), in a study of Welsh-English bilinguals in Wales, found results suggesting that perceived vitality predicted neither ethnolinguistic behaviour nor normative expectations about language use. Instead, degree of ingroup identification and perceptions of the stability of the intergroup situation were most predictive of Welsh language maintenance and norms about language use.

Interestingly, Giles and Johnson (1987) also reported that perceived vitality interacted with levels of ingroup identification in being predictive of anticipated language divergence from an outgroup speaker. Language divergence, dramatically demonstrated by Bourhis, Giles, Leyens and Tajfel (1979) in Belgium, refers to interlocutors accentuating linguistic differences between themselves and others. In Giles and Johnson (1987), the highest levels of anticipated divergence from outgroup speakers were reported by those who identified strongly as Welsh and who perceived ingroup vitality to be low, as well as by those who identified strongly less strongly as Welsh but who perceived ingroup vitality to be high. An inverse relationship between ethnolinguistic identity and subjective vitality was also obtained amongst Frisian-Dutch subjects (Ytsma et al., in press).

Such contrasting results about the relationship between subjective vitality and ethnolinguistic identification are difficult to explain and may well originate in interactions between motivational, cognitive and other elements of the situation such as changes in *objective* vitality. For instance, Harwood *et al.* (in press) suggest that Welsh subjects in Giles and Johnson's 1987 study, who identified strongly with their ingroup are likely to be more aware of the decline in Welsh vitality over recent years. Similarly, Gao *et al.*'s (1990) Mexican-Americans who identified highly with their ingroup may well be aware of the 'objectively' increasing demographic strength of their group in the USA.

Allard and Landry (1986) proposed that the predictive power of subjective vitality would be greatly increased if it were considered to be part of a belief system reflecting individual predispositions and orientations about vitality (also see Labrie & Clement, 1986). This reflected the empirically well-supported notion that generalized attitudes and perceptions are not reliable predictors of behaviour unless accompanied by specific behavioural intentions (see Ajzen, 1988).

Allard and Landry (1986) argued that studies using the SVQ (Bourhis *et al.*, 1981) lacked predictive power since the SVQ sampled only 'general beliefs' ('what is') about vitality, i.e. 'factual' beliefs about current vitality of ethnolinguistic groups. Using cognitive orientation theory (Kreitler & Kreitler, 1976), Allard and Landry (1986) found evidence that the predictive power of vitality was greatly increased when 'normative beliefs' ('what should be'), 'self-beliefs' ('what I think') and 'goal beliefs' ('my goals, wishes', etc.) about vitality were included in prediction equations (also see Allard & Landry, in press). 'General' beliefs, 'normative' beliefs, 'self' beliefs and 'goal' beliefs about individual vitality items had been incorporated into a 'Beliefs about Ethnolinguistic Vitality Questionnaire' (BEVQ: Allard & Landry, 1986).

Recently, Landry and Allard (1991; Allard & Landry, in press) proposed that 'self-beliefs' and 'goal beliefs' about vitality be considered under the rubric of 'ego-centric' vitality beliefs since the self is central as subject in such beliefs. In contrast, they propose that 'general beliefs' and 'normative beliefs', which do not have the self as subject, be referred to as 'exo-centric' beliefs about vitality. In analyses of responses to their BEVQ, Allard and Landry (in press) obtained some factor-analytic support for the distinction between ego-centric and exo-centric beliefs about vitality amongst francophone students across Canada. Moreover, their findings also showed that amongst francophone Canadians, ego-centric beliefs were more predictive of ethnolinguistic behaviour than 'factual' exo-centric beliefs about francophone vitality.

Sachdev (1991) reported preliminary findings amongst Polish speakers in London (UK) which supported Allard and Landry's (in press) results amongst francophones in Canada. Relative to exo-centric beliefs, ego-centric beliefs were not predictive of self-reported language use and attitudes amongst Polish-speaking Londoners. However, Sachdev (1991) also reported contrary findings amongst Tamil subjects: ethnolinguistic identifications and intergroup contact were more predictive of self-reported language use and opinions about language use than beliefs about vitality (cf. Giles & Johnson, 1987).

Assuming that subjects were striving for positive ethnolinguistic identities (Tajfel & Turner, 1986; Giles, 1978), Sachdev (1991) argued that the relatively high ethnic/racial 'visibility' of groups like the Tamils compared to the Polish in England, contributed to the differences between them (cf. 'hardness of boundaries': Giles & Johnson, 1981). It was proposed that if language was an important dimension of ethnic identity, then, for 'visible' groups like the Tamils, ethnolinguistic identification and contact might well be sufficient predictors of language use and opinions about language use. In contrast, for the 'not-so-visible' groups, such as the Polish in the UK and francophones across Canada, striving for ethnolinguistic distinctiveness may involve relying on beliefs about vitality to prop up their ethnolinguistic identities. Future research clearly needs to examine the relationship between vitality, identity and ethnolinguistic 'visibility' more closely.

5 Epilogue

Research on 'objective' and subjective vitality has been reviewed in this chapter showing that the vitality construct clearly remains an active and growing concern today. For instance, Currie and Hogg (in press) argued that since the foundations of subjective vitality lie in 'social belief systems' (Tajfel & Turner, 1986; Hogg & Abrams, 1988), subjective vitality should affect a broader range of behaviours than just language behaviours. Accordingly, they obtained evidence that educational achievement, occupational aspiration and life satisfaction among Vietnamese refugees in Australia were significantly related to aspects of subjective ethnolinguistic vitality. Mapping the impact of subjective vitality on non-linguistic aspects of behaviour and social relations thus promises to be an exciting avenue for further research.

Harwood et al. (in press), in a different vein, argued for discoursal extensions in research on ethnolinguistic vitality. They proposed that the communication of vitality beliefs is important to investigate as it is through such communications that individuals become aware of their own group memberships, and construct representations of relative group vitality which influence the visibility and activity of groups within their respective contexts (Allard & Landry, 1986; Farr & Moscovici, 1984). Currie and Hogg (in press) and Harwood et al. (in press) further point out that the subjects in vitality surveys, and the belief scales themselves, are part of an ongoing intergroup process that makes it theoretically difficult to disentangle assessment outcomes from elements of the situation. The act of completing vitality scales may thus reflect various motivational and rhetorical strategies (e.g. emphasizing deprived resources) as well as 'objectively' assessing a group's position (cf. Billig, 1987). Investigating the discoursal implications of group vitality is thus likely to provide interesting and fruitful perspectives on ethnolinguistic relations.

Subjective ethnolinguistic vitality has thus far been construed as a psychological construct subjected to various socio-cognitive-affective filters (also see Harwood *et al.*, in press). Motivational and cognitive processes underlying subjective vitality assessment and ethnolinguistic behaviour have been reviewed in this chapter. Giles, Scherer and Taylor (1979) had previously suggested that communication phenomena function psychologically for two main reasons: identity maintenance and cognitive organization (also see Thakerar, Giles & Cheshire, 1982). However, research on ethnolinguistic vitality has focused mainly on the identity maintenance function, while the cognitive organization function, involving the ordering of events into meaningful social categories, has generally been neglected.

In previous studies, identity maintenance has been discussed in terms of satisfying the need for positive self-esteem (Tajfel & Turner, 1986; Giles & Johnson, 1981; Sachdev & Bourhis, 1990a). However, Hogg and Abrams (1990) argued that the evidence for a self-esteem motive underlying intergroup behaviour and attitudes in previous studies was noticeably weak. They proposed that the 'search for meaning' was likely to be the most important motive underlying intergroup behaviour and outlined how this may be satisfied by the operation of *self-categorization* processes (Turner, Hogg, Oakes, Reicher & Wetherell, 1987; Hogg & McGarty, 1990). Following Bruner (1957), Turner *et al.* (1987) argued that individuals are motivated to represent their social world, including self, in terms of the categories which are most 'accessible' to their cognitive apparatus and which best 'fit' subjectively meaningful and salient contrasts in that situation (Oakes & Turner, 1990).

A re-evaluation of the literature on subjective vitality in terms of self-categorization theory may prove to be more integrative relative to previous conceptualizations. For instance, perceptual distortions of group vitality may be viewed as being the consequence of a cognitive process seeking to organize information in terms of the most meaningful and parsimonious set of self and other categories in their particular contexts. Relatedly, the results reported by Sachdev (1991) amongst 'visible' Tamil subjects in London (above) may be understood in terms of ethnic/racial self-categorizations providing the maximal contrast and fit between relevant intracategory similarities and intercategory differences.

In conclusion, we have argued that the motivational focus of previous group vitality research should be counterbalanced by assessing the cognitive processes underlying vitality perceptions and their impact on ethnolinguistic behaviour. Subjective vitality research would benefit from examining the impact of judgemental heuristics, self-categorization processes and discoursal elements on vitality theory and assessment. Coupled with the recent work of Sachdev and Bourhis (1991) emphasizing the value of conducting experimental studies of 'objective' vitality to complement the field survey research of previous studies, such an approach will allow the examination of vitality in a more integrative manner. Lacunae linking vitality research with the experimental social psychology of prejudice, discrimination and intergroup relations are thus likely to be filled using this approach.

4 Prejudice, intergroup behaviour and self-esteem: Enhancement and protection motives

Jennifer Crocker, Bruce Blaine and Riia Luhtanen

Membership in social groups provides an important source of self-esteem for many people. People can derive a sense of value, self-respect and self-worth from their memberships in high-status or successful social groups (cf. Brown & Lohr, 1987; Coleman, 1961; Cusick, 1973). Conversely, membership in a low-status, disadvantaged or devalued group may threaten self-esteem by suggesting that the individual has undesirable attributes, or is regarded unfavourably by others (cf. Allport, 1954; see Crocker & Major, 1989, for a review).

However, people are not merely passive victims of their group's social status. Membership in disadvantaged, low-status or stigmatized groups does not necessarily result in lowered self-esteem for the members of those groups. Indeed, people often actively try to protect their self-esteem from the damaging implications of membership in low-status, disadvantaged or poorly performing groups (cf. Crocker & Major, 1989). One strategy for protecting or enhancing self-esteem is derogating or discriminating against members of outgroups. The meaning of membership in a high-status, selective or successful group is, in part, derived from the fact that other groups are lower in status, less selective or less successful (e.g. Tajfel & Turner, 1979). Thus, by derogating other groups, one may elevate the *relative* status of one's own group, and hence elevate self-esteem (cf. Tajfel & Turner, 1979; 1986; Wills, 1981).

Psychologists have long recognized that feelings about the self may be related to prejudice and intergroup behaviour. Negative or insecure feelings about the self have been implicated as a cause of prejudice in the theory of the authoritarian personality (Adorno, Frenkel-Brunswik, Levinson & Sanford, 1950), in downward comparison theory (Wills, 1981), in social identity theory (cf. Tajfel & Turner, 1979), and in terror-management theory (Rosenblatt, Greenberg, Solomon, Pyszczynski

& Lyon, 1989). Of course, enhancement and protection of self-esteem are but two of several motives that may drive prejudice and discrimination (cf. Abrams & Hogg, 1988; Snyder, in press). Nonetheless, because prejudice and discrimination may sometimes result entirely or primarily from self-esteem concerns, we believe that it may be heuristically useful to apply the existing literature on self-esteem and self-serving biases to the domain of prejudice, discrimination and intergroup behaviour.

Research on the role of self-esteem in prejudice and discrimination has focused on two issues: first, whether derogating or discriminating against outgroups can enhance self-esteem; and second, whether individual differences in self-esteem are related to prejudice and discrimination (cf. Abrams & Hogg, 1988). Our focus in this chapter is on this latter question. We argue that not all people are equally likely to cope with threats to their self-esteem through prejudice and discrimination. Differences in individuals' level of trait self-esteem affect their use of various strategies designed to enhance or protect self-esteem from threat (cf. Baumeister, Tice & Hutton, 1989; Blaine & Crocker, in press; Crocker & Blaine, 1992, for reviews). In this chapter, we will evaluate the role of self-esteem as a predictor of prejudice and intergroup relations, with a particular focus on three issues: first, we will discuss the role of personal versus collective (or social) self-esteem in prejudice and intergroup relations. Second, on the basis of recent developments in research and theory on personal self-esteem, we reconsider the issue of whether high or low self-esteem people are more prejudiced and discriminatory. Third, we argue that the existing literature has been unnecessarily restricted in the types of dependent measures that have typically been included for study, obscuring many important effects of self-esteem on prejudice and intergroup behaviour.

Personal versus collective self-esteem

According to social identity theory (cf. Tajfel, 1982a; Tajfel & Turner, 1979; 1986; Turner, 1982), the self-concept has two distinct aspects. One is personal identity, which includes beliefs about one's skills, abilities or attributes such as attractiveness or intelligence. The second is social identity (or what we have called 'collective identity'), defined as 'that aspect of the individuals' self-concept which derives from their know-ledge of their membership in a social group (or groups) together with the value and emotional significance attached to that membership' (Tajfel, 1981a, page 255). Whereas personal identity concerns one's individual characteristics, social or collective identity concerns the characteristics of one's groups, which may or may not also characterize oneself as an individual. Just as there are stable individual differences in the tendency to have a positive personal identity (i.e., personal self-esteem), we have argued that there are also stable individual differences in the tendency to have a positive social or collective identity (i.e., collective self-esteem; see Luhtanen & Crocker, 1991; 1992). In other words, personal self-esteem is the self-evaluative (rather than self-descriptive) component of personal identity, and collective self-esteem is the self-evaluative component of social (or collective) identity (see Luhtanen & Crocker, 1992, for a scale to measure collective self-esteem).

Trait personal self-esteem should not be confused with temporary threats to self-esteem, and trait collective self-esteem should not be confused with temporary, or even relatively enduring, threats to collective self-esteem. Having enduring low personal self-esteem is not equivalent to suffering from a failure experience, and low trait collective self-esteem is not equivalent to membership in a low-status or unsuccessful group. For example, African-Americans, who are chronically disadvantaged and stigmatized in American culture, are not lower in personal or collective self-esteem than white Americans (Luhtanen, Blaine & Crocker, 1991). Furthermore, the way that people respond to threats to self-esteem may be determined by their level of trait self-esteem (cf. Baumeister et al., 1989; Crocker & Luhtanen, 1990; Crocker, Thompson, McGraw & Ingerman, 1987). Thus, we would argue that it is misguided to consider manipulations of group status to be equivalent to manipulating trait collective self-esteem; or to consider personal success or failure feedback to be equivalent to manipulating trait personal self-esteem. Rather, it is an empirical question when and for whom low ingroup status or personal failure results in low collective or personal self-esteem.

When are prejudice and intergroup behaviour driven by personal self-esteem, and when are they driven by collective self-esteem concerns? We have argued that negative feedback regarding the status, reputation or success of one's ingroup constitutes a threat to collective self-esteem. Conversely, negative feedback regarding one's personal competencies, reputation or success constitutes a threat to personal self-esteem. Although the personal and collective aspects of the self are relatively distinct (cf. Brewer, 1991; Luhtanen & Crocker, 1991; 1992; Tajfel & Turner, 1979), many situations may threaten personal and collective self-esteem simultaneously. For example, a group failure experience may suggest not only that one's group is incompetent, but that one is personally incompetent, if one contributed to the group failure. Conversely, a personal failure may reflect poorly on the private and public image of one's group. The challenge for researchers is to determine in advance which aspect of the self – collective or personal – is threatened in a particular situation.

We have argued that responses to personal threats should be predicted by the individual's level of trait personal self-esteem. Responses to collective threats are predicted by one's level of trait collective self-esteem (Luhtanen & Crocker, 1991; 1992). In support of this idea, we have shown individuals who are high in personal self-esteem responding to personal failure feedback by derogating outgroups (those who succeeded) in a way that should enhance or restore their personal identity (Crocker *et al.*, 1987). Individuals who are high in collective self-esteem respond to group failure feedback by derogating outgroups in a way that should enhance or restore their collective identity (Crocker & Luhtanen, 1990). When both personal and collective self-esteem are threatened by some negative outcome, both personal and collective self-esteem may predict responses to that outcome.

High versus low self-esteem as a predictor of prejudice

Who are more prejudiced, high or low self-esteem people? Theoretically, there are four possible outcomes for the effect of self-esteem on prejudice and intergroup discrimination. First, people who are low in self-esteem may be *more* likely to be prejudiced, because their need for self-esteem is greater (Wills, 1981). Alternatively, people who are low in self-esteem may be *less* likely to be prejudiced, because they lack the motivation to enhance self-esteem (cf. Abrams & Hogg, 1988; Alloy & Abramson, 1979; Brockner, 1983; Crocker *et al.*, 1987; Taylor & Brown, 1988), or their self-concepts do not support the use of self-serving biases such as ingroup bias (cf. Shrauger, 1975). Indeed, the failure to use self-serving biases in general, and to derogate outgroups in particular, may be a cause of low self-esteem (cf. Crocker *et al.*, 1987). This is the hypothesis that most frequently appears in the literature on self-esteem and intergroup behaviour (cf. Abrams & Hogg, 1988; Wills, 1981).

Third, if prejudice and discrimination have causes other than self-esteem concerns, there may be no differences between high and low self-esteem people. Finally, it is possible that both high and low self-esteem individuals are prejudiced and discriminate against outgroups, but under different circumstances. For example, Brown, Collins and Schmidt (1988) have argued that high self-esteem individuals self-enhance directly, whereas low self-esteem individuals self-enhance indirectly. Gibbons and McCoy (1991) have argued that high self-esteem individuals engage in active downward comparisons, whereas low self-esteem individuals engage in passive downward comparisons. Baumeister *et al.* (1989) have argued that people who are high in self-esteem are oriented towards self-enhancement, whereas people who are low in self-esteem are oriented towards self-protection (see also Arkin, 1981; Tice, 1991).

Empirical research on this issue has yielded conflicting results. Several studies have found that people who are low in self-esteem evaluate outgroups more negatively (i.e., are more prejudiced) than do high self-esteem individuals (cf. Ehrlich, 1973; Wylie, 1979; Wills, 1981, for reviews). Other studies have found that people who are high in self-esteem are more likely to derogate outgroups relative to ingroups (cf. Abrams & Hogg, 1988; Crocker et al., 1987; Crocker & Luhtanen, 1990; Luhtanen & Crocker, 1991). Others have found no relation between self-esteem and ingroup bias (e.g. Crocker & Schwartz, 1985; Wagner, Lampen & Syllwasschy, 1986). Still other studies have found that high self-esteem people show ingroup bias under some circumstances, whereas lows show it under other circumstances (e.g. Brown et al., 1988).

In sum, there has been a great deal of confusion regarding the role of self-esteem in prejudice and discrimination (cf. Abrams & Hogg, 1988; Hogg & Abrams, 1990, for reviews). However, recent research on the self-concepts and motivational orientations of high and low self-esteem individuals has begun to yield a coherent and integrated picture of the cognitive and motivational consequences of self-esteem. We have recently outlined a framework that we believe can account for the widely divergent findings on the role of self-esteem in self-serving biases (cf. Blaine & Crocker, in press; Crocker & Blaine, 1992). This framework may also help to clear up inconsistencies within the literature on self-esteem and prejudice, as well as suggest directions for future research.

Personal self-esteem, the self-concept, and motivation

Research clearly indicates that high and low personal self-esteem persons differ in their self-concept content. Relative to low self-esteem individuals, people who are high in self-esteem tend to believe that positive attributes describe them and negative traits do not (cf. Marsh, 1986; Pelham & Swann, 1989), they are quite certain in these self-perceptions (cf. Baumgardner, 1990; Campbell, 1990; Campbell & Lavallee, in press), and they expect positive outcomes in the future (cf. Brockner, 1983; and Shrauger, 1972, for reviews). People who are low in self-esteem, on the other hand, appear to believe that they have a mix of positive and negative qualities (cf. Brown, 1986; Marsh, 1986; Pelham & Swann, 1989), they tend to be uncertain about just what attributes characterize them (Baumgardner, 1990; Campbell, 1990; Campbell & Lavallee, in press), and they are less likely to expect positive outcomes in the future (cf. Brockner, 1983; Shrauger, 1972; Taylor & Brown, 1988, for reviews). However, high and low self-esteem people do not differ in the attributes and outcomes that are important to them (Coopersmith, 1967; Harter, 1986; cf. Crocker & Blaine, 1992, for a review).

These aspects of the self-concept have effects both on the motivational orientations of high and low self-esteem individuals in intergroup contexts, and on the ways that self-relevant information is processed. Because they believe it is important to have positive attributes and important not to have negative attributes, both high and low self-esteem people *want* to believe the best of themselves, and are motivated to enhance the self, or interpret outcomes in ways that are flattering to the self (cf. Allport, 1937; Baumeister *et al.*, 1989; Brown, in press; McDougall, 1933; Shrauger, 1975). Thus, both high and low self-esteem people are motivated to engage in prejudice and discrimination when such behaviour could lead to a more positive self-view. However, because they differ in the positivity and certainty of their self-concepts, and their expectations for the future, self-enhancing judgements are not equally plausible to both high and low self-esteem people. These self-concept differences place constraints on the believability of self-serving judgements and guide interpretations of information by high and low self-esteem people, as well as on the public selves they can plausibly claim to others (cf. Baumeister *et al.*, 1989; Brown, in press; Shrauger, 1975).

Because of their positive and certain self-concepts, people who are high in self-esteem are relatively unconcerned with the remote possibility of failure or humiliation. For them, an evaluative situation is, first and foremost, an opportunity to enhance the self (cf. Baumeister *et al.*, 1989; Baumeister & Tice, 1985; Blaine & Crocker, in press; Crocker & Blaine, 1992). They are oriented towards seeking glory, success, and emphasizing their positive qualities rather than protecting against failure.

People who are low in self-esteem desire positive attributes as much as high self-esteem people do, yet are not sure they have them and do not expect success. Consequently, they see evaluative situations primarily as posing the threat of failure or humiliation. They are primarily oriented towards self-protection, avoiding confirmation of their possible negative selves (cf. Arkin, 1981; Baumeister *et al.*, 1989; Blaine & Crocker, in press; Crocker & Blaine, 1992; Markus & Nurius, 1986).

Collective self-esteem, the self-concept, and motivation

Just as people who are high in personal self-esteem have very positive and certain views of themselves, we suggest that people who are high in collective self-esteem have highly positive and certain views of their social groups. Although we have provided evidence that high collective self-esteem individuals have positive views of their groups (cf. Luhtanen & Crocker, 1991), to our knowledge the certainty of those views has not been assessed empirically. Nonetheless, extrapolating from the literature on personal self-esteem, this seems a plausible prediction.

Conversely, people who are low in collective self-esteem typically evaluate their groups less positively, and should be less certain about the attributes that characterize their groups. However, given the universal desire for positive regard from oneself and others (cf. Allport, 1937; McDougall, 1933), we suggest that both high and low collective self-esteem people want their groups to have positive attributes and to be regarded favourably by others.

The positive and certain concepts that high collective self-esteem people have of their social groups should lead them to view positive information about their group, and its status relative to other groups, as highly credible, and to interpret information about the ingroup in a favourable manner. Because low collective self-esteem people have less positive and certain concepts of their social groups, they should be less likely to interpret information about their group in a favourable way.

Just as people who are high in personal self-esteem are motivated to seek personal success, glory and self-enhancement, we suggest that people who are high in collective self-esteem are motivated to seek glory, success and enhancement for their ingroups. Furthermore, just as people who are low in personal self-esteem are motivated to be self-protective, avoiding personal failure and humiliation, we suggest that people who are low in collective self-esteem are motivated to protect their ingroups, avoiding group failure and humiliation.

Implications for prejudice

What are the implications of these self-concepts and motivational orientations for behaviour in group and intergroup contexts? We argue that these self-concepts and motivational orientations affect social comparisons with outgroups, the types of groups that high and low self-esteem people wish to affiliate with, their reactions to group success and failure, and their public presentations of themselves and their groups.

Social comparisons

According to social identity theory, prejudice, discrimination and derogation of outgroups are motivated by the desire to enhance the self through downward social comparisons (Tajfel & Turner, 1979). Actually, downward social comparisons may be either self-enhancing or self-protective. Self-enhancing social comparisons emphasize the positive aspects of the ingroups. Self-protective social comparisons guard against failure by emphasizing that outgroups are worse off.

Social comparisons can be measured in several ways (cf. Wood, 1989;

Wood & Taylor, 1991). Subjects may rate ingroup and outgroup members on evaluative attributes (cf. Crocker & Schwartz, 1985; Crocker *et al.*, 1987), indicating their social comparison beliefs. Alternatively, comparison information-seeking may be assessed. In these studies, subjects typically receive feedback about their own standing on some dimension, and are given the opportunity to compare their scores with those of others who scored better or worse than the subject (cf. Friend & Gilbert, 1973; Wilson & Benner, 1971; Smith & Insko, 1987). In yet further studies, subjects are given the opportunity to *create* downward comparison targets, making outgroups worse off than the ingroup by actively discriminating against them (cf. Hogg & Sunderland, 1991).

Research on prejudice and intergroup behaviour has focused on beliefs about how one's ingroup compares to outgroups, and on creating downward comparison targets by discriminating against outgroups. To our knowledge, no studies have explored social comparison information-seeking, despite the fact that information-seeking is a major focus of the social comparison literature. The distinction between comparison beliefs, comparison seeking and discrimination is important, because the effects of self-esteem on social comparison depend on the type of measure that is used (Gibbons & McCoy, 1991; Wood & Taylor, 1991; Wills, 1991).

Social comparison beliefs

Social comparison beliefs, or ratings of ingroups and outgroups on evaluative attributes, may tap enhancement and protection motivations, as well as cognitions about the self, ingroup and outgroup members. When people hold certain beliefs about the self and the ingroup, cognitions about ingroups and outgroups should be assimilated to those beliefs. Because people who are high in collective self-esteem have more positive and certain views of their ingroups than do low collective self-esteem people, they should be more likely to evaluate their ingroups favourably, relative to outgroups (see Crocker & Blaine, 1992, for a related discussion of personal self-esteem and social comparison beliefs). When group memberships have clear implications for personal identity, people who are high in personal self-esteem should also evaluate their ingroups more favourably than outgroups.

Research is generally consistent with these predictions. Although Crocker and Schwartz (1985) found that personal self-esteem was unrelated to the magnitude of ingroup bias in a minimal intergroup situation, Crocker *et al.* (1987) found that subjects who were high in personal self-esteem who were threatened with personal failure feedback showed ingroup bias on measures directly related to the threat (ratings of above- and below-average scorers), but low self-esteem subjects did not. In a parallel study, Crocker and Luhtanen (1990) found that subjects who were high in collective self-esteem responded to group failure feedback with ingroup bias directly related to the threat.

Brown and his colleagues (Brown, in press; Brown et al., 1988) have argued that people who are low in self-esteem are not self-enhancing in their social comparisons because their relatively negative self-concepts make such comparisons difficult to defend to the self and others (see also Wills, 1991). However, they suggested that low self-esteem individuals may make self-serving comparisons between their groups and others when those comparisons are only indirectly related to the self, and hence not constrained by their negative self-concepts (see also Brown, in press). In their study, high and low self-esteem subjects were divided into two groups on the basis of a perceptual style (overestimating v. underestimating), so that for each subject there was an ingroup and an outgroup. The ingroup and outgroup were further divided into two, so that there was a subgroup of the ingroup that subjects actually belonged to, and one that they didn't (subjects obviously belonged to neither outgroup). Each of the four groups then participated in a problem-solving task. Subjects then either rated their own group's solution (to which they had directly contributed) and an outgroup's solution, or they rated the solutions of the other ingroup (to which they had not directly contributed) and an outgroup.

High self-esteem subjects showed more ingroup favouritism (rating the ingroup's solution as better than the outgroup's) when the ingroup was also their own group, and they had directly contributed to the solution. Low self-esteem subjects, on the other hand, showed more ingroup favouritism when they rated the other ingroup's solution compared to an outgroup, and they had not contributed to the solution. In a subsequent study (Brown et al., 1988, experiment 2), this effect was replicated. In addition, the effect was found to be weaker when subjects received positive feedback prior to rating the group products, suggesting that enhancement of the ingroup may be motivated by the desire for positive affect, or self-enhancement.

The results of this study indicate that both high and low self-esteem subjects enhance the self through ingroup bias. However, concerns with the plausibility or believability of favourable comparisons between ingroups and outgroups appear to constrain self-enhancing social comparisons by low self-esteem people. When relevant beliefs about the self or the ingroup do not constrain judgements, then both high and low self-esteem people should show ingroup bias.

Such a situation may be created by the minimal intergroup paradigm, when subjects are divided into groups on a clearly arbitrary basis (cf. Locksley, Ortiz & Hepburn, 1980; Crocker & Schwartz, 1985), have no other relevant information about ingroups and outgroups (such as performance or status information) and are asked to rate their ingroup (excluding the self) and the outgroup. In this situation there are no self- or ingroup-relevant cognitions available to constrain self-enhancing or self-protective cognitions, so both high and low self-esteem people should be expected to engage in ingroup bias in this situation. Results of a study by Crocker and Schwartz (1985) are consistent with this prediction.

Ingroup bias may be both self- or ingroup-enhancing (by emphasizing the positive qualities of the self or the ingroup), and self- or ingroup-protective (by emphasizing that others are worse off). When the focus is on the difference between ingroup and outgroup ratings, self-enhancement motives cannot be distinguished from self-protection motives. However, we suggest that ingroup ratings reveal enhancement motives, whereas outgroup ratings reveal protection motives. Thus, people who are high in self-esteem, because they are oriented towards enhancement of the self or the ingroup, should be more likely to rate the ingroup positively, rather than derogate the outgroup. Low self-esteem people, on the other hand, should be more likely to derogate the outgroup, rather than enhance the ingroup. Such a pattern would yield more positive ratings of both the ingroup and the outgroup by high self-esteem individuals relative to low self-esteem individuals, when both high and low self-esteem people show ingroup bias. In fact, this general pattern has been observed (cf. Crocker & Schwartz, 1985; Crocker *et al.*, 1987; Crocker & Luhtanen, 1990). Unfortunately, this main effect of self-esteem on ratings of both ingroups and outgroups is also consistent with other interpretations, such as mood effects on ratings (Crocker & Schwartz, 1985). Future research might profitably explore this distinction between enhancement and protection as motives for ingroup bias.

Ingroup bias in allocations

Research on ingroup bias has consistently shown that people who are divided into groups will not only rate the ingroup more favourably than the outgroup on personality attributes, they also allocate resources or rewards in such a way as to maximize the difference between the ingroup and the outgroup (Tajfel, 1978b). This pattern of ingroup bias in allocations has been interpreted as an attempt to create a positive social identity by actually making the ingroup more advantaged than the outgroup, thus creating favourable comparisons between the ingroup and the outgroup (cf. Tajfel & Turner, 1979). Thus, according to social identity theory, ingroup bias in allocations essentially represents an attempt to manufacture downward comparisons with outgroups. Typically, reward allocations are interpreted as revealing the same processes as ratings of the ingroup and outgroup on attributes (cf. Abrams & Hogg, 1988; Hogg & Abrams, 1990). That is, more resources may be allocated to the ingroup than to the outgroup, because more positive qualities are attributed to the ingroup than to the outgroup. We argue, however, that reward allocations may more purely reflect the motivation for enhancement or protection of personal or social identity, because allocations of resources or rewards are less directly related to cognitions about the self and the ingroup, and hence less constrained by them.

Like ingroup bias in evaluative ratings, ingroup bias in reward allocations may be both enhancing and protective of the self and the ingroup. We suggest that allocating rewards to the ingroup is enhancing, because it creates positive distinctiveness for the ingroup, whereas withholding rewards from the outgroup is protective, because it ensures that some other group is worse off than one's own. Of course, maximizing the difference between ingroup and outgroup typically produces both enhancement and protection, and should be a strategy that is appealing to both high and low self-esteem individuals. If forced to choose between enhancement or protection, however, we would suggest that people who are high in self-esteem would be more enhancing, whereas people who are low in self-esteem would be more protective. To our knowledge, however, although researchers have investigated the role of self-esteem threats such as failure or low group status (cf. Hogg & Sunderland, 1991; Sachdev & Bourhis, 1985; 1987; Wagner et al., 1986), no published studies have examined the role of trait self-esteem as a predictor of reward allocations, and specifically whether subjects prefer an ingroup-enhancing or protective allocation strategy when forced to choose one over the other.

Choice of social comparisons

Within the social comparison literature, research has also examined the types of comparison targets that high and low self-esteem individuals *choose*. Selecting a downward comparison target is self-protective, because it indicates interest in others worse off than oneself and provides the opportunity to compare with them. Selecting upward comparison targets, on the other hand, may be self-enhancing, because it may provide information about how to improve one's own (or the ingroup's) performance (cf. Major, Testa & Bylsma, 1991). To our knowledge, research on prejudice and ingroup bias has not examined the choice of upward v. downward comparison targets as a dependent measure. However, such choices may be an interesting and relatively subtle indicator of prejudice.

Who are more likely to choose downward comparison targets, high or low self-esteem people? People who are low in self-esteem are more likely than those who are high in self-esteem to choose a comparison target who performed worse (see Wills, 1981; 1991; Wood & Taylor, 1991, for reviews). The tendency for high self-esteem people to choose others ranking higher in comparison to themselves than do low self-esteem people reflects the motivational orientations arising from high and low self-esteem self-concepts (Crocker & Blaine, 1992). Specifically, high self-esteem people are more oriented towards enhancing themselves and seeking success. Consequently, they may be more interested in obtaining information about how to improve their performance, especially following failure. Upward comparison targets should provide more useful informa- tion about improving one's own performance than downward compari- son targets. Low self-esteem people, on the other hand, are more oriented towards avoiding failure. When given the opportunity to choose a comparison target, they may be most concerned with proving that they are superior to *someone* than with learning how to excel in the future. Consequently they are more likely to select a worse-off target. Because high self-esteem individuals are already confident in their superiority, they may be less motivated to seek information about their superiority to a worse-off outgroup.

The differing cognitions about the self and the ingroup, and the motivational orientations of high and low self-esteem people, may have implications for other types of intergroup behaviour as well. Although group affiliations, reactions to group success and failure, and public self-presentations have been studied less within the intergroup literature, and particularly with reference to self-esteem differences, we believe that extending research into these areas may prove interesting and fruitful.

Group affiliations

One of the most powerful effects of individual differences on social behaviour may lie in the kinds of situations that different types of people select for themselves (Snyder & Ickes, 1985). In intergroup contexts, choosing situations may involve choosing groups with which to affiliate or identify. Of course, some group memberships, such as one's gender and ethnic groups, are ascribed rather than acquired, and typically involve little choice. Many group memberships, however, are achieved – i.e., individuals actively choose to affiliate with those groups. The choice of which groups to affiliate or identify with, and which groups to avoid, may be a crucial way in which people's prejudices reveal themselves. People may identify with or seek membership in those groups they admire, and avoid identifying or affiliating with those groups they dislike. Yet, to our knowledge, this aspect of group behaviour has been neglected in the study of prejudice.

When people have a choice about which groups to affiliate or identify with, they typically choose upward or high-status groups (Ellemers, van Knippenberg, de Vries & Wilke, 1988; Ellemers, van Knippenberg &

Wilke, 1990; Snyder, Lassegard & Ford, 1986; see van Knippenberg, 1989, for a review; also see Chapter 2, this volume). Affiliation with higher-status groups may reflect both self-enhancement and self-protection concerns. That is, by affiliating or identifying with higher-status groups, people may be both avoiding the possible failure and humiliation associated with membership in a low-status group, and seeking the glory and prestige of affiliating with a high-status group. When these two motives can be separated, we suggest that people who are high in self-esteem, because they are more oriented towards self-enhancement, are motivated to *seek* affiliation and identification with high-status groups, while people who are low in self-esteem, because they are more oriented towards self-protection, are motivated to *avoid* affiliating or identifying with low-status, unsuccessful or stigmatized groups. For example, people high in self-esteem may be most concerned with joining the highest-status sororities on their campus, or the most exclusive private clubs, because such group memberships enhance their identities. People low in self-esteem, on the other hand, may be more concerned about avoiding any connections with low-status sororities or groups that are scorned by others, because such group memberships threaten to confirm their relatively negative and uncertain identities.

Because membership in many social groups has implications for both social identity and personal identity, we suspect that the choice of affiliating with groups is influenced by both personal and collective self-esteem. However, some group memberships or identifications may have relatively few implications for one's personal abilities. For example, Cialdini and his colleagues have shown that people tend to bask in the reflected glory of their school's winning football team, by wearing clothing that identifies them with their school, and using first-person pronouns to describe the team's performance (e.g. 'we won', but 'they lost': Cialdini, Borden, Thorne, Walker, Freeman & Sloan, 1976). A win by one's school team does not imply that all students at the school are high in football skills, so what is enhanced in this situation is one's *social* identity, not *personal* identity. In this case, collective self-esteem should predict basking in reflected glory.

On the other hand, some group memberships have direct implications for one's personal identity. Being admitted to a highly selective college, for example, implies that one has an outstanding academic record. Where personal identity is strongly implicated by affiliating with particular groups, then personal self-esteem should predict self-enhancing versus self-protective ingroup choices.

Reactions to ingroup success and failure

Success or failure by the ingroup also has implications for self-esteem. People are not merely passive receptacles for information about their group's performance. Rather, they actively interpret and react to this information. For example, people tend to attribute positive behaviours, outcomes and successes by the ingroup to internal factors, and discount or explain away negative behaviours, outcomes and failures by the ingroup, whereas their attributions are less flattering when these events happen to an outgroup (cf. Hewstone, 1990, for a review). People may have both affective and cognitive reactions to their group's performance.

Is self-esteem related to how people react to group feedback? We have argued that cognitive reactions to personal feedback are determined by the positivity and certainty of the self-concept. The more positive and certain the self-concept, the more people tend to distort feedback in a positive direction, remember positive feedback better than negative feedback, attribute positive outcomes to internal factors and negative outcomes to external factors, and find positive feedback more credible than negative feedback (cf. Blaine & Crocker, in press; Crocker & Blaine, 1992). Analogously, cognitive reactions to feedback about one's group should be determined by the positivity and certainty of one's concept of the group.

Because they have highly positive and relatively certain views of their social groups, we predict that people who are high in collective self-esteem will show similar cognitive reactions to feedback about their group. Specifically, people who are high in collective self-esteem should interpret feedback through the positive filter of their beliefs about their groups, distorting information in a positive direction. They should remember positive feedback better than negative feedback; attribute positive group outcomes to their group's positive attributes, and negative outcomes to external causes (including blaming other groups); and find positive feedback about their group more credible than negative feedback. Because their concepts of their groups are less positive and less certain, people who are low in collective self-esteem should be less biased in their cognitive responses to group feedback.

Affective or emotional reactions to group feedback, on the other hand, should be determined by the positivity of the feedback and the import-ance the individual places on the group having that attribute. Assuming that it is equally important to them that their groups have positive attributes, and not have negative attributes, both high and low collective self-esteem people should react to group success with positive affect, and group failure with negative affect. Indeed, Crocker and Luhtanen (1990) gave subjects high and low in collective self-esteem feedback that their group had either succeeded or failed at a task, and found that both high and low collective self-esteem individuals were more satisfied with their group's score when their group had succeeded, and wished that their group had scored better when their group had failed.

Presenting the ingroup to others

The desire to have important positive attributes and not have negative attributes that characterizes both high and low self-esteem people also extends to the desire to have others see oneself in a positive light (Arkin, 1981; Baumeister, 1986; Schlenker, 1980). The desire for a positive image may extend to desiring a positive public image for one's groups (cf. Abrams & Hogg, 1988). Consequently, both high and low self-esteem people may be motivated to present their ingroup in a favourable way, and claim desirable social identities, in public. However, people who claim to have positive attributes in public run the risk that their claims will be rejected by others, or disproven in the future. As a result, public self-presentations may be constrained by what one feels one can *plausibly* claim. High collective self-esteem people, who have highly positive and certain views of their ingroups, may believe that most positive claims about the ingroup can be justified and supported, and are unlikely to be disproven in the future. Low self-esteem people, on the other hand, are less positive and less certain about their ingroups, and may consequently be more concerned about the possibility of public humiliation should their claims about the ingroup be too positive. As a result, they may be less likely to present the ingroup in a positive light in public settings, particularly when an audience might disbelieve or disprove those public claims (cf. Baumeister *et al.*, 1989).

Claims about outgroups may also be constrained by what is plausible or defensible to the others (as well as to the self). Thus, highly successful outgroups will seldom be rated in uniformly negative ways. However, even successful outgroups may be derogated in areas unrelated to their success, where negative evaluations are not obviously contradicted by evidence. Because claims about outgroups are not constrained by what one believes about one's own group, high and low collective self-esteem people may find it equally plausible (or implausible) to derogate outgroups. However, if negative claims about outgroups primarily serve self-protective functions, people who are low in collective self-esteem should be more likely to make such claims in public.

We are not suggesting that all prejudice and ingroup bias represents public claims that are not privately believed. Rather, consistent with the self-presentation literature (cf. Crocker & Blaine, 1992), we suggest that self-presentation concerns may contribute to positive claims about the self, or negative claims about outgroups, in some circumstances. The tendency to enhance or protect the ingroup in public has its origins in the same motivational concerns with enhancement and protection as does private behaviour.

Conclusions

Although the idea that prejudice and discrimination have their origins in concerns with self-enhancement and protection has been around for decades, empirical research on this topic has been scant and has yielded contradictory results. We have argued that the effects of trait self-esteem on intergroup behaviour depend on what aspect of the self is salient or threatened in a particular situation: personal or collective self-esteem.

We have argued that people who are high and low in self-esteem differ both in their cognitions about the self and ingroups, and in their motivational orientations. Although both high and low self-esteem people are concerned with self-esteem, high self-esteem individuals are primarily concerned with enhancing the self, whereas low self-esteem people are primarily concerned with protecting the self from possible failure or humiliation. These different motivational orientations, we have argued, have consequences for social comparisons with outgroups, choice of groups with which to affiliate or identify, affective and cognitive reactions to group outcomes, and public claims that people make about their groups.

Although the cognitive and motivational consequences of self-esteem have been well documented in the realm of personal identity, the extension of these findings to social or collective identity is admittedly somewhat speculative. Nonetheless, we believe that a consideration of both the relevant cognitions and the motivational orientations of high and low self-esteem people may be heuristically useful in at least two respects. First, it may lend some coherence to the contradictory and confusing literature on the role of trait self-esteem in prejudice and intergroup behaviour. Second, it suggests intriguing directions for future research.

5 Freezing intergroup evaluations: Anxiety fosters resistance to counterstereotypic information

David A. Wilder

As reason is a Rebel unto Faith, so Passion unto Reason
Sir Thomas Browne, Religio Medici ɪ, xix.

The heart has its reasons, which reason cannot know
Pascal, Pensées.

And reason panders will
Shakespeare, Hamlet ɪɪɪ, iv.

Each of the quotations above shares the theme that our rational beliefs ('reason'), feelings ('passion', 'heart') and motives ('will') may not accurately reflect one another. Browne and Shakespeare imply that affect and motives can distort and control our thoughts. Pascal suggests that rational thought may never be able to explain our feelings. None of these misgivings about the unity of our 'minds' surprises the jaded psychologist who has suffered the indignities of studying subject matter that refuses to sit still on the laboratory table and act predictably. The lack of correspondence between what people say and what they actually do is legendary in our field (e.g. Ajzen, 1982). So too is the ability of persons to mask their thoughts, feelings and motives from others and even from themselves (e.g. Festinger, 1957; Goffman, 1967; Orne, 1962).

Social motivations

Despite frequent inconsistencies among beliefs, affect and behaviour, social psychologists and lay persons alike believe that people should display consistency among those three constructs. In social psychology the assumption that people are motivated to achieve and maintain consistency among thoughts, feelings and actions is well illustrated by the many cognitive consistency theories that arose in the 1960s (e.g. Abelson, Aronson, McGuire, Newcomb, Rosenberg & Tannenbaum, 1968). Most of these derived from either Heider's (1958) balance model or Festinger's (1957) theory of cognitive dissonance.

A second motivation that many social psychologists would agree on is the desire to maximize rewards. This is a direct application of basic principles of conditioning to social behaviour. However, the desire to maximize one's outcomes often conflicts with the same motive in others. To minimize conflict, societies have developed rules that regulate the exchange of rewards and punishments. This is the crux of social exchange theory and the concepts of distributive justice, fairness and equity which are acquired algorithms to determine satisfaction in a relationship (Blau, 1964; Homans, 1961; Thibaut & Kelley, 1959; Walster, Walster & Berscheid, 1978).

A third motivation is to create and maintain a positive self-image or positive self-identity. In social settings that can be achieved by the acquisition of a positive identity for groups that we are associated with or with whom we identify (social identity theory: Tajfel & Turner, 1979, 1986). In-group favouritism at the expense of outgroups can be a result of the quest for a positive social self.

These three motivations are certainly not independent of one another. If, for example, one possesses a positive self-concept, then information consistent with that belief is likely to be preferred and behaviour that reinforces that belief should be enacted. Nevertheless, these motivations parallel the three kinds of outcomes that social psychologists study: affect, cognition and behaviour. Desire for a positive social identity is manifested largely through affective evaluations. Desire for consistency among beliefs is cognitively based. Finally, desire to maximize material outcomes is revealed largely in our actions. Another way of putting this is to say that motivations for positive social identity, cognitive consistency and rewards are manifested in the domains of affect, cognition and behaviour, respectively.

To these three motives a fourth will be added that reflects reactions to strong demands such as those imposed when persons are highly aroused. This is a need to reduce high levels of stimulation. (See, for example, Berlyne's (1971) work on levels of arousal and affect or the older, classic work by Yerkes & Dodson (1908) on arousal and performance.) To do so, simplifications may be made in social perception and judgements. These simplifications can encourage a structural inertia characterized by rigid adherence to existing cognitive structures and habits (Kahneman, 1973). Consequently, when we are aroused, schema-discrepant information may be especially vulnerable to distortion or discounting. This prediction can be derived from several well-established lines of reasoning. For example, the social facilitation literature has consistently shown that arousal facilitates the performance of well-learned or dominant responses while inhibiting the acquisition of novel responses (e.g. Allport, 1920; Zajonc, 1965). From a different perspective, cognitive psychologists have argued that arousal can interfere with performance by consuming precious degrees of attentional freedom. Distracted by increased arousal, persons are less adept at monitoring the external world (e.g. Easterbrook, 1959; Kahneman, 1973) and may be more likely to freeze their cognitive structures and resist new, discrepant information (Anderson, 1983; Anderson & Sechler, 1986; Kahneman & Tversky, 1973). Recall Piaget's (1952) classic contention that we first attempt to assimilate discrepant or novel information to existing cognitive structures. Only if assimilation fails do we modify our schemata.

Combining these literatures yields the central thesis of this chapter: arousal induced by anxiety fosters reliance on existing beliefs and evaluations of outgroups. When persons are anxious, information that appears to disconfirm opinions and stereotypes of an outgroup will have less impact than when persons are not so aroused (anxiety-assimilation hypothesis). The following sections consider the issue of when stereotypes are likely to be used as well as evidence that heightened arousal facilitates stereotyping. Subsequent sections focus on the effect of subjective anxiety on the impact of counterstereotypic information. Finally, implications are drawn for the role of anxiety in contact situations involving members of antagonistic groups.

Stereotypes and stereotype change

Social stereotypes are beliefs persons have about the attributes of members of social groups (e.g. Ashmore & DelBoca, 1981; Hamilton, 1979). The content of these beliefs generally includes personality traits, physical characteristics, values and habits. While stereotypes may come in all sorts of shapes and sizes, those that are of concern in this chapter satisfy two minimum requirements. First, to be called an outgroup stereotype, the belief must be applicable to a significant number of the target group. Second, the belief must be shared by others, but not necessarily everyone, in one's ingroup.

Research on stereotypes has addressed four questions: What is the content of stereotypes about a particular group? How are stereotypes formed? How are they changed? When are they likely to be used? The latter two questions are of most concern in this chapter – specifically the influence of an individual's affective state on the use of stereotypes and their susceptibility to change in response to disconfirming information.

Use of stereotypes

One way of addressing the issue of when stereotypes are likely to be employed is to distinguish between active, conscious decisions to rely on a stereotype versus non-conscious, subtle usage. Recent work by Devine (1989) exemplifies the latter. In her research, some subjects were exposed to stereotype-related words at durations below conscious recognition. When compared to control subjects, they interpreted a target's ambiguous behaviour in a manner consistent with the stereotype. Thus, cueing of stereotypes appeared to have been automatic and nonconscious. However, when stereotype-relevant cues were made obvious, subjects actively inhibited their responses so as not to appear biased.

At the other extreme, when little information is available about persons, other than one or more social groups to which they belong, we are likely to consider stereotypes in a more conscious way as we attempt to make our best guesses about them. Again, we may not want to admit it publicly, but we will be likely at least to consider the stereotype in predicting and analyzing another's actions.

We are also likely to employ stereotypes, particularly unfavourable stereotypes of outgroups, to justify discrimination and/or to make us feel better about ourselves. Justification of actions helps to maintain a positive social identity.

Finally, we are likely to employ stereotypes when there are cues that cause us to define ourselves as belonging to the complementary ingroup to the outgroup that contains the stereotype in question. Arguing from social categorization and identity theories (Tajfel, 1982b; Turner, 1984; Turner, Hogg, Oakes, Reicher & Wetherell, 1987), one's identity as a member of a social group should be particularly salient when fellow ingroup members are present to cue that identity. Salience of an ingroup identity encourages the categorization of others into ingroups and outgroups relevant to that identity. That, in turn, should make salient beliefs about those groups, including stereotypes, which can influence judgements of those others. Wilder and Shapiro (1992) reported that subjects were more likely to make stereotypic judgements of a stimulus person when their ingroup identity had been made salient by the presence of other ingroup members. In their studies stereotypes of an outgroup were created by exposing subjects to several representative members of a fictitious outgroup who possessed some common traits. Then subjects viewed information about another outgroup member who violated those expectations. Evaluations of him were more in agreement with outgroup stereotypes when subjects viewed the deviant in the presence of other ingroup members than when they were in the presence of others who did not belong to the ingroup or outgroup or when they were alone.

Changing stereotypes

Much of the research on changing stereotypes has approached this subject from the perspective of cognitive consistency motives and information integration (e.g. Hewstone, Johnston & Aird, 1992). Whether obtained first hand through direct experience or second hand by observing videotapes or reading about others, information that disconfirms a social stereotype either forces some modification of the belief, or the information is dismissed as deficient in some manner. Presumably, credible information causes modification of the stereotype to maintain an accurate and consistent belief structure.

Following Rothbart (1981), Weber and Crocker (1983) tested three models of stereotype change in a series of experiments with college students. According to the conversion model, instances that disconfirm a stereotype are more effective when they are extreme; slight discrepancies from the stereotype have little impact. According to the bookkeeping model, stereotype change occurs through the accumulation of counter-stereotypic instances; thus, the number of disconfirmations is critical. According to the subtyping model, counterstereotypic instances do not directly change stereotypes; rather, they create subcategories to accommodate the exceptions. Change in the stereotype occurs if the number of subtypes accumulates and renders the stereotype useless as a diagnostic tool.

The Weber and Crocker experiments generated some support for each of the models, with the lion's share claimed by the bookkeeping and subtyping hypotheses. Gurwitz and Dodge (1977), however, reported outcomes in line with the conversion model. In experiments such as these, the procedures have been contrived so that subjects respond only to the manipulation of counterstereotypic information before them. Arousal generated by an affective response to the material is neither encouraged nor assessed. On the contrary, the procedures encourage subjects to play the role of a 'cold' processor of information. Thus, subjects either view or read about members of a social category (e.g. occupation or fraternity/sorority). The experiments then manipulate the degree to which the stimulus material disconfirms outgroup stereotypes. Subjects' judgements are then compared with their pre-test data or results from a comparison sample of others.

While appreciating the contributions of these efforts, it should be noted that their restricted methodology raises some concern about generalizability. Presenting subjects with discrepant information about social categories and then asking them to make judgements about those categories can cue subjects to the purpose of the experiment. Although they may not be aware of the specific independent variable (e.g. number of disconfirmations, extremity of disconfirmations, number of target groups), surely subjects are aware that their opinions of those social groups are being assessed after exposure to relevant information. One might well expect subjects to experience some evaluation apprehension or, at minimum, a concern to present a positive impression. In addition, subjects are instructed to digest passively the information listed on their *prix fixe* menu. To minimize 'error', they are asked to attend only to the information presented to them.

In natural settings, however, persons often find themselves in a different set of circumstances. When engaged in direct contact with an outgroup, they may very well assume a more active role in the selection of stimuli and performance of tasks. Information relevant to outgroup stereotypes may be incidental to, rather than the focus of, the task. Thus, persons may not actively consider the stereotypically relevant information unless it is cued by the task. If attention is not drawn explicitly to the stereotype, there is no need to force a resolution – either integration of the counterstereotypic information and some change in the stereotype or rejection of the discrepant examples. Rather than dealing with counter-stereotypic information to satisfy a motive for cognitive consistency, natural situations are more likely to be guided by 'hotter' self-identity concerns.

Social categorization and identity theorists have argued that people desire and act to maintain a positive social identity (Hogg & Abrams, 1990; Tajfel & Turner, 1979; Turner et al., 1987).[1] Moreover, as mentioned at the outset of this chapter, arousal encourages dependence on well-established schemata. Combining these points yields the anxiety-assimilation hypothesis. Anxiety increases the assimilation of external stimuli to existing cognitive schemata. This effect should be even stronger when the new information threatens one's positive identity. Put in the context of intergroup relations, information that runs counter to expectations or stereotypes of an outgroup will be assimilated to the stereotype when persons are anxious. Thus, counterstereotypic behaviour by an outgroup member will have less impact when subjects are aroused by anxiety than when they are relatively calm.

In a series of experiments Warren Cooper, Peter Shapiro, John Thompson and I have found that anxiety lessens the impact of counter-stereotypic information (Wilder, Cooper & Thompson, 1981; Wilder & Shapiro, 1989a; 1989b). In those experiments subjects were given information that led them to expect certain behaviours in a group they were to observe. They also observed one group member behave in a counter-stereotypic manner. Overall, when subjects were anxious, they reported the deviant outgroup member's actions to be more similar to the majority (i.e., less counterstereotypic) than when they were not anxious. Before plunging into our research programme, let us briefly review a growing body of research that indicates a relationship between emotional arousal and stereotyping.

We embarked on these experiments because of our interest in the question of when favourable contact with members of an outgroup would be effective in promoting intergroup harmony. As researchers have noted across several decades, contact effectively reduces bias under limited conditions (e.g. Allport, 1954; Amir, 1969; 1976; Cook, 1984; Pettigrew, 1986). These include co-operative interaction in pursuit of a common goal, equal-status relationships in the contact setting, institutional support for the contact, and relatively intimate as opposed to superficial interaction. When one or more of these criteria are satisfied, the contact experience may yield a more favourable evaluation of those outgroup members. However, there is no guarantee that successful contact will generalize to evaluations of the outgroup as a whole. As Pettigrew (1986) and others (Miller & Brewer, 1984; Hewstone & Brown, 1986; Wilder, 1986) have noted, a central problem for the contact hypothesis is how to encourage generalization from a specific positive instance to the entire outgroup.

A facile way of responding to a pleasant encounter with a small subset of a disliked outgroup is to dismiss the episode as an atypical instance, an exception to the rule. Discounting of positive contact can be readily justified if one concludes that the contact persons are atypical or unrepresentative of others in the outgroup. Discounting may also occur if there is evidence that their positive actions reflect some aberration that deflects them from their true dispositions, such as strong social pressure to act positively in that situation. (This point will be discussed in more detail towards the end of this chapter.)

Emotional arousal and stereotyping

In addition to the conditions mentioned above, some recent research suggests a relationship between heightened arousal and the use of stereotypes. An increase in arousal can overload or distract us so that we rely more heavily on well-established, dominant schemata including stereotypes. For example, Kim and Baron (1988) reported that arousal can enhance reliance on stereotypes. They reported that arousal induced by exercise led to increased stereotyping in an illusory correlation paradigm (Hamilton & Rose, 1980). Subjects viewed word pairs at different frequencies of presentation. Aroused subjects had better recall for word pairs composed of stereotypically associated words even though those pairs did not occur more often than non-stereotypic pairs. In agreement with other work on the relationship between arousal and information-processing, their research suggests that heightened arousal can decrease cognitive capacity and increase reliance on already acquired expectations and response strategies (e.g. Broadbent, 1971; Easterbrook, 1959; Hasher & Zacks, 1979).

Turning to instances of specific emotional arousal, results of several investigations indicate that anxiety can disrupt performance and decrease careful rumination. For instance, Darke (1988) reported that anxiety reduces both the storage and processing capacities of working memory. Gur, Gur, Skolnick, Resnick, Silver, Chawluk, Muenz, Obrist and Reivich (1988) have offered some supportive physiological data. They found that high levels of anxiety were correlated with reduced performance and reduced cerebral blood flow.

Effects of sadness on information-processing are variable (Bodenhausen, in press). If sadness discourages or distracts from thought, then we are likely to rely on habits or well-learned schemata. For example, Ellis and Ashbrook (1988) reported impaired memory performance when subjects were in a depressed mood state. On the other hand, other researchers have concluded that sadness can induce a more careful, considered response (e.g. Gotlib, McLachlan & Katz, 1988; Sinclair, 1988). For instance, Bless, Bohner, Schwarz and Strack (1990) reported that sad subjects attended to a persuasive message more carefully and processed it more systematically than did control subjects.

Similar to the sadness literature, some studies have shown that happiness promotes superficial processing (Clark, 1982) while others have demonstrated that the happy subject attends more closely and makes careful judgements (Forgas, 1989). Bodenhausen (in press) has noted that a critical determinant of the effect of happiness may be how the quality of our judgement affects our welfare. If the judgement has ramifications for our welfare, a happy mood appears to make us more careful and deliberate. But if the judgement lacks personalism, we are more likely to be careless in our attention, content perhaps to bob in the joy of our buoyant mood.

A few studies have directly examined the relationship between affect and stereotyping. Using excerpts from films, Mackie, Hamilton, Schroth, Carlisle, Gersho, Meneses, Nedler and Reichel (1989) induced happiness or sadness in subjects. Happy subjects showed more evidence of stereotyping on an illusory correlation task than did control (neutral) subjects, but only for negative group attributes.

Bodenhausen and Kramer (1990) asked subjects to recall events that were either happy, sad or angry as a means of creating affective arousal. The subjects read cases of a student accused of cheating or assault and who either did or did not fit subjects' expectations for that action. Happy and angry subjects rated the stereotypic defendant as more likely to be guilty than subjects in the control condition.

Gilbert and Hixon (1991) examined the relationship between stereotyping and cognitive overload by manipulating how cognitively active their subjects were. Subjects who were made 'busy' following activation of a set of stereotypes were more likely to rely on those stereotypes in the interpretation and recall of a target's behaviour. However, being 'busy' before the stereotypes were salient inhibited their influence because the augmented cognitive activity interfered with initial activation of the stereotypes. Subjects in their research made a series of judgements in the presence of either a Caucasian or Asian experimenter. When subjects had to attend to multiple tasks at the outset ('busy' condition), they were not likely to stereotype the Asian experimenter. However, they were more likely to stereotype her when they were overloaded with task demands later in the experiment, after they had categorized the Asian experimenter.

Baron, Burgess, Kao and Logan (1990) reported a relationship between anxiety and superficial processing of information. Subjects in their first experiment who were anxious while waiting for dental work exhibited pronounced illusory correlation effects. They significantly overestimated the number of associations between stereotypic traits and members of the corresponding occupational group. In a second experiment subjects rated the strength of a persuasive message. The authors constructed a weak message but presented it forcefully with interruptions from an applauding audience. A person who carefully examined the message would judge it to be weak and unpersuasive. However, a person who focused on superficial cues such as presentation style and audience reaction would find the message convincing. Prior to evaluating the message, subjects were exposed to a description of dental procedures that were designed to generate relatively high or low fear. Subjects in the high fear condition judged the message to be more persuasive than those in the low fear condition.

Overall, the studies reviewed above suggest that emotional arousal influences the use of cognitive schemata and stereotypes to the extent that the arousal interferes with careful attention to the external field. In addition, valence of the affect should be important because it cues similarly valenced cognitions and schemata. Negative stereotypes may become more salient to a person who has experienced negative affect whereas positive affect should stimulate more pleasant cognitions. Some research indicates a consistency of affective cueing such that positive mood induces positive thoughts while negative mood encourages negative thoughts (Clark, Milberg & Erber, 1984; Isen, 1987; Isen & Levin, 1972).

In an intergroup context, anxiety should cue negative stereotypes of the outgroup. Information consistent with those negative expectations may receive preferential processing while inconsistent information (e.g. instances of counterstereotypic behaviour) has diminished impact as we rely on the salient stereotypes to structure our judgements in response to the demands created by the heightened arousal. This thesis is developed more fully in the next section and becomes the focus for the remainder of the chapter.

Anxiety and stereotype change

Effects of anxiety on information-processing reviewed above suggest a reason why positive contact with a few outgroup members frequently does not significantly alter negative stereotypes and attitudes towards the outgroup. The prospect of contact with a disliked outgroup generates anxiety (as well as other emotions that may include disgust, loathing, fear and anger). Anxiety can increase arousal and interfere with the processing of information about the contact experience. Anxiety can distract persons and encourage them to misperceive the actions of a favourable contact member in a manner more consistent with prevailing stereotypes of the outgroup and with the negative affect being experienced in the contact setting (anxiety-assimilation hypothesis). Thus, anxious perceivers should underestimate the degree to which a counterstereotypic outgroup member has challenged their negative beliefs about the outgroup. As mentioned above, this can come about by two separate yet complementary means. Anxiety may distract persons so that they process actions of the favourable outgroup member less completely or accurately. Ambiguities and gaps in information are resolved by reliance on existing outgroup stereotypes. In addition, anxiety may cue similarly valenced, negative beliefs and increase sensitivity to evidence that fits with negative outgroup stereotypes. These effects should be accentuated when a positive outgroup member is viewed in a predominantly negative context: for instance, when a favourable outgroup member is surrounded by other members who reinforce the negative stereotypes of the group.

Anxiety-assimilation experiments

In the first set of experiments in this research programme, small groups of subjects participated in an alleged investigation of communication between groups (Wilder, in press; Wilder & Shapiro, 1989a). They were given a problem to work on and sent their solution to another group situated in an adjacent room. Actually there was no outgroup: subjects received feedback from the experimenter. We manipulated subjects' level of anxiety by making the relationship between the ingroup and outgroup either a co-operative or competitive one. In the co-operative condition the cover story stated that their success was dependent on the joint outcome of the ingroup and outgroup. The pair of groups from a single session with the best combined effort would receive the highest score and a joint prize. Subjects were told to expect critical feedback as the outgroup would be interested in providing constructive criticism. However, in the competitive condition subjects were led to believe that the group in each session that did best would be eligible for a prize. Each group could benefit only at the expense of the other, so subjects expected the relationship with the outgroup to be relatively acrimonious. Subjects in the competitive condition reported feeling more uncomfortable during the experiment than did subjects in the co-operative condition.

After the relationship between the groups had been established, subjects worked on a second task that required them to assemble information and make a recommendation for an urban transportation system. Their recommendation was sent to the outgroup for its reaction. In all conditions subjects received identical feedback from the outgroup. Three of the four outgroup members gave critical, negative reactions while one member responded favourably. After receiving this feedback, subjects expected a face-to-face interaction with members of the outgroup to discuss their solution and any revisions they chose to make. At this point subjects completed the dependent measures. We were particularly interested in how subjects would perceive and respond to the positive outgroup member who had offered a favourable evaluation of the ingroup product when other outgroup members responded in the anticipated negative manner.

Reaction to the positive outgroup member was significantly affected by the co-operation/competition manipulation. When subjects expected to compete with the outgroup, they underestimated the favourableness of his comments, remembered less information that differentiated him from the others, and were more prone to make errors in assigning some of the negative comments to him that were actually made by the other outgroup members. Moreover, subjects' self-reports of discomfort were significantly correlated with the primary dependent variables. The more anxious subjects reported themselves to be during the experiment, the less positively they evaluated the favourable outgroup member, the less constructive they found his comments to be, the more similar they judged him to be to the outgroup majority, and the more errors they made in recall of his actions. When anxiety was used as a covariate in analyses of covariance, differences between the co-operative and competitive conditions were significantly reduced or eliminated on the main dependent measures.

In a follow-up experiment anxiety was manipulated using the same paradigm (Wilder & Shapiro, 1989a). In addition, for some subjects in the competitive condition there was an attempt made to lessen anxiety prior to receiving the predominantly negative feedback from the outgroup.

These subjects were exposed to humorous cartoons before receiving outgroup evaluations of the ingroup solution. Otherwise this condition was identical to the standard competitive condition. As reported in the first experiment, when expecting competition, subjects experienced more discomfort at the prospect of interacting with the outgroup and evaluated the positive comments from a favourable outgroup member more negatively and more like the unfavourable majority than did subjects in the co-operative condition. However, when subjects in the competitive condition viewed the amusing cartoons prior to receiving the outgroup comments, they behaved like subjects in the co-operative condition. Subjects in the 'relaxed' competitive condition felt less discomfort and rated the favourable outgroup member more positively and more accurately than subjects in the standard competitive condition.

Overall, findings from these experiments provide evidence for a link between anxiety and perception of outgroup members. Using both direct manipulations of anxiety and correlational analyses, anxiety was shown to be a causal agent in determining the effectiveness of disconfirming information on judgements of an outgroup member. When outgroup behaviour contradicted expectations and subjects were anxious, they biased judgements and recall in the direction of the expected negative behaviour. In short, they assimilated the deviant outgroup member in the direction of how he 'should' have acted.

A second set of experiments addressed the question of whether the anxiety-assimilation finding would also occur when expectations about the outgroup were positive and the deviant behaved in a negative manner (Wilder & Shapiro, 1989b). Moreover, we wanted to see if the effects observed in the first series of experiments would generalize to other operationalizations of anxiety. In the first series of experiments described above, anxiety was created at the prospect of a hostile encounter with an unfavourable, disliked outgroup. In the follow-up experiments described in Wilder and Shapiro (1989b), anxiety was manipulated by threatening subjects with the prospect of either performing an embarrassing task or receiving electric shocks.

To sketch the procedure briefly, subjects viewed a videotape of four members of a mock jury deliberating a case. Three members of the jury behaved in a competent manner while one member (deviant) behaved incompetently and was unsure of himself. (To test for generalizability, behaviour patterns were reversed in one experiment of this series. In that study the majority of the group behaved incompetently while the deviant appeared to be competent.) Prior to observing the stimulus persons, subjects' levels of anxiety were manipulated by leading them to anticipate that they would be performing an embarrassing act (i.e., make a speech about their bodies or pose for pictures in infant attire) or experiencing shocks later in the experiment. The pattern of outcomes was essentially the same regardless of anxiety manipulation. When subjects were made anxious, they distorted their judgements of the deviant group member in the direction of the expectation created by the majority's actions. Thus, anxious subjects underestimated the incompetence (or competence) of the deviant when the majority behaved in a highly competent (or incompetent) manner. As with the first series of studies (Wilder & Shapiro, 1989a), when subjects were anxious, they assimilated judgements of the deviant in the direction of the majority. Furthermore, compared to calm subjects, anxious ones reported thinking more about their feelings and the anticipated anxiety-provoking task while viewing the outgroup. Biased judgements of the deviant group member in the direction of outgroup expectations were significantly correlated with self-reports of anxiety and self-reports of time spent thinking about their feelings and the upcoming noxious task. These findings suggest that anxiety distracted subjects from careful observation and integration of information about the deviant outgroup member. Apparently, they relied on their general beliefs about the outgroup (generated by the majority's actions) to fill in gaps in information about the deviant.

Limitation of the anxiety-assimilation hypothesis

In all of the experiments in our research programme, anxiety has fostered an assimilation of judgements of a deviant group member in the direction of the majority's actual or presumed behaviour. However, the opposite pattern of outcomes might be expected if anxiety limits the field of judgement by narrowing a person's attention span. If persons focus more closely on the deviant when anxious, judgements of the deviant member might well be polarized and differences between the deviant and the majority accentuated. Note, though, that subjects in our studies were told to observe the outgroup as a whole. If we had encouraged them to focus initially on the deviant member, narrowing of attention induced by anxiety may have prompted them to focus all the more on the deviant with the result that differences from the majority would have been accentuated. Anxiety might also lead to polarization if deviants appear so atypical of the outgroup that they draw attention to themselves at the outset of the interaction before the majority can establish normative behaviour. Furthermore, if the deviants are portrayed to be members of a different outgroup than the majority, anxiety should not foster assimilation to the majority. If categorized into mutually exclusive groups, the perceiver should accentuate differences between the deviants and the majority when anxious and prone to make simplistic judgements.

We tested these predictions in a set of studies (Wilder & Shapiro, 1992) employing the procedures from some of our earlier experiments (Wilder et al., 1981; Wilder & Shapiro, 1989b). Anxiety was created by giving some subjects the expectation that they would be making an embarrassing speech about themselves to an audience of peers. Subjects then viewed a group of confederates discussing a legal case. Some subjects were instructed to focus on the deviant outgroup member; others were asked to attend to the group as a whole; and a control group was given no explicit instructions on where to focus attention. Subjects given no instructions or asked to focus on the entire group showed the pattern of findings reported in our previous research – when anxious, they assimilated the deviant to the outgroup majority. However, subjects who were instructed at the outset to focus on the deviant did not show the anxiety-assimilation effect. When anxious, these subjects rated the deviant somewhat more different from the majority than control (non-anxious) subjects.

In another experiment the deviant outgroup member was presented either as a typical group member in good standing or as an atypical, marginal member. In the typical condition, while the deviant acted differently from the majority, he appeared similar to them and professed allegiance to the group. But in the atypical condition he dressed differently and indicated that he was considering a change in group membership. When portrayed as atypical, the anxiety manipulation did not lead to assimilation of judgements towards the majority. On the contrary, the deviant member was judged accurately in both the high and low anxiety conditions. Finally, in a third experiment subjects viewed the behaviour of four confederates, one of whom behaved differently from the others. For some subjects all four were explicitly categorized as members of a common group. For other subjects the deviant was categorized into a group different from the others. The typical anxiety-assimilation effect occurred when all confederates belonged to the same group. However, when the deviant belonged to a different group, anxious subjects did not bias their judgements of the deviant in the direction of expectations for the majority.

The pattern of findings from these follow-up investigations indicates that anxiety facilitates an accentuation of the field. The anxious observer assimilates within salient cognitive categories, so discrepancies among relatively typical group members are underestimated. On the other hand, differences between group or between markedly different members of a single group are maintained and even enhanced. Members of different groups who act differently are judged to be even more different when observers are anxious.

Explanatory mechanisms

In our work anxiety has been consistently shown to lessen the impact of counterstereotypic behaviour and, thereby, to reduce the effectiveness of positive contact between members of different groups. We have attributed these findings to a motive to lessen stimulation by relying on dominant, extant schemata (such as stereotypes) when persons experience heightened arousal. Furthermore, in the case of arousal induced by anxiety, negative affect may cue negative stereotypes about the target outgroup. If anxiety fosters holding on to stereotypes and negative evaluations of an outgroup in the face of contrary information, how is it that schema-discrepant information is overlooked? Three possibilities come to mind, each of which acts at different points in the processing of information. First, perceivers may be distracted and simply miss some of the contrary information (Abrams, 1985). Second, they may be aware of the discrepant information but misconstrue it and judge it to be stereotype-consistent. Third, they may perceive the contrary information accurately but discount it as not indicative of the outgroup as a whole.

Distraction

Data from one set of our studies generated evidence for an explanation of the anxiety-assimilation effect in terms of distraction (Wilder & Shapiro, 1989b). Subjects estimated the amount of time they spent thinking about the upcoming anxiety-provoking task while observing the outgroup (including the counterstereotypic actions of the deviant member). Although subjective reports of locus of attention suffer from some ambiguity, nevertheless subjects' estimates did predict responses to the major dependent measures. The more distracted subjects reported themselves to have been, the less effect the counterstereotypic behaviour had on their evaluation of the deviant and the outgroup. In addition, in most of our experiments subjects were asked to recall what they could about the counterstereotypic outgroup member. Anxious subjects generally made more errors of recall.

Distortion

A second possibility is that subjects attended to the behaviour of the counterstereotypic outgroup member as well when anxious as when relatively calm. Rather than overlook the positive (or negative) actions of the deviant member, subjects may have interpreted his actions as more stereotypic than they actually were. Anxiety-induced errors, therefore, occurred at the point of interpretation and information integration (distortion explanation) rather than at the point of information selection (distraction interpretation). The free recall measures referred to in the last paragraph can also support this interpretation. Subjects remembered fewer distinctive features and actions of the deviant outgroup member than of the modal members. Of greater relevance to a distortion interpretation, errors of recall were not simply random. When anxious, subjects were more likely to misattribute behaviour and features of a modal member to the deviant. This pattern of errors did not occur in the reverse direction: characteristics of the deviant were hardly ever mistakenly assigned to a modal outgroup member. A substantial literature from social cognition research has demonstrated that expectations can influence interpretation of behaviour in a schema-consistent manner (Fiske & Neuberg, 1990; Fiske & Taylor, 1991; Hamilton & Trolier, 1986; Rothbart, 1981). It should be pointed out, of course, that these distortions are often subtle and most likely to affect behaviour that is somewhat ambiguous in the first place. Thus, in our studies it may have been relatively easy to reinterpret a constructive criticism as a hostile comment. It is less likely, however, that an overt gesture of friendship can be interpreted as an openly hostile act unless it is attributed to Machiavellian or malicious motives. That possibility brings us to a third disruption that may have contributed to our findings.

Discounting

Even if the counterstereotypic outgroup member is attended to faithfully and his actions are interpreted without substantial distortion, those actions can still be discounted in either of two ways. First, the behaviour may be attributed to something other than the individual's intent or disposition. To the extent the counterstereotypic behaviour can be rationalized as a response to situational pressure or a temporary anomaly, it can be dismissed as unrepresentative of how that person would normally act. (For example, they have to behave co-operatively because the authorities are watching, or they are acting constructively because 'they are not like themselves today'). Furthermore, even if the behaviour is viewed as representative of the outgroup member's true beliefs, she or he may still be dismissed as atypical of others in the outgroup. Consequently, any beneficial impact of the contact is limited to that specific setting with that specific individual. Indeed, the 'exception to the rule' is often pointed to as proof of the legitimacy of the stereotype. While it is critical, of course, that the specific contact setting yields a favourable interaction, it is also essential that any benefits be generalized beyond that setting to the outgroup at large.

There are several ways to enhance the impact of counterstereotypic information. First, the source of the information must be presented as representative or typical of the outgroup (Johnston & Hewstone, 1992; Pettigrew, 1986; Rothbart & John, 1985; Wilder, 1984; 1986). Second, the information must be seen as intentional and indicative of the true beliefs of the outgroup member (Wilder & Faith, 1992). Multiple contacts with the deviant outgroup member can help ensure that his or her actions will be attributed to stable, dispositional properties (Allport, 1954; Pettigrew, 1986). In addition, multiple contacts with multiple counterstereotypic members should be most effective in changing general expectations of and attitudes towards the outgroup. Some of the literature from persuasion indicates that multiple communicators are more effective persuaders than single communicators when they are viewed as relatively heterogeneous (Harkins & Petty, 1981; Wilder, 1977; 1978). For instance, ingroup members may be more influential than outgroup members, in part, because they are seen as a collection of more heterogeneous individuals than their counterparts in the other group (Wilder, 1990).

The challenge, then, is to create counterstereotypic information that is both credible and generalizable to outgroup members not present. This can be accomplished by presenting counterstereotypic outgroup members who are sufficiently similar to one another so that they cannot be summarily dismissed as atypical members yet who are also sufficiently dissimilar so that they cannot be discounted as an unusual subtype. This is not so contradictory as it may first appear. Impact can be maximized and discounting minimized by making the 'exceptions' similar in their counterstereotypic actions yet dissimilar on more peripheral characteristics. For example, stereotypes about football players should be more susceptible to change if counterstereotypic examples are all active players (typical) yet come from a variety of teams and play a variety of positions (heterogeneity of peripheral cues).

Finally, multiple contacts also should be more effective when they occur across a range of situations as well as a range of outgroup members. This expectation follows from Kelley's (1967) analysis-of-variance model of the attribution process. The desired attribution for counterstereotypic information is that it reflects something about the outgroup. Similar actions by multiple outgroup members across multiple situations should encourage a strong attribution to a stable property that they share – a property of the outgroup.

The distraction, distortion and discounting hypotheses offer different, but not mutually exclusive, interpretations for the anxiety-assimilation phenomenon found in the research presented in this chapter. It is likely that each of these factors reduces the impact of counterstereotypic information. The challenge is to specify the contexts that minimize them. These biases are likely to lose potency when anxiety is reduced and persons are encouraged to focus carefully on the deviant outgroup member, and when that member's actions are judged to be representative of the outgroup. Furthermore, beneficial impact of an accurately perceived counterstereotypic encounter is most likely to generalize to the outgroup as a whole when multiple contacts occur with multiple outgroup members across multiple situations.

Implications for the contact hypothesis

Research reviewed in this chapter demonstrates that anxiety can promote the use and maintenance of stereotypes even in the face of disconfirming information. Intergroup conflict can be a source of anxiety. Reliance on outgroup stereotypes should, therefore, be especially likely when interpreting and responding to actions of members of a disliked outgroup. Given that stereotypes of disliked outgroups are mostly negative, their salience to the anxious perceiver may well poison the interaction and undermine a potentially successful contact experience (Stephan & Stephan, 1985). Might not the spotty success of apparently positive contact between disliked groups be partly attributed to the disruptive role of anxiety in person perception? Alternatively stated, do the conditions that promote successful intergroup contact also reduce anxiety in the contact setting?

From Allport (1954) and Sherif (1966) through Amir (1969, 1976) and Cook (1984) to Pettigrew (1986) and Stephan (1985), successful intergroup contact has been characterized by some subset of the following conditions: co-operation between the groups in pursuit of a superordinate goal; intimate as opposed to superficial interaction; contact supported by outside authorities or institutions; contact between persons of equal status in the setting; and multiple contact experiences that include one or more of the preceding conditions. Each of these conditions for successful contact should also lower anxiety in the contact setting. Certainly, compared to competitive relationships, those characterized by co-operation are likely to minimize anxiety (Wilder & Shapiro, 1989a). Intimate contact should lessen anxiety generated by the strangeness of outgroup members and may also reveal points of similarity between the groups that have been hidden by superficial differences (e.g. Byrne & Wong, 1962; Rokeach, 1960; Stephan & Stephan, 1985). Equal-status contact can minimize anxiety based on the supposition that one party may dominate the other. Institutional and authoritative support for contact (e.g. schools, government) can lessen anxiety both by providing social support and role models and by ensuring that neither party will be vulnerable to exploitation. Finally, multiple positive contact experiences can desensitize one to the outgroup. Negative affect attached to the outgroup diminishes as a result of repeated, pleasant interactions with its members.

In short, those conditions that have been found to promote successful contact with members of an outgroup are also conditions that are likely to reduce anxiety in the contact setting and anxiety associated with the outgroup category. Of course, this argument does not demonstrate that diminished anxiety is a primary mediator of successful intergroup contact. Future research might profitably assess the degree to which contact situations generate anxiety and might directly manipulate some of the variables that have been shown to promote successful contact to see if their absence increases anxiety while their presence diffuses it. Reports of subjective anxiety could then be statistically controlled to see if anxiety has a causal role in the success of contact under the favourable conditions set forth by the classic research in this area.

Note

1. The relationship between intergroup bias and desire for a positive identity is not clear-cut. One might expect ingroup favouritism to enhance a person's self-esteem. Similarly, when self-esteem has been lowered, one might expect persons to engage in ingroup favouritism as a means of boosting their self-esteem. As Hogg and Abrams (1990) point out in a recent review, these predictions have not received consistent support. Part of the difficulty may be methodological in that several investigations have measured self-esteem with global indices while the effects of intergroup bias may be limited to more transitory feelings present in the intergroup context. In any event the relationship between self-esteem and bias is not critical to the anxiety-assimilation argument advanced in this chapter.

6   On the failure to see oneself as disadvantaged: Cognitive and emotional components

Faye Crosby, Diana Cordova and Karen Jaskar

It is fall 1989, and a group of a dozen women are gathered at the alumnae house of Smith College. The group is attending a reunion of women who had joined the Waves during World War II, and had trained together at Smith before moving on to further training in engineering at Harvard and MIT. At the prompting of a resident professor of psychology, the women reminisced about their wartime experiences:

> *Wave member*: 'All the women had to take care of themselves. The men had quarters, we did not. So we lived where we could . . . Which was very hard . . . We had to get rooms and live there and commute into Cambridge every day.'

> *Professor*: 'And at that time did you think of that as a problem? Did you say "this is sex discrimination"?'

> *Wave member*: 'No, not really . . . No, it wasn't . . . Though the funny thing which we were talking about this morning, is that Harvard had no rest-room facilities for us.'

No rest-rooms. No rest-rooms! Think about it. Surely the allocation to one gender only of the ability to meet one's basic biological functions is sex discriminatory. And yet, to these women who were serving their country in World War II, the gender imbalance went virtually unnoticed.

This small anecdote recalled by a working woman as she spoke of her experiences in American culture, illustrates not only the existence of sex discrimination over time, but also the extent of self-delusion. Although the women being interviewed expressed great sympathy and interest in the struggles of working women and declared themselves advocates of gender equality, they were unable to frame their own experiences in terms of sex discrimination. What was occurring at the alumnae house of Smith College in the fall of 1989 was but one instance of a phenomenon that has come to be known as the *denial of personal disadvantage*.

The denial of personal disadvantage, i.e. the phenomenon of perceiving discrimination at the societal level but denying its occurrence at the personal level, has been the subject of a few recent reviews (Clayton & Crosby, 1992; Crosby, Pufall, Snyder, O'Connell & Whalen, 1989; Nagata & Crosby, 1991). As the reviews show, the work on the denial of personal disadvantage falls into two types. First, there is the empirical literature. Second, are the analyses that focus on the policy implications of the existence of the phenomenon. In this review we focus on both conceptual and empirical issues, and leave to the side any questions of policy. What is novel about the current review is that we address the distinction between the cognitive and the emotional bases of the phenomenon.

We start the chapter by describing briefly the studies that have shown the existence of the phenomenon. We then move to those experiments that indicate the possible cognitive basis of the phenomenon, and end by examining how one might demonstrate an emotional component as well. To date, no one has yet demonstrated in a rigorous fashion that the denial of personal discrimination is a motivated behaviour and yet both anecdotal information and our general understanding of how human beings operate lead us to believe that it is only a matter of time until we can do so.

The phenomenon of denial

The phenomenon of the denial of personal disadvantage was first noted in a survey of employed men and women in the Boston suburb of Newton over a decade ago (Crosby, 1982). The survey contained indisputable evidence of sex discrimination. The 182 employed men in the survey earned significantly more money, on average, than the 163 employed women of exactly comparable age, education, training and occupational level. Also, the majority of the working women in the study acknowledged sex discrimination as a serious concern. Indeed, on most measures the employed women in the study were reliably more concerned with sex discrimination as a problem than were either the employed men or a control sample of housewives from the same community. Yet, these same women were equal to the men in measures of job satisfaction. Here was a clear case of denial: the employed women of Newton felt themselves personally exempt from the obstacles of sex discrimination, although the objective data showed they had not been as fortunate as they had imagined.

The Newton study was neither the first nor the last empirical demonstration of the denial of personal discrimination. Prior to the study, Abeles (1976) had found that black activism and optimism were correlated with an awareness of group deprivation, but not with personal discrimination. Around the same time that the data were being collected in Newton, Canadian researchers were finding that francophones there minimized the degree to which they were discriminated against by the larger business community, even as they acknowledged ethnic and language prejudices and injustices in their society (Guimond & Dube, 1983). More recently, this phenomenon has been observed among working women in Canada (Hafer & Olson, 1993), gay men in England (Birt & Dion, 1987), and minority MBAs in the US (Ford, 1988), all of whom acknowledged the discrimination facing their group as a whole but did not see it as applying to their personal situation. In one study of 181 minority (mostly black) MBA graduates, for example, researcher Ford asked the participants to compare their career progress to that of their white colleagues. Ninety-five per cent of the respondents saw their career progress as being equal to or faster than their white counterparts. Yet, when Ford examined the objective data concerning the respondents, it was found that the black subjects were significantly disadvantaged in terms of promotion and salary. In addition, a recent study of unemployed workers in Australia further confirmed the distinction between resentments felt about one's own personal situation, on the one hand, and resentments about the situation of one's social group on the other hand (Walker & Mann, 1987). These studies accurately reflect the existence of the phenomenon in respondents suffering from discrimination outside the issues of gender usually surveyed in current experiments on denial.

Variations within the Newton sample

Were all the women in the Newton study equally susceptible to the denial of personal disadvantage? In fact, some of the women felt as upset about their own situations as they did about the situation of working women in general (Crosby, 1982). Each of the female respondents was asked to rate the extent to which she believed she received less from her job than she deserved, and then to rate the extent she felt women in general received less from their jobs than they deserved. The majority of women in the study believed that working women in general received less than they deserved from their career and also believed that as individuals they received as much from their jobs as they deserved. Only thirteen women in the study were able to see their experiences in relation to women as a whole, as they gave approximately equal ratings for unmet deservingness on both the personal and gender scales. The findings were consistent with relative deprivation theory, a theory that posits that individuals feel dissatisfied only when comparing their own situation to that of a better-off subjective reference group (Merton & Rossi, 1957). This sub-group of women did, in general, have a different comparison group than the majority of the Newton women, and thus were more dissatisfied with their situation.

Subsequent analyses by Crosby and her colleagues substantiated that the choice of comparison persons was extremely important (Zanna, Crosby & Lowenstein, 1987). In a secondary analysis of the data collected in the Newton survey, Crosby and her co-workers examined the rela-tionship between a woman's reported job satisfaction and her choice of comparison other. Of the employed women in the Newton study, twenty-five subjects used a male-dominated reference group as the basis for measuring what they felt they deserved from their career and their job satisfaction. Another thirty-eight women used a reference group that was predominantly female.

These two groups were found to have differences outside the choice of comparison others. Generally, those women who used a male-dominated reference group were more likely than others to express feelings of deprivation in their careers, as they perceived a large gap between what they had and what they felt they deserved. The women of this subgroup were also more likely than others to express pessimism about the future and to perceive a gap between their personal outcomes and outcomes of others. Although the women with male-dominated reference groups differed significantly from those women who used other females as their comparison others with regard to job attitudes, the two groups did not differ in their attitudes towards the position of women in society in general. Thus, the use of a male reference group seems to be correlated to a comparative acknowledgement of personal disadvantage among the working women in the Newton study.

Variations in other studies

Given the variation evident in the women of the Newton survey, it seemed plausible that the phenomenon of denial was a process that applied more to some people than to others. The logical question then became: are there some groups of people who appear to be more susceptible to the phenomenon of denial and other groups who appear to be less susceptible? It was this question which was at the basis of three additional sets of data analyses.

The quest for groups who would be immune to the phenomenon of denial began in Western Massachusetts in 1985 and 1986 (Crosby *et al.*, 1989). Through a network of personal contacts, Crosby and her coworkers made contact with fifteen 'out' lesbians. Each of the lesbians was interviewed both in depth and in person about her own personal situation and about the situation of lesbians in the United States generally. It seemed likely that if anybody would be immune to the phenomenon of denial, it would be these highly politicized individuals, who had strong group identification and who were no strangers to the feminist dictum 'the personal is the political'.

Surprisingly, the results of the survey showed that the women also had significant differences in the perception of personal disadvantage and group discrimination. These women generally believed themselves to be exempt from the discrimination they thought to affect lesbians through-out the United States.

Of course, the possibility existed that the lesbians in the Western Massachusetts sample were not deceiving themselves about the extent to which they were discriminated against, but were, in fact, the lucky exceptions to the consequences of homophobia that they acknowledged to be a problem for lesbians throughout the rest of the United States. It was possible, in other words, that the region in which these women were living did allow them a better life than most lesbians in other parts of the country. Similarly, one could argue that our sample consisted of lesbians who had exerted an extraordinary amount of energy and effort in order to surmount the obstacles which stood in the path of their career goals and personal aspirations. In other words, they recognized that things are generally stacked against women – especially against lesbians – yet they felt that, as a result of their efforts, they had accomplished everything they had originally set out to achieve. Because the sampling design was one that did not involve a control group, it was not logically possible in the first study of lesbians to say for certain whether the women were self-deluding or were, in fact, very privileged.

A second study was designed to settle the geographical issue. If the lesbians were in fact privileged, they ought to have felt that the lesbians living in their own region were equally privileged. If, on the other hand, the women in the first lesbian study were exhibiting the denial of personal disadvantage, then they would be expected to imagine that they were better off than other lesbians in their own region.

Analysis of the data from the second sample of lesbians gave extremely strong support to the denial explanation. The thirteen lesbians surveyed for the second survey responded to questions asking them to assess how much they felt they had suffered personally from discrimination, the extent to which lesbians in their region suffered from discrimination, and the degree of discrimination encountered by lesbians nationally. The results confirmed the hypothesis of the original lesbian study: the lesbians in the second sample did not perceive the existence of personal dis-crimination as a problem for themselves, yet they saw such discrimination as a greater problem for lesbians in their region, and an even greater problem for lesbians on the national level.

In Western Massachusetts, as in Newton, variations existed within the sample. The greater the identification the women felt with the larger lesbian group, the greater was their sense of personal disadvantage. This finding is not an isolated one. For instance, utilizing a Canadian sample, Tougas and Veilleux (1988, 1989) found that those women who strongly identify themselves as 'employed women' were significantly more discontented with the position of women in the economy and were more positively disposed towards the policy of affirmative action relative to those women for whom employment was not such a strong component of their social identity. Thus, both in the Newton and Western Massachusetts studies, and in the research of Tougas and Veilleux, it appears that the greater the identification a respondent has with a disadvantaged group, the more likely it is for her/him to recognize the presence of personal discrimination.

This set of findings is consistent with social identity theory (Tajfel, 1978b; Turner, 1982; Hogg & Abrams, 1988). The theory conceives of the self-concept as a collection of self-images which may vary in terms of the length of their establishment, their complexity and the richness of their content. However, the important emphasis is that self-images can be construed as falling along a continuum, with individuating characteristics at the personal extreme and social categorical characteristics at the social extreme (Turner, 1982). To the extent that personal identifications are salient (e.g. 'I like to play tennis'; 'I am tall'), one is aware of features distinguishing oneself from other individuals. In contrast, when social identifications are salient (e.g. 'I am a social psychologist'; 'I am a woman') one becomes aware of features distinguishing one's own relevant category from others. As a result, when a person's self-image as a group member becomes salient, he or she will behave as a group member. There are some instances, however, in which a strong identification with a given group will incur a personal cost. For instance, in their recent study of British and Scottish adolescents, Abrams and Emler (1992) found that the stronger the identification the adolescents felt with their region – even if this region was disadvantaged in terms of employment opportunities – the more prone they were to act at a group level and the less inclined they were to change their own personal situation to avoid the disadvantage.

While the lesbian studies, by and large, failed to identify the parameters of the denial of personal discrimination, a third study provided us with some additional insights. Noting that both the Western Massachusetts and the Newton survey were predominantly middle class, Crosby et al. (1989) chose to examine the relevance of social class as a factor in the denial of personal disadvantage by surveying over 200 students at a technical college in Springfield, Massachusetts. It seemed intuitively likely to Crosby and her research team that people who have the expectation of upward mobility, but who are not yet privileged, might be willing to perceive the extent to which they have been individually harmed by certain demographic characteristics.

The respondents in the Springfield survey included 130 women and 92 men, of whom approximately 16 per cent were ethnic minorities. A nine-page questionnaire asked students about the extent they and their families had suffered from discrimination in the last year or ever. The questionnaire asked the respondents to view discrimination in terms of employment, education and recreation. The participants then rated the extent to which they had been discriminated against in the above categories over the past year and ever. Subsequently, the students were asked to estimate their families' experiences with discrimination in these same categories over the past year and ever. The comparison of scores for personal discrimination and the scores of the family was used to test for the denial of personal disadvantage.

The results showed there was no difference between the students' perceptions of their own suffering and their family's suffering. Nor were there any differences between ethnic groups. Most of the women, and many of the men, admitted to more suffering 'ever' than in the past year. None of these findings was particularly surprising.

More surprising was the fact that the majority of the subjects saw themselves as suffering as much as, if not more than, most people. Three-quarters of the male students perceived that they had suffered from discrimination more than most men, and a third of the male students felt that they had experienced greater discrimination than most women. Eighty-eight per cent of the women felt they were more discriminated against than most men, and 60 per cent viewed their suffering as greater than that of most women. Clearly, among the aspirant working class, people were not so blind to their own categorical disadvantages that they claimed to have suffered less than other people.

Yet even among the Springfield sample, denial reared its head. The students in the sample felt they had a far greater chance for success in life than most people; and they believed that they were coping well despite the disadvantages they faced. When asked to rate their chances of success in life as compared to other men and women as a group, nearly a quarter of the women expected to have a better chance of success than most men, and nearly three-quarters believed they would be more successful in life than other women.

One reason why the working-class respondents in Springfield may have resisted the temptation to imagine that they had suffered less than other people in the past is that working-class subjects may have different cultural norms or mores than the middle-class subjects previously studied. Moreover, the reason why the upwardly-mobile working-class respondents may have imagined themselves as especially adept at coping, and in this way exhibited the symptoms of denial, could spring from their partial adherence to – or at least emulation of – some of the mythology of the American middle class. Certainly, culture seems to play a part in the extent to which the denial of personal discrimination exists.

It was to test the influence of cultural norms on the denial of personal disadvantage that Nagata and Crosby (1991) reanalyzed data collected by Nagata's Sansei Research Project (1987, 1988, 1990, 1992). Sansei are third-generation Japanese-Americans and, as such, may endorse values different from the mainstream of white America. To be sure, Japanese-Americans are known for their commitment to group identification and ideals of connection rather than separateness. Perhaps such people are less willing than Caucasians, with their adherence to rugged individualism (Crosby, 1991), to see themselves and their immediate families as different from the larger ethnic group in the experiences of suffering.

As part of a much larger study, questions were posed to 600 Sansei about the suffering and coping of Japanese-Americans during World War II. All of the respondents in the survey had at least one parent who had been interned in a detention camp during World War II. The respondents were asked to rate on a 1 (much less than most) to 5 (much more than most) scale the extent to which their parents suffered from the internment. They also rated on a 1-to-5 scale how well their parents had coped with the experience. On the same scale, the respondents compared their own families to other interned Japanese-Americans, both in terms of suffering and in terms of coping. Additional questions determined the degree to which the respondents chose to associate with other Japanese-Americans.

Analyses of the data from Nagata's Sansei Research Project showed that the Sansei did not minimize the suffering of their own parents. The respondents felt that the suffering of the Japanese-American community during the internment was very great. On a five-point scale, with 5 being the maximum suffering, the average response by Sansei rating the suffering of Japanese-Americans was 4.63. Most Sansei reported that their own parents had suffered to the same degree as others and also that their parents had coped with the situation in much the same manner as most Japanese-Americans. These results are consistent with the idea that there is a cultural pressure not to differ from the group among Japanese-Americans.

There was, however, one group of respondents who did appear to deny their family's disadvantage, consisting of those Sansei who believed that their parents had suffered less than others interned. Approximately 66 of the respondents rated their parents' suffering as less in comparison with that of other Japanese-Americans. This subgroup of Sansei also had a lower degree of identification with Japanese-Americans as a group, assessed by their scores on attitudinal tests measuring the respondents' ethnic preference of Caucasian-Americans as their reference group. As with the lesbian studies, so with the Sansei study: it appears that close identification with a group helps people to become more politically active (Gurin, 1987).

In sum, the denial of personal disadvantage occurs frequently, yet it is not a universal and immutable phenomenon. That is, sometimes it exists more and sometimes it exists less. Cultural norms seem to be especially important and the phenomenon probably exists most among those cultures in which individualism is emphasized, and exists least in those cultures where the group is privileged over the individual.

The cognitive basis of the phenomenon

Given the robustness of the phenomenon, the impulse exists to understand what causes it. Two aspects of the denial of personal disadvantage seem immediately apparent: the cognitive and the emotional. Consider the original Newton study. In that study, it was found that people could not see disadvantage in their own case, but could see it in the case of the group to which they belonged. Two different dimensions operate in the contrast between one's own situation and the situation of one's own group. As illustrated in Figure 6.1, the two dimensions are: number and identity. From anecdotal data reported in a number of sources, it seems plausible to infer that people have a harder time recognizing problems that relate to the self than to others (Crosby & Stewart, 1991). The more distant the others, the easier it might be to visualize problems. Alternatively, or additionally, people may have difficulty perceiving disadvantage, and especially discrimination, when they are examining one datum,

		Identity dimension	
		self	other
Number dimension	one datum	a	b
	many data	c	d

The Newton study and subsequent studies have demonstrated a contrast between cells a and d. The number dimension is essentially a cognitive dimension; identity involves emotion.

Figure 6.1 Contrasting number and identity dimensions.

or a few data, rather than an array of data. For the purposes of this review, the number dimension of the phenomenon of denial will represent the cognitive component, and the dimension of identity will relate to the emotional component.

The cognitive basis of the denial of personal disadvantage has received a considerable amount of research attention for a couple of reasons. First, it is important in a political sense to determine if the blindness that most people experience to their disadvantage is susceptible to change and can be explained by simple information-processing, because such an approach allows us to reform people's behaviour without having to alter their attitudes or restructure their psyches. Second, cognitive factors are accessible through clever laboratory manipulations in a way that may not be true for the emotional factors.

The original study that examined the cognitive factors of information-processing in the perception of discrimination was conducted at Yale University with thirty male undergraduate subjects (Crosby, Clayton, Hemker & Alksnis, 1986). These subjects were presented with information concerning a fictitious company consisting of ten different departments. The materials instructed the students to evaluate whether sex discrimination was or was not practised at the fictitious company, Company Z. Information was given concerning a randomly selected male manager and a randomly selected female manager from each of the ten departments of the company. The subjects were given information about four 'input' variables which they were instructed to take as the valid measure of the contributions of each employee. These variables were education, seniority, level of job and assessed motivation. Moreover, the subjects were instructed that in a totally fair world, these four variables – and only these four variables – should determine the employee's salary. Salary was the only variable by which subjects could measure rewards.

The materials were constructed in such a way that the company was, in fact, practising sex discrimination. In the fabricated materials, the male managers and female managers had, on average, equivalent inputs, and yet they had vastly different salaries. It should be noted that the fictitious materials represented a conceptual replication of the situation documented in the Newton study.

To search for cognitive effects on the perception of discrimination, the experimenters presented the information to subjects in two different formats. Half of the time the information was presented in aggregate form. In this format, the information for all ten departments was arranged on a single, large table. The other half of the time the information was presented in sequences, department by department.

Half of the subjects in the Yale study viewed the materials of Company Z, first in the aggregate form, then in the segmented form. The other half of the subjects viewed the materials in segmented form first, and in aggregate form second. In both conditions, the subjects were asked to give their assessment of the extent, probability and seriousness of the sex discrimination. When the subjects examined the information in segmented form, they made their assessments of each particular department before proceeding to the materials on the next department.

The results of the Yale study show that, while order of presentation was generally unimportant, the format in which the relevant information had been presented greatly influenced subjects' discrimination ratings. Information provided in the aggregate form allowed the subjects to perceive a greater degree of discrimination than did this same information presented in the segmented form. There were three main effects for format, as subjects rated the degree of discrimination, the probability of discrimination and the seriousness of the discrimination as significantly higher in the aggregate format than in the segmented condition.

Experimenters in the Yale study also examined the possibility that individuals who considered themselves to be feminists might be more likely to perceive the presence of sex discrimination than those students who were not involved in the women's movement. Subjects were asked questions to measure the degree of their self-reported feminism and this was correlated to their discrimination ratings. No significant correlation between the two variables was found.

Most subjects in the Yale study did not consider themselves to be involved in the women's movement overall. Despite the general lack of involvement in women's issues among the subjects in the Yale study, it is possible that the very words 'sex discrimination' could have raised emotional red flags. Certainly the words are not neutral. Perhaps the intelligent men of the Yale study were not as detached from the materials as the researchers had supposed.

Because of the possibility of emotional involvement, it was important to test whether the same effects would be obtained among people who were more emotionally involved than the Yale subjects, and among people who were less emotionally involved. A replication of the Yale study was performed at Smith College, a women's college known for its commitment to feminism (Twiss, Tabb & Crosby, 1989). Half of the subjects in the Smith study received the standard materials documenting the sex discrimination at Company Z and using the words 'sex discrimination'. The other half were instructed to review and rate data between 'plant A' and 'plant B', rather than between male and female managers.

Analyses showed that in both conditions subjects were adept at perceiving the discrimination when they received the information in the aggregate form and were unable to perceive the discrimination when they received the materials in the segmented form. There was no difference between the results obtained in the 'sex discrimination' condition and the 'plant A/plant B' condition. Nor was there any difference between the ratings of the by-and-large feminist Smith students, and the ratings of the generally uninvolved Yale students. Clearly, there is evidence that the cognitive component of the denial of personal discrimination phenomenon can operate independently of emotional factors when the subjects' attention has been drawn to the relevant comparison.

There has also been criticism of the Yale study on the basis of methodological issues. Despite an instruction to subjects to weigh each department equally when judging the company as a whole, there is a possibility that subjects would weigh a discriminatory department more heavily than the rest when determining the company's overall discrimination ratings, and thus rate the company higher in discrimination than was instructed.

Cordova (1992) redressed the problems of the Yale study by including three conditions. In the first condition, subjects received information on each department on a single, large sheet and then assessed the extent of sex discrimination in the company. This condition was an exact duplicate of the aggregate condition in the original study. Second was the condition in which the subjects reviewed the material from each department and made a rating about each specific department. This condition was the same as the segmented form of information presentation in the original study. Finally, a third and new condition had subjects review the information department by department but delay their ratings of discrimination until they had reviewed all of the departments. Subjects in the third condition made a rating about the level of sex discrimination as a whole, as did those in the first condition, but they did so after seeing the information sequentially.

Results of Cordova's study confirmed the original findings. Subjects were better able to perceive sex discrimination in the aggregate condition than in either of the case-by-case conditions. There were no significant differences between the two segmented conditions. Cordova's study serves to reiterate the importance of cognitive factors in the perception of discrimination.

One final study, serving as a variation of the Yale experiment, deserves mention. Crosby, Burris, Censor and MacKethan (1986) designed an experiment to test the possibility that some patterns may make discrimination easier to perceive than others. They presented their subjects with a fictitious scenario involving an institution that had to make eight choices between male and female candidates. For each of the eight choices, there were four input variables in which the man could be superior, the woman superior, or they could be equal. In the different versions of the scenario, the man was superior twelve times, the woman twelve times, and they were equal eight times. These versions differed in how the scores were distributed between the male and female candidate – either they were spread out, making it difficult for the subject to notice the discrimination, or they were close together, allowing the subject to see two or more blatant cases of discrimination.

Results showed that people can perceive the existence of sex discrimination when there are at least two cases in which the female candidate was unfairly passed over for the job. With less than two obvious cases, the atomized view of discrimination fails to enter people's perceptions. This finding is highly consistent with the literature on stereotype change (e.g. Gurwitz & Dodge, 1977; Rothbart, 1981; Brewer, Dull & Lui, 1981; Weber & Crocker, 1983; cf. Chapter 5, this volume). For instance, in a series of experiments designed to test the applicability of the three leading models (the bookkeeping model, in which each instance of stereotype-relevant information is used to modify the stereotype; the conversion model, in which stereotypes change radically in response to dramatic or salient instances; and the subtyping model, in which new subtypes are developed in order to accommodate instances not easily assimilated by existing stereotypes), Weber and Crocker (1983) found that stereotype change followed the bookkeeping model when the stereotype-inconsistent information had been dispersed among many individuals and the subtyping model when the inconsistent information had been concentrated on just a few individuals. Certainly, one could argue that subjects in Crosby's aggregate conditions are processing the relevant company data in a manner consistent with the bookkeeping model whereas subjects in the segmented or atomized conditions process the information in a manner consistent with the subtyping model of stereotype change. The importance of Crosby *et al.* (1986) lies in its further confirmation of the significance of the format of information in people's impressions of justice and injustice: how people are told to process information about sex discrimination influences whether or not they will perceive the existence of sex discrimination.

Emotional factors

The demonstration of a cognitive basis for the denial of personal disadvantage established through laboratory experiments does not imply the universal lack of emotional factors. Indeed, in the real world, outside the laboratory, it is highly likely that emotional factors combine with information-processing to make people more prone to denying the extent to which they are personally harmed by the systematic cultural biases that they acknowledge are harmful to their reference groups. If nothing else, the variation among different populations suggests that there are people for whom denial is more common, and people for whom it is less common, or conditions under which it will exist and other conditions that decrease the likelihood of it existing. The inability to draw strong inferences on the basis of one datum or a few data is a relatively universal phenomenon. So something – most likely a person's emotional involvement – is probably operating to explain why people are sometimes more and sometimes less able to see the political as the personal. Thus, we believe, as do Walker and Pettigrew (1984) and Martin and Murray (1983), that important insights can be gained by emphasizing the distinction between the cognitive and the affective components of the phenomenon.

There are several reasons why women might be motivated to avoid a face-to-face confrontation with their own personal disadvantage. Three have been identified (Crosby, 1982; 1984). First, it may be emotionally aversive to see anyone, including oneself, as a victim because such a vision challenges a person's ability to believe in a just world. Second, it may be emotionally aversive to imagine that one's co-workers and supervisors are anything less than totally admirable. Finally, it may be a threat to self-esteem to see oneself as someone who does not live outside of history.

Need to see the world as just

Approximately twenty years ago Melvin Lerner and his colleagues (Lerner, 1980; Lerner & Miller, 1978; Lerner, Miller & Holmes, 1976) identified a phenomenon they labelled 'the just world theory'. The core proposition of Lerner's theory is that people have a need to believe that the world is a just place. This need is related to our basic human desire to think that we are living in a predictable world in which we will be rewarded for our efforts and abilities and punished for our wrong-doings. Any observations that challenge the vision of the world as just are threatening to people, implying as they do that anyone, including the people themselves, might fall victim to unexpected and undeserved misfortune. Thus, for example, the sight of an innocent person suffering is an emotionally arousing event and one that we are motivated to avoid or decrease.

Numerous laboratory studies have documented Lerner's just world phenomenon. One series of studies, for example, found that people are so invested in the belief that the world is fair that they will react to a positive outcome by praising the winner and to a negative outcome by derogating the victim. In each of these cases, the affected individual is perceived as deserving his or her specific outcome.

One representative study involved showing college students a videotape in which a fellow student – in reality a confederate – was ostensibly participating in another psychology study. Some subjects were led to believe that the videotaped student was going to receive painful shocks, while other subjects were told that she would be in a control condition in which no shocks would be administered. The students who watched the videotape rated the confederate as having a less attractive personality when they believed she was going to be shocked than when they thought she was in the harm-free condition (Lerner, 1980).

Additional studies have shown that when subjects were given the opportunity to end the victim's suffering by discontinuing the shocks, they unanimously chose to do so. Also, their ratings of the victim were much less negative if they had been permitted to help than otherwise. Clearly, rationalization and not sadism was at play when subjects decided that harmful outcomes are not an injustice after all, but rather are simply the deserved outcomes, which is to say the fair and just ones.

How does a person's emotional need to believe in a just world contribute to the tendency to see the self as exempt from the misfortunes known to affect one's reference group? All of Lerner's (1980) experiments were conducted looking at individuals, and not groups, that were falling victims of injustice. It seems likely that the vision of a group being victimized lacks the immediacy of the vision of an individual. Even more remote is the news of a whole category of people (say, women) being unfairly treated.

Through what strategy might we test the proposed connection between the need to believe in a just world and the denial of personal disadvantage? One strategy might be to test for an association between the two across a variety of people. Early researchers showed that there was variation in the degree to which people need to believe in a just world (Rubin & Peplau, 1975). More recent investigators (i.e., Hafer & Olson, 1989) have empirically demonstrated that women with a strong need to believe in a just world are less likely than others to advocate either personal or collective actions to correct unfair employment situations. It would be interesting to extend Hafer and Olson's survey and see if the tendency to deny one's own personal disadvantage increases as the need to believe in a just world increases. If the phenomenon has an emotional component to it, then we should find substantial differences between extent of denial among ideologues on the one hand and cynics on the other.

Other as villain

A second reason why people might be motivated to imagine that they are personally exempt from disadvantage also relates to their discomfort with perceptions of injustice. It seems likely that people experience emotional distress when they contemplate the possibility that their co-workers and their superiors wish them ill. While situations involving an entire category of people do not seem to evoke images of specific harm-doers, individual cases of disadvantage – and especially individual instances of discrimination – may lead us to think about individual harm-doers. It has been suggested that one reason women avoid the perception of their own personal disadvantage is that they wish to avoid the emotionally distasteful thought that someone wishes them ill (Crosby, 1984). Cold logic would allow people to recognize that personal harm can result from systemic factors; but here is one instance where psycho-logic and rational logic fail to coincide.

How might we test the proposition that the avoidance of villains contributes to the phenomenon of denial? A couple of different ideas come to mind. First, we might present subjects with information either about an individual who is at a disadvantage or about a group or category at a disadvantage and ask the subjects to generate possible reasons for the disadvantage. If the hypothesis about psychological matching is correct, then the account of the individual victim should pull for an individual villain while the account of a group should not.

Complementing the first strategy is a second. We might attempt to break down the denial phenomenon by educating (reminding) people about how systems can cause suffering, even unjust suffering, through the fault of no specific individual or specific set of individuals. If the (emotional) reluctance to identify villains in one's world is part of the reason why people do not see their own disadvantage, then we should be able to detect a greater readiness to see the political in one's personal situation among those who have been educated than among the others not so educated.

Self as exempt from harm

The final motivational factor contributing to the denial of personal disadvantage is the need to see oneself as special, as someone who is somehow unaffected by the law of averages and outside the march of history, as someone to whom good things happen and bad things do not. The final way, therefore, to determine if there is a motivated basis for the denial of disadvantage is to see if people have a harder time recognizing discrimination (i.e., disadvantage based on categorical attributes) when the individual in question is closely related to the self than when the individual in question is unrelated to the self. In the terms used in Figure 6.1, the issue is this: does cell 'a' differ from cell 'b'? If the answer is yes, then we can conclude that there is an affective component to denial. If the answer is no, then the processes are solely cognitive.

Designing an experiment in which the materials sometimes relate to self and sometimes are distant from the self is, in principle, a simple matter. We might, for example, develop materials like those depicting fictitious Company Z used to test for cognitive bias. We could present the materials to female medical students and to female law students so that half of the time the materials refer to gender discrimination in the field of medicine and half of the time to gender discrimination in the field of law. If denial has an affective component, then the medical students should react to the materials about medicine in the same way that the law students react to the materials about law and both of these conditions should differ from the other two conditions.

Choice of a dependent measure is considerably more complicated than the selection of an experimental design. We already know that the simple measure of ability to perceive discrimination is too gross to detect the sort of differences in which we are interested. After all, Cordova (1992) found no gender differences when she presented her subjects with materials about sex discrimination. Nor were there obvious differences between scores of the male subjects at Yale (Crosby, Clayton et al., 1986) and the female subjects as Smith College (Twiss et al., 1989). More appropriate would be a more subtle measure, such as reaction time (in milliseconds) of subjects as they 'study' materials that are or are not relevant to the self.

Another way to establish the motivational component of the denial phenomenon would be to adapt the methodology of Ziva Kunda (1987) who has conducted research on motivated inferences. In a very interesting experiment, Kunda informed subjects, all of whom were unwed college students, that the divorce rate in the United States is currently 50 per cent. She then studied the mechanisms whereby the students convinced themselves that they would not fall victim to divorce. Some subjects remembered that they had been in a series of romantic relationships. They reasoned that their experiences in these relationships had given them insights into interpersonal processes that would make it especially easy for them to establish a solid relationship with their spouse. Other subjects recalled that they had not been involved in any previous relationships, and they took comfort in the belief that they would enter matrimony without unresolved emotional issues, left over from broken relationships. Thus, no matter what the subjects' attributes were, people inferred that their particular attributes would help them achieve desirable outcomes and avoid undesirable ones.

Following Kunda, we could present female subjects with information about a set of women who had graduated from their school ten years previously and had then encountered sex discrimination on the job. All of the victims would have a set of attributes in common. They might all be: (a) economics majors; (b) who had a high grade point average; but (c) mediocre scores on standardized tests; and (d) come from liberal families in which (e) the mother was employed outside the home and (f) the father travelled on business and so was away from home a great deal. We would then ask the subjects to explain how it was that the target women came to experience adverse treatment on the job and to decide which, if any, of the women's attributes contributed to their misfortune.

If denial has a motivational component, we would expect the subjects to explain the targets' victimization in terms of attributes that they themselves did not share with the victims. If denial is entirely a matter of cognition, no such pattern would appear.

Distinguishing between motivational and cognitive components

Why does it matter what the bases of denial are? As long as the phenomenon has been demonstrated – and it has been – why should we care whether the processes underlying it are wholly cognitive, wholly motivational, or partly both? As Tetlock and Levi (1982) argued a decade ago, the distinction between emotion and cognition may be arbitrary and not very useful.

We feel the distinction matters in at least two ways. First, at the practical level, it matters whether the denial of personal disadvantage is a purely cognitive phenomenon or is, at least in part, affectively driven. While 'unrealistic optimism' may prove healthy in a number of situations (Perloff, 1983; Weinstein, 1980; 1984), it is surely unhealthy for individuals to pretend that they are exempt from all suffering when a frank recognition of their situation could lead them to ameliorate it. If people are blind to personal discrimination wholly because of the difficulty of processing one datum or one comparison, then all we need to correct the situation is to present an array of data. But what if people are defensively avoiding the array of data? Then some 'emotional education' may be in order.

Second, at a basic, theoretical level, it also matters whether we see human beings as 'intuitive scientists' whose heuristic judgements may be flawed but who essentially progress through life in the cold pursuit of understanding (Nisbett & Ross, 1980) or as creatures full of needs and defences whose thinking errs in ways that maintain self-esteem (Bradley, 1978; Weinstein, 1980; Zuckerman, 1979). Probably people are, as Fiske and Taylor (1991) maintain, 'motivated tacticians' who will sometimes choose among information-processing alternatives in a way that enhances accuracy while choosing at other times in the interests of speed or self-esteem. Knowing which model best describes people seems a worthy goal, and thus distinguishing between the cognitive and the emotional underpinnings of denial is surely one aspect of the larger goal of describing and understanding human beings.

7 Group socialization: The role of commitment

Richard Moreland, John Levine and Marie Cini

Over the past few years, there has been a renewed interest among social psychologists in studying small groups. Much of this work has been cognitive in nature, focusing on how people encode, process and retrieve information about groups and their members (cf. Messick & Mackie, 1989; Mullen & Goethals, 1987). Although such work is intriguing and has produced some valuable discoveries, it often seems artificial. Many researchers rely on brief descriptions of hypothetical groups or individuals as stimuli, and even when real groups are studied, they usually meet in laboratory settings where the interactions among members are severely limited. Under these conditions, it is not surprising that cognitive processes have such powerful effects. But what about other processes that might influence groups and their members – processes that are behavioural or motivational in nature? We believe that these processes deserve more attention from researchers, because they are likely to be critical for any comprehensive analysis of small-group behaviour.

This chapter focuses on the motivational process of commitment. We have studied commitment in the context of group socialization, a complex phenomenon involving temporal changes in the relationships between a group and its members. We will begin by presenting a theoretical model of group socialization that both describes and explains those changes. Then we will consider three alternative views of commitment, drawn respectively from social exchange theory, self-categorization theory and identity theory. The nature of commitment and its potential role in group socialization will be analyzed from each theoretical perspective, and some suggestions for future research reflecting those perspectives will be made. Finally, we will offer a few concluding remarks about the broader lessons that work on commitment can teach us about studying other motivational processes in small groups.

Group socialization

Several years ago, we became intrigued by the passage of individuals through groups. What forces propel people into and out of groups? After reviewing theoretical and empirical work on this issue from a variety of disciplines, we developed a general model (Moreland & Levine, 1982) of group socialization that accounted for what was already known and suggested some promising directions for future research. Our model is based on three psychological processes: evaluation, commitment and role transitions. According to the model, both the group and the individual engage in an ongoing evaluation of their relationship together, comparing its value to that of other relationships that are available to them. On the basis of these evaluations, feelings of commitment arise between the group and the individual. These feelings change in systematic ways over time, rising or falling to previously established decision criteria. When a decision criterion is reached, a role transition takes place, the individual enters a new phase of group membership, and the relationship between the group and the individual is transformed. Evaluation proceeds, often along different dimensions than before, producing further changes in commitment and subsequent role transitions. In this way, the individual can pass through five phases of group membership (investigation, socialization, maintenance, resocialization and remembrance), separated by four role transitions (entry, acceptance, divergence and exit).

Figure 7.1 illustrates the typical passage of an individual through a group. Group membership begins with a period of investigation. During investigation, the group engages in recruitment, looking for people who can contribute to the achievement of group goals. Meanwhile the individual, as a prospective member, engages in reconnaissance, looking for groups that can contribute to the satisfaction of personal needs. If the commitment levels of both parties rise to their respective entry criteria (EC), then the individual undergoes the role transition of entry and becomes a new member.

Entry marks the end of investigation and the beginning of socialization. During socialization, the group attempts to change the individual so that he or she can contribute more to the achievement of group goals, while the individual attempts to change the group so that it can better satisfy his or her personal needs. When these activities are successful, the individual experiences assimilation and the group experiences accommodation. If the commitment levels of both parties rise to their respective acceptance criteria (AC), then the individual undergoes the role transition of acceptance and becomes a full member of the group.

Acceptance marks the end of socialization and the beginning of maintenance. During maintenance, there is negotiation between the group and the individual as they search for a special role (e.g. group

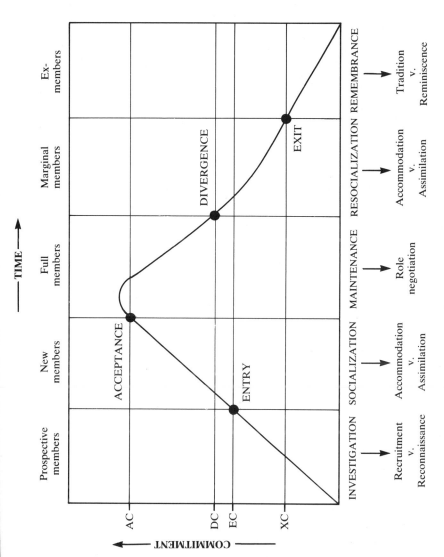

Figure 7.1 A model of group socialization (Moreland & Levine, 1982).

leader) that maximizes both the achievement of the group's goals and the satisfaction of the individual's needs. If these role negotiations succeed, then the commitment levels of both parties remain high. But if role negotiations fail and the commitment levels of both parties fall to their respective divergence criteria (DC), then the individual undergoes the role transition of divergence and becomes a marginal member of the group.

Divergence marks the end of maintenance and the beginning of resocialization. During resocialization, the group attempts again to change the individual (assimilation) so that he or she can contribute more to the achievement of group goals, while the individual attempts again to change the group (accommodation) so that it can better satisfy his or her personal needs. If the commitment levels of both parties rise again to their respective divergence criteria, then a special role transition (convergence) occurs and the individual regains full membership in the group. But if the commitment levels of both parties fall to their respective exit criteria (XC), then the individual undergoes the role transition of exit and becomes an ex-member of the group. This second and more common outcome is shown in the figure.

Finally, group membership ends with a period of remembrance, when both the group and the individual evaluate their prior relationship together. These evaluations become part of the group's traditions and the individual's reminiscences. If both parties continue to have contact with one another, then they may evaluate their current relationship as well. As more time passes, feelings of commitment between the group and the individual stabilize eventually at some low level.

As this brief review of our model suggests, commitment plays a central role in group socialization and thus deserves to be analyzed in more detail. Any such analysis must acknowledge two key features of commitment. First, commitment is a *reciprocal* process that operates at both the group and individual levels. Just as an individual can feel committed to a group, so a group can feel committed to an individual. Moreover, these feelings are often interdependent. The group and the individual can communicate their commitment to one another in a variety of ways, and when one party seems more committed to a relationship than does the other, attempts are usually made to reduce that imbalance (see Moreland & Levine, 1982; 1984). Second, commitment is clearly a *dynamic* process. Feelings of commitment rise and fall over time, reflecting changes in the relative value of the relationship between the group and the individual. These changes may involve developments in that relationship itself, or in alternative relationships that are available to the group or the individual.

Commitment can be analyzed from several theoretical perspectives. We have chosen social exchange theory, self-categorization theory and identity theory, all of which offer useful insights into commitment and its role in group socialization. Our analyses of commitment required 'stretching' the three theories in certain ways, which is hardly surprising, as none of them was developed with group socialization in mind. The fact that these theories were indeed useful for analyzing commitment attests to their scope and power, and we hope that whatever liberties we may have taken will be forgiven.

Social exchange and commitment

Social exchange theory has a long tradition within the social sciences (see Clark, 1985; Gergen, Greenberg & Willis, 1980; McClintock, Kramer & Keil, 1984; Rusbult, 1980; Thibaut & Kelley, 1959) and has undergone many changes over the years. However, at the heart of the theory are a few simple ideas. First, every relationship generates rewards and costs for its participants. The balance between these rewards and costs is a critical factor in determining a relationship's value. Second, the participants in most relationships are motivated to maximize their rewards and minimize their costs. These goals can be accomplished in several ways, such as increasing the rewards and/or decreasing the costs actually generated by the relationship, re-evaluating those rewards and costs so that the relationship seems more valuable, or becoming more involved in other relationships whose value seems greater. Finally, people can participate in several relationships simultaneously, so the relative value of a given relationship depends in part on the value of any other relationships that are available to the participants.

Our original analysis of commitment (Moreland & Levine, 1982) was influenced by social exchange theory and thus reflected many of these ideas. We argued that both the group and the individual judge the value of every relationship that is available to them, including their relationship with one another. The value of each relationship depends on the number, strength and frequency of whatever rewards and costs it generates. Relationships are very rewarding when they generate many strong and frequently occurring rewards. Conversely, relationships are very costly when they generate many strong and frequently occurring costs. The balance between the rewardingness and costliness of a relationship is thus critical – relationships become more valuable as their rewardingness exceeds their costliness.

Judgements about a relationship's value can focus on the past, the present or the future. Commitment for both the group and the individual thus depends on three important comparisons. First, both parties compare the value of their past relationship with the value of other prior relationships in which they were or could have been involved. Second, both parties compare the value of their present relationship with the value of other relationships in which they are or could be involved. Finally, both parties compare the expected value of their future relationship with the expected value of other future relationships in which they will or could become involved. Commitment between the group and the individual is thus higher when (a) their past relationship is remembered as more valuable than prior alternative relationships; (b) their present relationship is perceived as more valuable than current alternative relationships; and (c) their future relationship is expected to be more valuable than future alternative relationships.

Feelings of commitment clearly change as time goes by. One source of change is the accumulation of memories about the prior relationship between the group and the individual, and about any other prior alternative relationships. These memories affect the relative value of group membership in the past. Ongoing developments in the current relationship between the group and the individual, and in any current alternative relationships, represent another source of change in commitment. New rewards and costs may emerge within a relationship, and even old rewards and costs may change their frequency or strength. These developments affect the relative value of group membership in the present. Finally, new or altered expectations may arise about the future relationship between the group and the individual, and about any future alternative relationships. These expectations affect the relative value of group membership in the future.

Changes in commitment are important because they regulate an individual's passage through the group. Both the group and the individual develop decision criteria for determining when role transitions should occur. These decision criteria are the minimal (for entry and acceptance) or maximal (for divergence and exit) levels of commitment needed for movement from one phase of group membership to another. Decision criteria are derived from a variety of sources, including prior experiences in other relationships, observations of the socialization process in other groups, cultural norms about group socialization, and so on. Whatever their sources, decision criteria are used in much the same way by the group and the individual. When the commitment level of either party crosses its decision criterion, an attempt is made to produce the relevant role transition. Role transitions proceed smoothly when the group and the individual are equally committed to one another and share the same decision criteria. However, serious conflicts can arise when either one of these conditions is not met (see Moreland & Levine, 1984).

This analysis of commitment raises many interesting issues (see Moreland & Levine, 1982). For example, if commitment depends on judgements about the relative value of group membership in the past, present and future, then which of those judgements is most important? Because present relationships are generally more salient than past or future ones, we suspect that they have more impact on commitment. And past relationships probably have more impact than do future relationships, because judgements about the latter relationships are usually less certain. The impact of past, present and future relationships on commitment may also vary as a person moves from one phase of group membership to another. For example, future relationships are probably more important during investigation and socialization, when membership in the group is just beginning. Past relationships are probably more important during resocialization and remembrance, when group membership is ending.

Another interesting issue is whether judgements about the relative value of group membership in the past, present and future have independent effects on commitment. Suppose, for example, that membership in a group seems quite valuable at present, in comparison to other relationships that are available to the group or the individual. This might create an assimilation or 'halo' effect, causing judgements about the relative value of group membership in the past or the future to become more positive as well. There are other ways too in which judgements about the relative value of group membership that are made at different times could become interdependent. For example, some costs that the group and the individual have experienced in their past or present relationship with one another, along with some rewards that they have missed in past or present alternative relationships, might be perceived as *investments* (see, for example, Becker, 1960; Kanter, 1972; Rusbult, 1980). Investments are negative experiences that seem necessary for the attainment of future rewards or the avoidance of future costs. As a result, investments increase the relative value of group membership in the future, rather than decreasing its relative value in the past or present.

The best way to resolve these and other issues is to study the rewards and costs that groups actually exchange with their members over time. Many researchers have, in fact, studied commitment from a social exchange perspective. Some of this work can be found in organizational psychology, where researchers study the commitment of workers to business organizations (see Mathieu & Zajac, 1990; Reichers, 1985). Other work can be found in social psychology, where researchers study the commitment of friends and lovers to intimate relationships (see Levinger, 1980; Rusbult, Johnson & Morrow, 1986). Unfortunately, there has been little work in either field on commitment within small groups. As a result, almost nothing is known about such basic matters as the types of rewards and costs that are exchanged in those groups, the possible role of individual and group differences in the exchange process, and the causes and consequences of temporal changes in commitment levels.

We have begun to study commitment and its role in group socialization in several research projects involving campus groups. Although our efforts so far have been modest, they have produced some intriguing results. One of our first projects was a survey of all the freshmen who entered our university several years ago. These students participated in a summer orientation session held just before the fall semester began. During that orientation, we distributed a brief questionnaire to the new students. This questionnaire, which took about twenty minutes to complete, assessed the students' previous experiences in high-school groups and their expectations about future experiences in college groups. About 85 per cent of the questionnaires were filled out and returned to us. Some questionnaires were set aside because they were not filled out completely or correctly, or because the students who filled them out were unusual in some way (e.g. older adults returning to school). The remaining questionnaires, more than 1,100, were then coded and analyzed.

On one portion of the orientation questionnaire, students were asked to list up to five college groups that they had already considered joining and to choose which group (if any) they were most likely to join in the future. Students who could name such a group ($N = 549$) were then asked to list up to five rewards and five costs that they might experience in that group and to rate the probability (expected frequency) and strength (positivity/negativity) of each reward and cost. A variety of groups was chosen by the students. Sports and recreation groups (181), fraternities and sororities (105) and fine arts or media groups (86) were the most popular. Many students also chose pre-professional (57), student governance (47) or service groups (31). Finally, honoraries, nationality clubs and political or religious groups were chosen by a few students (42 altogether).

The expected rewards and costs of membership in these groups are summarized in Figure 7.2. Social rewards, such as meeting people with shared interests or making new friends, were by far the most common, but personal rewards, such as enhancing one's self-esteem, developing self-discipline, helping others or becoming more sociable, were often mentioned as well. Other rewards that many students expected to experience were intellectual (e.g. learning new skills or information), physical (e.g. improving or maintaining personal fitness) or professional (e.g. developing an impressive résumé or networking). Finally, a number of students simply expected to have fun in their chosen groups. Nearly all of these rewards (99 per cent) were direct rather than indirect: students almost never described the avoidance of costs (negative reinforcement) as a type of reward.

Among the expected costs of group membership, lost time (e.g. time wasted or diverted from other activities) and financial expenses (e.g. paying dues and buying special materials/equipment or uniforms/costumes) were by far the most common. Other costs that students expected

REWARDS

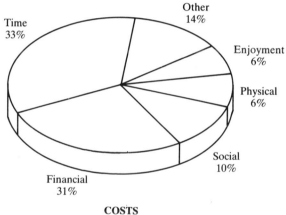

COSTS

Figure 7.2 Students' expectations about the types of rewards and costs associated with membership in campus groups.

to experience were social (e.g. conformity pressures, conflicts with other group members or limited contact with outsiders) or physical (e.g. fatigue, illness or injuries) in nature. Finally, some students expected their chosen groups to be boring, frustrating or too demanding, and thus not much fun. Although most of these costs (65 per cent) were also direct, a substantial number were indirect: many students described the loss of rewards from other relationships as a type of cost.

The mean frequency and strength ratings for the various types of rewards and costs are summarized in Figure 7.3. The most interesting

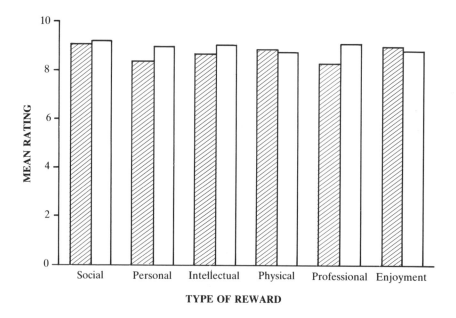

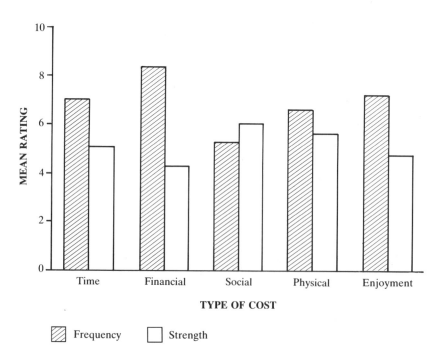

Figure 7.3 Students' frequency and strength ratings for the expected rewards and costs of membership in campus groups.

aspect of these results was the remarkable optimism displayed by the students (see Brinthaupt, Moreland & Levine, 1991). The mean ratings for the expected rewards of group membership were all quite high and did not vary much from one type of reward to another. In contrast, the mean ratings for the expected costs of group membership were much lower and varied considerably from one type of cost to another. In addition, there seemed to be a negative relationship between the frequency and strength of costs – stronger costs were expected to occur less often. To verify the students' apparent optimism, we first calculated for each student the total number of rewards and costs that he or she listed, as well as the mean frequency and strength ratings for those rewards and costs. (All of the students listed at least one reward, but many of them listed no costs. The mean frequency and strength ratings for the latter students' costs were set to zero.) A series of within-subjects t-tests revealed that the average student expected to experience significantly more rewards than costs in his or her chosen group [$M = 2.47$ v. $M = 1.34$, t (548) = 22.76, $p < 0.01$] and expected the rewards of membership in that group to occur more often [$M = 8.75$ v. $M = 5.32$, t (548) = 19.81, $p < 0.01$] and to be stronger [$M = 9.07$ v. $M = 3.71$, t (548) = 35.18, $p < 0.01$] than the costs.

Additional analyses of how individual or group differences affected these students' expectations about the rewards and costs of group membership could be performed. However, a more relevant issue for us was the students' commitment to their chosen groups. Because none of the students had yet joined those groups, membership had no past or present value for them. However, it was possible, by examining the expected rewards and costs of group membership for each student, to assess its future value for that person. We began by multiplying the frequency rating for each reward by its strength rating, then summing across rewards to produce a measure of how rewarding that person expected group membership to be. Similar computations on the cost ratings produced a measure of how costly group membership was expected to be. Finally, the future value of group membership was assessed by subtracting its expected costliness from its rewardingness. Scores on this measure ranged from a low of -147.50 to a high of $+415.50$, with a mean of $+153.61$ and a standard deviation of 98.68. The mean score was significantly greater than zero, t (548) = 36.49, $p < 0.01$, suggesting that the average student was quite committed to his or her chosen group.

According to our analysis of commitment, however, it is the *relative* value of a group that determines a person's commitment to it. Perhaps we should have asked the students to describe not only the expected rewards and costs of membership in their chosen groups, but also the rewards and costs that they expected to experience in all the other groups to which they might belong at college. We lacked the courage, however, to pose such a difficult task. Yet some information about the students' alternative relationships was available from their responses on the orientation questionnaires. Recall that the students were asked to list up to five campus groups that they had already considered joining. Our analysis of commitment suggests that the availability of these alternative group memberships should have *decreased* the relative value of the students' chosen groups.

To test this hypothesis, we first counted how many alternative campus groups each student listed on the orientation questionnaire. To qualify as an alternative, a group had to come from the same general category as the student's chosen group (e.g. fraternity or sorority, student governance, political or religious). About 79 per cent of the students listed no alternatives to their chosen groups. Most of the remaining students listed just one alternative, though some listed two or even three. We then divided the students into two sets, those who had considered joining alternative groups (118) and those who had not (431). A between-subjects t-test revealed that the mean commitment scores for these subjects were not significantly different [$M = +154.35$ $v.$ $M = +153.40$, t (547) = 0.09, $p < 0.05$]. Several explanations for this (non-)finding could be offered. Merely asking the students to list alternative group memberships may have led them to adjust their expectations about the rewards and costs of membership in their chosen groups. In other words, the students may have described the relative rather than absolute value of future membership in those groups. Another possibility is that our decisions about which groups qualified as alternatives did not reflect the students' opinions about such matters.

There are probably better ways to measure the relative value of group membership for the individual. Perhaps people could be asked not only to describe the rewards and costs of membership in a target group, but also to evaluate how unusual those experiences are in the general context of other groups available to them. For example, how often do people experience the same rewards and costs in those other groups, and how strong are those rewards and costs there? Or one could ask people to make comparative judgements about whether the rewards and costs of belonging to the target group occur more or less often, and are stronger or weaker, than the same rewards and costs in other groups that are available to them. The relative value of the target group would be greater insofar as membership in that group generated unique rewards and common costs, or rewards that were relatively frequent and strong and costs that were relatively infrequent and weak. Another tactic might be to ask people how they would feel if membership in their target group were not possible. The relative value of that group would be greater insofar as people regretted not belonging to it. Finally, people could be asked to select just one group that seemed similar to their target group and then describe the rewards and costs of membership in that comparison group. The relative value of the target group would be greater insofar as it generated a better set of rewards and costs.

We stressed earlier in this chapter that commitment is both a reciprocal and a dynamic process. The study just described focused on the commitment of individuals towards groups, but ignored the commitment of groups towards individuals. We have not yet attempted to study the reciprocal nature of commitment, partly because of the methodological challenges associated with such research. How could one assess the value of an individual to a group? One obvious tactic might be to ask every other member to describe the rewards and costs generated for the group by the target person. However, this would be cumbersome in most groups, and the problem of weighting evaluations from different group members would have to be solved. An alternative might be to ask the group's leader to describe the rewards and costs generated by the target person, or simply to assess how valuable that person is to the group. These tactics, of course, would not capture the *relative* value of the individual for the group. Perhaps some of the methods just suggested for measuring the relative value of group membership for an individual could be modified to measure the relative value of individual membership for a group. For example, one might ask either the members of a group or its leader about how they would feel if the target person were not a member. The relative value of the individual would be greater insofar as other members regretted his or her absence from the group.

Studying the dynamic aspects of commitment is also quite challenging, but we have made some progress in this regard. A subsample ($N = 100$) of the students who filled out our orientation questionnaire were recontacted about three months after school began and then again about three months later. At these follow-up sessions, the students described their recent experiences with campus groups. For example, they were asked to list any groups they had contacted or that had contacted them, when those contacts occurred, and what methods of contact (e.g. personal visits, telephone calls, letters or mailings) were used. Students' estimates of how committed they were to these groups, and how committed those groups were to them, were also obtained. Finally, students who had chosen a special group on the orientation questionnaire were asked whether or not they had joined that group yet. Students who had not yet joined their chosen groups described again the future rewards and costs that they expected to experience in those groups. Students who had joined their chosen groups described the rewards and costs that they were presently experiencing in those groups, as well as the future rewards and costs that they expected to experience there.

Preliminary analyses of these data have produced some intriguing findings regarding the students' feelings of commitment during the first three months of the study. First, initial levels of commitment were higher among students who later joined their chosen groups than among students who did not join such groups. Second, students who joined their chosen groups became less committed to those groups afterwards. This decrease in commitment, which is consistent with other research (e.g. Wanous, 1980) on the disappointments felt by overly optimistic newcomers, was especially clear in the students' expectations about the future rewards and costs of group membership. Finally, levels of commitment among students who did not join their chosen groups increased somewhat over time. Further analyses of these data should help to clarify some of the causes and consequences of temporal changes in commitment.

Self-categorization and commitment

We have devoted considerable attention to the social exchange perspective on commitment, because it has guided our own work. However, other theories can also provide useful insights into the nature of commitment and its role in group socialization. An example is self-categorization theory, developed by Turner and his colleagues (see Hogg & McGarty, 1990; Turner, 1985; Turner, Hogg, Oakes, Reicher & Wetherell, 1987; Turner & Oakes, 1989; also see Chapter 10, this volume). This theory arose from research on intergroup relations, but now has been extended to a variety of other group phenomena, including group formation, conformity and deviance, decision-making, and cohesion. We believe that the theory also can be extended to the process of commitment.

Although self-categorization theory is complex, a few central ideas can again be identified. First, people are motivated to understand the world around them, so that they can cope more effectively with whatever problems occur. Categorization is helpful for achieving that goal, because it permits more rapid responses to environmental stimuli, without exhaustive evaluations of all their characteristics. Second, social as well as non-social stimuli can be categorized, and the categorization of social stimuli involves the self as well as others. Self-categorization plays an important role in guiding many forms of social behaviour. Finally, self-categorizations can be carried out at different levels of abstraction. A sense of social identity develops when people categorize themselves as members of one group rather than another. When people categorize themselves as unique individuals within some group, a sense of personal identity develops. Choosing one level of self-categorization rather than another depends on both the accessibility of the relevant category and how well it 'fits' the situation. A categorization scheme that maximizes the *meta-contrast ratio* (the mean difference between categories divided by the mean difference within categories) provides the best level of fit for a given situation.

Social categorization, which focuses a person's attention on similarities within and/or differences between groups, encourages the use of *prototypes* to characterize group members. A prototype (in this context) is a mental image of the type of person who best represents some group. Any characteristic (e.g. appearance, background, abilities, opinions, personality traits) that makes a significant contribution to the meta-contrast ratio on which the social categorization was based will be incorporated into the group prototype. The prototypical member, whether real or imaginary, is thus someone who embodies whatever characteristics make a group distinctive.

Hogg (1987, 1992, 1993) has argued that cohesion within a group may be related to how well its members match the group prototype. Hogg distinguishes between personal attraction and social attraction as possible sources of group cohesion. Personal attraction among group members reflects their levels of similarity to one another, whereas social attraction among group members reflects their levels of prototypicality. These two forms of attraction are often correlated, but need not be identical. For example, group members could be similar to one another in ways that do not make their group distinctive. As a result, their levels of personal attraction would be high, but their levels of social attraction would be low. Hogg claims that group cohesion really depends more on social attraction than on personal attraction, with higher levels of social attraction producing greater group cohesion. The results of several experiments by Hogg and his colleagues (e.g. Hogg & Hardie, 1991) provide some support for this claim.

Hogg's work on group cohesion suggests that self-categorization theory could be used to analyze commitment as well. Suppose that group members indeed evaluate both themselves and one another to determine how well each person matches the group prototype. The group's commitment to an individual might thus depend on how prototypical that person seems to all the other group members; and an individual's commitment to the group might depend on how prototypical that person seems to himself or herself. Social identity, or the psychological acceptance of group membership by the individual (cf. Turner & Oakes, 1989), thus could be the basis for personal commitment. Alternatively, someone's commitment to a group might depend on the average perceived prototypicality of all the other group members, as judged by the individual.

This view of commitment suggests at least two ways in which it might change over time. First, commitment might change because the group prototype is unstable. As time passes, the composition of a group (see

Moreland & Levine, 1992) can change through (a) the arrival of prospective members and/or departure of marginal members and (b) the personal development (e.g. improved abilities, new opinions) of everyone in the group. Even if a group's composition were constant, temporal changes could occur in the social categorization process that yields the group prototype. For example, group members might compare their own group to a different set of outgroups, or the composition of a given outgroup might change. Second, commitment might change because the characteristics of individual group members are unstable as well. As we just noted, personal development can occur as time goes by; and time can allow group members to learn more about one another, so that even if their actual characteristics were constant, their perceived characteristics might change. Any changes in the group's prototype and/or the characteristics (real or perceived) of its members could alter the perceived prototypicality of every person in the group. As a result, each person's commitment to the group, and the group's commitment to him or her, would be altered.

These changes in commitment again serve to regulate an individual's passage through the group. We claimed earlier that both the group and the individual develop decision criteria for determining when role transitions should occur. These decision criteria were described as minimal or maximal levels of commitment associated with movement between different phases of group membership. When the commitment level of either the group or the individual crosses a decision criterion, an attempt is made by that party to produce the relevant role transition. These same ideas can be borrowed for the present analysis, except of course that commitment now depends on perceived prototypicality rather than the exchange of rewards and costs. Alternatively, decision criteria for both the group and the individual might involve judgements about prototypicality, rather than feelings of commitment. The role transition of acceptance, for example, may occur only when the degree of match between a newcomer's characteristics and the group prototype reaches some level that both parties regard as suitable for full membership. Whether decision criteria involve levels of commitment or prototypicality, serious conflicts are still likely to arise unless the group and the individual are equally committed to one another and share the same decision criteria.

A self-categorization analysis of commitment also raises many interesting issues. For example, the characteristics that make members of a group distinctive are not always clear. There may be few such characteristics or they may be subtle and hard to assess. As a result, it could be difficult to develop a strong group prototype. Moreover, more than one prototype might emerge within a group, producing conflicts among members who disagree about what makes their group distinctive. Even if a single, strong prototype emerges, its content may not be entirely positive. The members of some groups may be distinctive primarily because they are somehow worse than the members of other groups. If so, then it seems unlikely that commitment, for either the group or the individual, would increase as perceived prototypicality rises. Perhaps groups refuse to incorporate negative characteristics into their prototypes (cf. Tajfel & Turner, 1986), or somehow suppress the use of such characteristics when prototypicality evaluations are made. Alternatively, separate evaluations of prototypicality may be made for positive and negative characteristics. The balance between positive and negative prototypicality would thus be critical – commitment would increase as the positive prototypicality of group members exceeded their negative prototypicality.

Another interesting issue is whether group prototypes are really based on the characteristics that make group members *distinctive*, as self-categorization theorists believe. Several other kinds of prototypes that could emerge within groups can be imagined. For example, the prototypical group member might be someone who embodies whatever characteristics are *typical* of the group, or whatever characteristics group members regard as *ideal*. These alternative prototypes would affect commitment at both the group and the individual levels. For example, if the group prototype were based on typical characteristics, then both group and individual commitment would depend on how 'normal' the person was in comparison to other group members. If the group prototype were based on ideal characteristics, then the group's commitment to an individual would depend on how closely he or she approximated the ideal, whereas an individual's commitment to the group would also depend on how closely he or she approximated the ideal. Some groups might even develop separate prototypes (involving distinctive, typical or ideal member characteristics) for every phase of group membership. If so, then commitment would depend on how closely each person matched the prototype for someone in his or her membership phase.

Finally, self-categorization is such a rapid and flexible process that it may provide an ephemeral basis for commitment. At any given moment, people may choose to categorize themselves at the individual rather than the group level, making their personal rather than social identities more important. In addition, even when people categorize themselves at the group level, their social identities may be quite unstable. As the social context shifts, so will the categories that provide the best levels of fit, as determined by the meta-contrast ratio. Different categories may become salient, causing a variety of social identities to emerge and then recede. When someone belongs to a group, but is not currently thinking about himself or herself as a member, does that person feel any commitment to the group? And when a group is not currently thinking about someone as a member, does it still feel some commitment to that person, even though he or she still belongs to the group? If not, then one can imagine curious situations in which many rewards and costs are being exchanged among group members, yet self-categorizations focus everyone's attention on other social identities, so that neither the group nor the individual feels any commitment to their relationship.

Once again, the best way to resolve these and other issues is through research. Only a few researchers have studied group prototypes, but interestingly much of their work seems relevant to group socialization. For example, Niedenthal, Cantor and Kihlstrom (1985) found that new students' attitudes towards various campus housing options (e.g. apartments, dormitories) reflected a prototype-matching process – students assessed how similar they were to the typical person living in each setting and then chose options that provided the best matches. Several organizational psychologists (e.g. Dalessio & Imada, 1984; Rowe, 1984) have studied the role of group prototypes in the hiring of new employees. Their work suggests that recruiters match the characteristics of job applicants to prototypes that describe the typical, or often the ideal, worker. Applicants who match those prototypes more closely are more likely to be hired. Finally, Hogg and Hardie (1991) studied the members of a local sports team and found that perceived prototypicality (as judged by the self or by others) was associated with more positive evaluations of the team, greater popularity and longer tenure.

Although work of this sort is fascinating, there is a clear need for further research on group prototypes. In order to study the role of these prototypes in group socialization, people should be asked to evaluate both their own prototypicality and the prototypicality of every other group member. These evaluations should be collected on several occasions, so that temporal changes in prototypicality can be related to each person's passage through the group. At any given moment, an individual's commitment to the group would depend on that person's evaluation of his or her own prototypicality (or perhaps the prototypicality of all the other group members), whereas the group's commitment to an individual would depend on how prototypical (on the average) he or she seems to the other members.

The key to such research is developing adequate techniques for the measurement of group prototypes. One obvious tactic is simply to ask group members, either individually or collectively, to describe what makes their group distinctive (see Charles, 1982; Hogg & Hardie, 1991). This information could be supplemented by archival analyses of written statements about the group's goals, values or ideology (Bar-Tal, 1990). Members could also be asked to name someone who embodies the unique spirit of their group. That person's characteristics could then be measured directly, or group members could be asked to describe the person. Finally, ratings of ingroup and outgroup members (real or hypothetical) on some standard set of characteristics could be used to measure a group prototype. The most direct approach would be to collect comparative ratings, but one might also collect separate sets of ratings and then search for characteristics that distinguish between groups. An even better choice might be the 'diagnostic ratio' procedure developed by McCauley and Stitt (1978) for the measurement of stereotypes. Their procedure, derived from Bayesian statistics, assesses the extent to which prior knowledge about someone's group membership affects probability judgements about that person's characteristics. All of these tactics assume, of course, that group prototypes are sets of characteristics that make members distinctive, rather than characteristics that are typical of the group or that describe the ideal member.

Identity and commitment

Identity theory, developed by Stryker and his colleagues (see Stryker, 1968; 1987; Stryker & Serpe, 1982; Wells & Stryker, 1988), offers yet another perspective on commitment and its role in group socialization. This theory is also complex, but once again a few central ideas can be identified. First, social roles (representing the expectations of significant others) have a powerful impact on behaviour. At any given moment, several roles (e.g. father, husband, accountant, golfer, neighbour) may be available to an individual. However, some roles are incongruent with others, and even when roles are congruent, the person may lack the time and energy to perform them all. As a result, choices must be made about which role to perform. Second, social roles are often internalized by the individual as possible selves or *identities*. These identities are organized into a hierarchy reflecting their relative salience. Identities that are more salient are more likely to be activated, producing the relevant role behaviour. Finally, the salience of an identity depends primarily on the individual's commitment to it. This commitment arises from various pressures associated with the person's position within a social network.

A simple social network is illustrated in Figure 7.4. The focus of this network is Person A, who belongs to a small work group containing two other members (B and C). However, each member of that group has relationships with other people who are not group members. For example, A, D, E and F are all members of the same family; B, G and H play golf with one another; and C, I and J are neighbours. Some of the people who belong to these other groups may have relationships with one another as well. For example, D and G are friends, while F and J are enemies. The point of all this is that every group is embedded in a complex web of relationships, all of which can influence the thoughts, feelings and behaviours of group members.

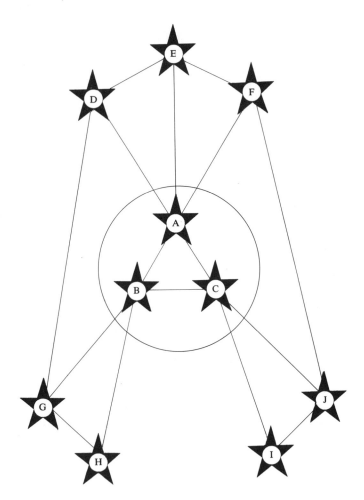

Figure 7.4 A simple social network.

According to identity theory, commitment to an identity depends on the number, intensity and value of whatever relationships would be lost by abandoning the relevant role. Suppose, for example, that Person A left his or her work group. That would clearly alter A's relationships with the other group members (B and C); but it might also affect his or her direct relationships with family members D, E and F, and indirect relationships with B's golfing friends (G and H) or C's neighbours (I and J). Some of these relationships are probably more intense than others, in the sense that they involve more frequent interaction across a wider variety of settings. The value of these relationships may vary as well, in the sense that some of them are more rewarding and/or less costly than others. As the total damage associated with the loss of all these relationships increases, Person A should become more committed to his or her identity as a group member (i.e., more concerned about maintaining membership in the work group).

A similar analysis could be made of the group's commitment to Person A. If he or she left the group, then a variety of people would be affected. For example, B and C would lose their relationship with A, and their relationships with the members of A's family probably would be weakened. Changes might also occur in the relationship between B and C, as they adjust to A's absence. In fact, the work group might not survive A's departure. As the number, intensity and value of all these lost relationships increase, both B and C should become more concerned about maintaining A's membership in the group. That is, their commitment to his/her identity as a group member should rise. The mean of their individual commitment levels represents the group's commitment to Person A.

As time passes, changes are likely to occur in the social network, producing corresponding changes in commitment between the group and the individual. For example, the composition of the network may change as new participants enter and old participants leave it. As new relationships form and old relationships lapse among current participants, the structure of the network may change as well. Finally, the intensity or value of various relationships within the network may rise or fall over time. All of these changes could affect commitment, if they are linked in some way to the individual's membership in the group. As more network relationships become contingent on that membership and/or those relationships grow more intense or valuable, levels of commitment between the group and the individual should rise. In effect, social pressure from network participants would force the group and the individual to remain together.

Our model of group socialization suggests that changes in commitment serve to regulate an individual's passage through a group. That passage is, however, difficult to explain from an identity-theory perspective. Group membership is viewed by identity theorists as an all-or-none phenomenon – someone is in or out of the group. Distinctions among the various phases of group membership are thus overlooked, making the occurrence of role transitions rather puzzling. Within a social network, a few relationships among participants could be contingent on an individual's presence in a particular membership phase. For example, a boy's parents might be quite happy if their son were an ex-member of a rock-and-roll band, but quite unhappy if he were a new or full band member. However, it would be surprising if many such contingencies arose. Perhaps network participants are most concerned about full group membership, because it has the greatest impact on a person's relationships with others. If so, then they may evaluate how far someone is from full membership at any given moment. Role transitions could thus mark significant shifts in an individual's perceived distance from the group's core.

This analysis of commitment, like its predecessors, raises many interesting issues. For example, is commitment always based on the desire to please people who approve of someone's membership in a group? There may be an alternative source of commitment, arising from the desire to annoy people who disapprove of group membership. A boy might join a rock-and-roll band, for instance, because he wants to annoy his parents and knows that they will disapprove. In any case, both (a) the motivation of an individual or group to please the other participants in a social network and (b) the attitudes of those participants towards the individual's group membership, may be important variables that influence commitment.

Another interesting issue is whether relationships within a social network are really contingent on one another. Some relationships may indeed be mutually exclusive, producing the contingencies described by identity theorists. Most relationships are probably more flexible. A college student who quits her sorority, for instance, may lose a few friends, but most of her relationships will be unaffected, and those that are harmed may suffer little damage and/or recover quickly. This suggests another important variable that might influence commitment, namely the tolerance of network participants for someone's loss of group membership. This tolerance not only varies across relationships, but might also vary within a relationship over time. Both the group and the individual may have difficulty assessing how tolerant other people would be if the individual left the group. Some people may be ambivalent about the individual's group membership, and thus send mixed messages, misleading messages or no messages at all about their tolerance to the group or the individual. Even if clear messages about tolerance are sent, they may be overlooked or misinterpreted.

Finally, there are several ways in which an awareness of the various pressures imposed on each party by its social network might affect the relationship between a group and an individual. For example, suppose a group discovers that one of its members is under pressure from friends and relatives to stay in the group. Expressions of commitment to the group by that individual are likely to be discounted, and the group may try to take advantage of the situation by demanding more from the person. Similarly, a group might demand less from an individual, and be quite impressed by his or her expressions of commitment, if it discovers that the person is being pressured to leave the group. All of this suggests that groups and their members may be quite interested in *all* the social pressures affecting their relationship, and that each party might try to control what the other knows or believes about those pressures.

Once again, research is the best way to resolve these and other issues. Only a few direct tests of identity theory have been performed (e.g. Hoelter, 1983; Stryker & Serpe, 1982), but their results indicate that commitment is indeed related to beliefs about how the loss of one relationship might affect other relationships in which someone is involved. Some research on commitment in social and organizational psychology also seems consistent with an identity-theory analysis. For example, there is ample evidence that friends and relatives can affect the relationship between a group and an individual by expressing their opinions about that relationship, creating problems or helping to solve them, offering advice, and so on (see Moreland & Levine, 1989). In addition, recent research on romantic relationships has demonstrated the importance of investments as sources of commitment. Rusbult (1980), for instance, has distinguished intrinsic investments (costs already experienced to build a relationship) from extrinsic investments (costs that would be experienced if a relationship ended). The latter investments are reminiscent of identity theory. Research by Rusbult and her colleagues (e.g. Rusbult, 1980; 1983; Rusbult et al., 1986; but see Sprecher, 1988) indicates that both forms of investment can strengthen commitment to a relationship. Finally, many organizational psychologists have studied the effects of 'side-bets' (Becker, 1960) on commitment among workers. Side-bets are accumulated investments, such as financial sacrifices, time and effort spent learning special skills, or relationships with colleagues, that might be lost or devalued if someone left an organization. Side-bets also seem reminiscent of social identity theory, but the available evidence indicates that they are not strongly related to workers' commitment (see Cohen & Lowenberg, 1990). This may reflect a tendency among researchers to use such variables as age or job tenure as proxies for side-bets, rather than measuring side-bets directly (Meyer & Allen, 1984).

Although an identity-theory view of commitment has some research support, few studies have focused on commitment within small groups, and studies of temporal changes in commitment (within any relationship) are even more rare. Once again, a need for further research is apparent. Research on commitment from an identity perspective requires information about the social network surrounding the group and the individual. Ideally, people should be asked to list any of their own relationships that would be harmed if (a) they were not group members and (b) every other person in the group were not a member. All of those relationships should then be evaluated for such characteristics as intensity, value, tolerance (for each lost membership), and so on. These data should be collected on several occasions, so that temporal changes in commitment can be related to each person's passage through the group. At any given moment, an individual's commitment to the group would depend on the total damage that his or her relationships might suffer if group membership were lost; and the group's commitment to an individual would depend on the total damage (averaged across members) that his or her loss of membership might cause everyone else in the group to suffer.

The problem with this approach, of course, is that collecting such data would place enormous and probably intolerable demands on respondents. Perhaps people could be asked to list and evaluate just a few of their relationships, namely those that would be most affected by the individual's loss of group membership. Another tactic, used by some researchers (e.g. Rusbult, 1983), is to offer people a prepared list of possible costs associated with the loss of group membership (for themselves or others) and then ask them to evaluate the overall strength of each cost if membership indeed were lost. Commitment would increase as those costs grew stronger. Finally, at a very general level, people could be asked to evaluate how harmful the loss of group membership (for themselves or others) would be for their social lives. Again, commitment would increase as the loss of group membership grew more harmful.

Conclusions

The purpose of this chapter was to analyze the nature of commitment and its role in group socialization from several theoretical perspectives. Three such perspectives – social exchange theory, self-categorization theory and identity theory – were selected. Each perspective offered a unique view of commitment and provided some useful insights into group socialization. Social exchange theory, for example, clarified the kinds of experiences that can affect the relationship between a group and an individual. Self-categorization theory revealed the potential importance of socially shared beliefs within a group about what makes it distinctive from other groups. Finally, identity theory affirmed the role of social networks in shaping the relationships between groups and their members.

Our analyses suggested many directions for future research on commitment and group socialization. It is apparent, however, that actually performing such research can be very challenging. Many social psychologists prefer to study small groups in the laboratory, where events are readily controlled. Unfortunately, most laboratory groups are poorly suited for research on group socialization, because their lives are so brief, their composition is so stable and their social context is so ambiguous. Researchers who hope to study the role of commitment in group socialization must therefore gain access to natural groups, and those groups must be studied over time periods that are long enough for the socialization process to unfold. Work of this sort can become a nightmare, combining the most difficult features of field research, groups research and longitudinal research. Nevertheless, such work *has* been performed, as witnessed by our own efforts and those of many others whose work we have cited. The effort required is amply rewarded by the information generated about social phenomena whose theoretical and practical importance seems indisputable.

A few final remarks about studying motivational processes such as commitment are in order. Although commitment is clearly an *affective* experience for both the group and the individual, our analyses of commitment and its role in group socialization were all rather *cognitive* in nature. Social exchange theory, for example, suggests that commitment depends on the relative value of group membership in the past, present and future. In order to assess that value, groups and their members must perform complex mental computations, using information about the rewards and costs (of varying frequencies and strengths) generated by all the relationships available to them. Self-categorization theory suggests that commitment depends on the perceived prototypicality of everyone in a group. Judgements about prototypicality require not only the identification of characteristics that distinguish ingroup from outgroup members, but also the evaluation of how well various individuals match the resulting prototype. Finally, identity theory suggests that commitment depends on how group members believe their relationships with other people would be affected by the departure of someone from the group. These beliefs reflect an extensive analysis of the social network in which the group is embedded. Information regarding the number, intensity, value and tolerance of all the relationships in which group members participate must be considered.

Do feelings of commitment always arise from such elaborate cognitive processing? The answer depends on one's views regarding the relationship between affect and cognition. A few theorists (e.g. Zajonc, 1980a) have argued that affect can have non-cognitive sources. If so, then other analyses of commitment, derived from theories that better reflect its affective nature, may deserve to be explored. Given the current emphasis within social psychology on cognitive theories, it is unlikely that any affective theories of commitment will be developed quickly or easily. In the meantime, researchers should at least consider some alternative ways of measuring commitment within groups. Rather than just collecting self-reports from group members about their cognitive processes and/or products, why not obtain behavioural (e.g. Dabbs & Ruback, 1987; Tickle-Degnen & Rosenthal, 1987) or even physiological (e.g. Blascovich & Kelsey, 1990; Cacioppo, Petty & Tassinary, 1989) measures of commitment as well? Such measures could provide valuable clues about the nature of commitment and its role in group socialization – clues that otherwise would be overlooked.

8 Working on collective tasks: Social loafing and social compensation

Kipling Williams, Steven Karau and Martin Bourgeois

The effect of working in groups on individual motivation and effort has long been a focus of social psychological interest. Indeed, two of the earliest experiments in social psychology dealt with this issue. In the 1890s, Triplett (1898) found that children exerted more effort (reeled in fishing-line more rapidly) on a coactive task with other children present than when they worked alone. In the 1880s, Ringelmann examined adults' rope-pulling performances individually and collectively and noted a decrease in effort with increasing group size (see Kravitz & Martin, 1986). Whereas Triplett's findings were replicated early (not without difficulty) and eventually explained in terms of social facilitation (Zajonc, 1965), Ringelmann's findings were essentially ignored, regarded with scepticism, or interpreted as a mere artefact of inco-ordination among group members rather than motivation loss (Steiner, 1972). It wasn't until 1974 that Ringelmann's findings were replicated (Ingham, Levinger, Graves & Peckham, 1974), and not until even later that the motivational component of this effect was understood as an important and reliable phenomenon unto itself, now called 'social loafing' (Latané, Williams & Harkins, 1979).

Comparisons with social facilitation theory and research have been made elsewhere (Geen, 1991; Harkins, 1987; Jackson & Williams, 1985). One important contribution of the social loafing literature is that we now know it is too simplistic to suggest that people are always aroused or made anxious by the presence of others (Zajonc, 1980a). There is a variety of instances in which the presence of others appears to be comforting or arousal-reducing (Jackson & Williams, 1985; Schachter, 1959). The apparent distinction may lie in how the others in the group are perceived – either as sources of influence or as co-targets of influence (Latané, 1981). For the purposes of this chapter, it will suffice to say that social facilitation is an increase in individual effort when working on coactive tasks (in which one works on an individual task in the presence of other group members) compared to when working alone. Social loafing is a reduction in individual effort when working on a collective task (in which one's outputs are pooled with those of other group members) compared to when working either alone or coactively. In most social facilitation studies, the other group members (coactors) are perceived as sources of influence or evaluation. In contrast, because social loafing research uses collective tasks, the other group members (coworkers) are perceived as co-targets of influence, hence reducing the impact of the source. We propose that most group tasks are collective. Athletic teams, committees, juries, work crews, manuscript coauthors, orchestras and choirs all provide everyday examples of groups that must work together collectively to accomplish their goals.

Indeed, Geen (1991) included social loafing as one of only three active research areas that pertain to social motivation. Because many group tasks are indeed collective, determining the conditions under which individuals do or do not engage in social loafing has theoretical, as well as significant practical, importance. At a theoretical level, specifying which variables moderate or mediate social loafing is central to developing a fuller understanding of the dynamics underlying the motivation and performance of both individuals and groups. At a practical level, the identification of moderating variables may suggest means for devising interventions by which social loafing may be reduced or overcome in everyday groups and organizations.

A brief review of the social loafing literature

Since the experiment by Ingham *et al*. (1974), nearly 80 studies on social loafing have been conducted. These studies have used a wide variety of tasks, including physical tasks (e.g. shouting, rope-pulling and swimming), cognitive tasks (e.g. generating ideas), evaluative tasks (e.g. quality ratings of poems, editorials and clinical therapists) and perceptual tasks (e.g. maze performance, vigilance performance). Both laboratory experiments and field studies have been conducted using a variety of subject populations. Given the relatively large empirical literature that is now available, a coherent understanding of the social loafing effect is beginning to emerge. Recently, Karau and Williams (1991a) conducted a meta-analytic review of this research. We will briefly review their findings, which cast light on the strength and generality of social loafing, and the extent to which various parameters moderate or mediate the effect.

Across all studies, there was a statistically reliable and moderately strong (i.e., a mean-weighted d of 0.44) social loafing effect: people produced lower effort levels when working collectively than when working coactively. Subjects' self-reports of their efforts, however, tended to fail to acknowledge this difference or to underestimate the magnitude of the difference. In addition, a number of factors were found to moderate social loafing. We will briefly consider each factor.

Evaluation

Evaluation potential was an especially potent determinant of collective effort. As expected, individuals were less likely to loaf on collective tasks when evaluation potential was held constant (either high or low) across the coactive versus collective comparisons. In fact, only when inputs could be evaluated coactively, but not collectively, did the social loafing effect reach significance. These findings are consistent with the claim made by Harkins (1987) and others that evaluation mediates the social loafing effect.

Task valence

A number of studies manipulated how involving or interesting the task was to the participants. The tendency to engage in social loafing decreased as task valence increased. Individuals loafed when task valence was moderate or low, but did not loaf when task valence was high. Consistent with their actual efforts, individuals were less likely to report that they engaged in social loafing when task valence was high than when task valence was moderate.

Group valence

Studies were classified according to how well acquainted group members were to each other. Individuals did not loaf when group valence was high, but loafed in all other conditions. The magnitude of the social loafing effect was highest when subjects worked with strangers but was lowest when subjects worked with close friends or team-mates. Thus, enhancing group cohesiveness might serve to reduce or eliminate social loafing. Similarly, the tendency to engage in social loafing was reduced when participants were provided with a group-level comparison standard.

Expectation of coworker performance

Several studies manipulated subjects' expectations for how well their coworkers would perform, usually by manipulating perceptions of the effort or ability of the coworkers. Individuals engaged in social loafing when working with coworkers whom they expected to perform well or when working with coworkers for whom no performance expectations were provided, but did not loaf when working with coworkers whom they expected to perform poorly. Interestingly, an examination of the individual studies involved suggests that self-reported effort in these studies tends to reflect the actual effort levels when individuals have expectations for how well their coworkers will perform (we elaborate on this point in the 'Strategic or non-conscious?' section below).

Uniqueness of task

Individuals worked just as hard collectively as coactively when their individual inputs to the collective product were unique, but loafed when their inputs were either potentially redundant or completely redundant.

Task complexity

Individuals performed better coactively than collectively when working on simple tasks (and on tasks for which complexity was unclear) but performed just as well collectively as coactively when working on complex tasks.

Group size

Group size was positively related to size of the social loafing effect. Effect sizes were larger (i.e., a greater tendency for subjects to engage in social loafing) for studies that combined more individual inputs into the collective product and for studies that had more individuals to perform the task at each session. The group size finding is consistent with social impact theory predictions (see Figure 8.1). Furthermore, the tendency for individuals to report working harder coactively than collectively was larger for studies that combined more individual inputs into the collective product.

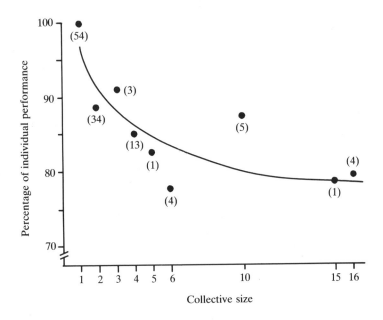

Note: Numbers within parentheses refer to the number of studies conducted in each collective size.

Figure 8.1 Social loafing as a function of group size across 54 studies. Taken from Jackson and Williams (1986).

Population differences

Third-graders and younger students tended to loaf less than either fourth- through sixth-graders or college students. In addition, organizational employees tended to loaf less than fourth- through sixth-graders, junior-high or high-school students or college students. It is possible that this may be indicative of a developmental trend whereby children do not become attentive to strategic concerns in task performance until they reach a certain age (see Williams & Williams, 1981, for a discussion). The latter finding might reflect either age differences or individuals' commitments to performing well within contexts related to their occupations.

The social loafing effect was also greater for studies that used samples of only male subjects than for studies that used either mixed samples or samples of only female subjects. In addition, social loafing was exhibited in a variety of cultures. The social loafing effect was stronger in magnitude, however, for subjects from Western cultures than for subjects from Eastern cultures (whose group orientation could be described as more 'collectivistic' than 'individualistic'; see Triandis, 1989).

Lab versus field studies

Although the effect emerged in and out of the lab, the magnitude of the social loafing effect was larger in laboratory experiments than in field studies.

Additional factors

Also relevant to the generality of the social loafing effect were the findings that the magnitude of the effect did not vary depending on whether (a) the coactive/collective comparison was made within-subjects or between-subjects, (b) maximizing or optimizing tasks were used, (c) tasks were additive or compensatory, and (d) physical, cognitive, evaluative or perceptual effort was measured.

The finding that the magnitude of the social loafing effect did not vary depending on whether the coactive/collective comparison was made within-subjects or between-subjects suggests that social loafing does not occur simply because subjects allocate greater effort to coactive trials than to collective trials (see Harkins, Latané & Williams, 1980; Kerr & Bruun, 1981). If allocational strategies alone accounted for social loafing, the effect would be found only for the within-subjects comparisons. Finally, the findings that the size of the social loafing effect was not dependent on (a) whether maximizing or optimizing tasks were used, (b) whether additive or compensatory tasks were used, and (c) the type of effort measured, suggests that the effect is robust across tasks.

With regard to subjects' self-reported effort, people were less likely to acknowledge that they had engaged in social loafing when (a) the cover story used informed subjects that the purpose of the experiment was to examine effort or task performance, (b) a within- rather than a between-subjects comparison of the coactive and collective conditions was used, and (c) when maximizing rather than additive tasks were used. These three moderating variables seem to suggest that participants may have been unwilling to admit that they had reduced their collective efforts on the task. When participants are told the general purpose of the experiment and can report on both their coactive and collective performances, they appear to report having worked equally hard on the task. Similarly, participants also appear to report having worked hard on the collective task when the instructions focus on producing as much as possible. Perhaps participants are more willing to admit reduced effort when task demands are not so strongly tied to productivity. On the other hand, people may not be as sensitive to their own motivation losses in conditions that focus on simply working hard collectively and coactively. Perhaps when other factors become salient (i.e., increased evaluation potential, partner contributions, etc.) then people are more cognizant of their efforts.

Robustness of the effect

The social loafing effect was very consistent across studies: 79 per cent of the comparisons were in the direction of reduced collective effort. Although a minority of the comparisons did not evidence social loafing, this should not be taken as an indication that the effect is not robust. Instead, an examination of the social loafing literature suggests that researchers have consistently adopted a problem-solving approach, seeking to determine the conditions under which the effect will and will not occur. This focus on limiting conditions (which, of course, results in null effects for those conditions predicted to eliminate loafing, such as making inputs identifiable in the collective condition), combined with the wide range of tasks and subject populations employed, contributes to the heterogeneity of findings.

Conclusions

The Karau and Williams (1991a) meta-analysis clearly demonstrates that the social loafing effect is strong and robust across tasks and subject populations, and documents the existence of a number of moderating and mediating variables. Although the prior research on social loafing leaves many questions unanswered, it also provides an initial understanding of the dynamics of motivation losses in groups and provides a firm foundation for future research efforts. It seems clear that working on collective tasks is often demotivating. However, individuals do not always reduce their efforts when working collectively. Indeed, some collective conditions might actually inspire motivation gains in groups.

Social compensation: social loafing's counterpart

Recently, Williams and Karau (1991; Karau & Williams, 1991b) have demonstrated conditions under which people may actually *increase* their efforts when working collectively compared to when working individually. They call this effect 'social compensation'. Consider an example of a teacher who divides a class into small groups and assigns them to work together on a project, hand in one paper and share the grade. The social loafing literature leads us to expect that each student's motivation and effort would decrease compared to a situation in which the teacher assigned individual papers and projects. In fact, the first author is currently teaching a small-groups class and part of the class requirement is for them to form groups of four persons and to design and write up an experiment, coauthored by each member of the group, for which they will share the grade. At mid-point through the course, class members were asked how much they were contributing to their respective group projects. Four per cent (one person) of the class indicated a tendency to loaf; 35 per cent said they were compensating for other group members; whereas the remaining 61 per cent said it was not affecting their motivation or performance. Putting labels aside, when examining the per cent self-reported contribution to the group project, 77 per cent of the class perceive themselves as putting more effort in than would be expected from an equal-contribution model. After combining each member's per cent contribution, one group saw itself as contributing a total of 294 per cent to the group effort! The average response in the class was that each person felt he or she was exerting over *twice* as much effort as would be expected.

It is easy to view this response as an example of students desiring to present themselves in a favourable light, of engaging in self-serving attributions. It is also likely, however, that certain people *do* exert more effort on collective tasks, or that under certain circumstances most people will feel it necessary to shoulder the burden for others. In a previous small-groups class with a similar requirement, a student who had done exceptionally well in the prerequisite course approached the instructor after class and, fighting back tears, stated that she knew she would end up doing all the work for the others in her group. She felt that she could not rely on the others because she had learned that people couldn't be trusted to hold up their end of the job. She thought they would reduce their efforts and that her coworkers were probably less capable than she was. From her perspective, she had no choice but to do everything that the group was supposed to do (even beyond that which an individual working alone would be expected to do) in order merely to share an A on the paper. Despite attempts to assure her that this didn't have to happen, she ended up doing almost all of the work.

We are proposing that, under some conditions, people may actually work harder in a collective setting than in a coactive setting in order to compensate for the others in their group, an effect we refer to as 'social compensation'. One factor that might produce social compensation is the expectation that other group members are performing insufficiently. Under these circumstances, we propose that individuals will feel compelled to contribute more to the collective goal. By compensating for the inadequate contributions of their coworkers this will enable them to maintain a favourable (albeit diffused) evaluation for themselves. The perception of inadequate coworker contributions may be derived from (a) a general lack of trust in the reliability of others to perform well when their contributions are pooled with those of others, (b) direct knowledge of coworkers' insufficient efforts or (c) inabilities.

The second factor that we believe may be necessary to produce compensation is that the group product is in some way important to the individuals involved. If the task or the group product is seen as meaningless, then there is no need to compensate for poorly-performing coworkers, because the evaluation of the group product simply doesn't matter to the individual. If, however, the evaluation of the group product is important to the individual, then he or she will be motivated to avoid a poor group performance by compensating for the poorly-performing coworkers.

In order to examine the effects of expectations of coworker performance on individual effort in a collective task, Williams and Karau (1991) designed three studies that varied different aspects of these expectations. In each experiment, participants worked either coactively or collectively on an idea-generation task that was designed to be viewed as meaningful. In all three studies, it was hypothesized that, when working on a task that was considered meaningful, participants would compensate for a coworker whom they expected to perform poorly and would actually work harder collectively than coactively.

In Experiment 1, expectations of coworker performance were inferred from participants' interpersonal trust levels. Participants scoring high or medium on trust, who might expect others to carry their own weight on group tasks, engaged in social loafing. In contrast, participants scoring low on trust, who might expect others to loaf on collective tasks, engaged in social compensation. In Experiment 2, expectations of coworker effort were manipulated by having a confederate coworker announce that he thought the experiment sounded interesting and that he either was or was not going to try hard on the task (thus evaluation of the task remained high while effort varied). Participants were also told that the task was related to intelligence, to ensure that the task was viewed as meaningful. Participants loafed when working with a high-effort coworker, whereas participants tended to compensate when working with a low-effort coworker. In Experiment 3, expectations of coworker ability were manipulated in a manner similar to Experiment 2 (i.e., the confederate said he either was or was not very good at the task). In addition, task meaningfulness was also manipulated. In the high-meaningfulness condition, the experiment was presented as important and related to intelligence. In the low-meaningfulness condition, the experiment was presented as rather useless and trivial. Participants socially compensated when working with a low-ability partner on a meaningful task, but socially loafed otherwise. Taken together, these studies provide compelling support for the social compensation hypothesis and suggest that social compensation is likely to occur only on tasks that are at least somewhat meaningful.

These results have also been replicated in a recent study (Karau & Williams, 1991b). A slightly different paradigm was used in which ability was manipulated by using a bogus note-passing technique, and no confederates were used. The social loafing and social compensation effects again emerged with pairs of opposite-sex strangers. (A different pattern of data, which was found for opposite-sex friends and couples, is discussed in the 'Social comparison in groups' section, below.)

In conclusion, social compensation has been demonstrated in four different experiments. There appear to be conditions under which people will exert more effort on a collective task than on a coactive task, despite the fact that individual inputs cannot be monitored collectively. The effect appears to be restricted to tasks that are at least somewhat meaningful or self-relevant, and in which participants expect that their coworkers will not contribute adequately to the group product. A number of other factors might influence whether social loafing or social compensation might occur. For example, Williams and Karau (1991) suggest that the social compensation effect is not likely to persist over time, unless reciprocated in some form, and may be more likely in small rather than large groups. Future research in this area will examine other conditions that may produce compensation. For example, assignments to either leader or follower roles may result in social compensation and social loafing, respectively. Additionally, people may be motivated to compensate in some cases for their own prior shortcomings rather than for shortcomings of other group members. A number of issues remain unresolved regarding motivation on collective tasks. What follows is a discussion of several of these issues.

Theoretical issues and directions for future research

Strategic or non-conscious?

In most social loafing studies, participants either do not appear to be aware that they loaf or are unwilling to report that they loaf. In some studies, however, participants seem to be more attentive to their individual effort levels. In particular, participants' self-reports of their efforts are more likely to be consistent with their actual performances when they have an expectation for how well their coworkers will perform on the task. This suggests that some factors might lead to a conscious decision to reduce one's collective effort, but that usually social loafing reflects non-conscious processes. Thus, it is possible to distinguish between reductions in effort on collective tasks that are strategic (i.e., deliberate, intentional, purposeful, controlled or decision-based) versus non-conscious (i.e., unintentional, automatic, out-of-awareness, mindless).

We propose that the results of most social loafing studies are not the result of conscious effort reductions for several reasons. First, whereas people exert less effort collectively, they usually do not report that they have done so. Second, from observation of over a thousand participants in the cheering and clapping paradigm, the first author remembers only one participant who was clearly strategically loafing. When cheering alone, he cheered loudly (around 95 decibels); when he believed he was cheering in groups, he made all of the contortions and expressions of a hard-working contributor, but made virtually no noise! For the rest of the participants, their group efforts were in the range of 80 dBs and up. To the ear, it was difficult to tell that they were reducing their efforts. We are arguing that if someone is strategically trying to loaf, they would act more like our lone participant and dramatic reductions would have been demonstrated. The smaller, yet consistent reductions in efforts characterize most of the social loafing literature. Swimmers swim the relay a few seconds slower, typists type collectively three words per minute fewer, people combining their contributions think of five fewer ideas for a knife. It would be implausible to think that someone would recognize the opportunity to loaf and yet still work as hard as they do in these experiments. Third, Harkins et al. (1980) found that the social loafing effect was equally large regardless of whether a between-subjects or within-subjects design was used. As mentioned earlier, these results were found to replicate across studies in the meta-analysis by Karau and Williams (1991a). If subjects were merely allocating more effort to individual trials, then social loafing should have been reduced or eliminated in between-subjects studies. Yet, the type of design used had no impact on the magnitude of social loafing, suggesting that the effect was not simply an artefact of effort-allocation strategies.

The strategic versus non-conscious distinction is also useful in clarifying the relationship between social loafing and a related phenomenon referred to as the 'free rider' effect. Kerr and colleagues (e.g. Kerr, 1983; Kerr & Bruun, 1983) have demonstrated that collective effort reduction can be found under some conditions even when individuals' inputs are completely identifiable. In the free-rider paradigm, individuals' effort alone is compared to their effort collectively on disjunctive, threshold tasks (in which the task requirement is for any one of the group members to reach a criterion, and once this is accomplished all group members are considered to have succeeded, making further effort unnecessary). In these studies, each individual's contribution is made identifiable to themselves, their partner and the experimenter, regardless of whether they are working individually or collectively. In this paradigm (pumping air through a hand sphygmograph), participants tend to reduce their efforts when working collectively.

Because social loafing and free riding both describe the same effect (a reduction in individual effort when working collectively compared to when working coactively), it is worth asking whether free riding really represents a separate effect at all. Some researchers (e.g. Harkins & Szymanski, 1989; Kerr, 1983) have argued that social loafing is defined as motivation loss as a result of lack of identifiability, whereas free riding is not. However, a number of other causes of social loafing have been identified including perceived redundancy of contributions (Harkins & Petty, 1982) and lessened responsibility (Petty, Harkins, Williams & Latané, 1977). Additionally, although an experiment failed to support the hypothesis that social loafing may occur because of reduced individual control over the group product, a significant social loafing effect was obtained even when participants were fully identifiable (Williams, 1977). Thus, it seems premature to define social loafing in terms of only one of many of its potential causes. The real distinction might lie in the degree to which an individual's collective effort-reduction is strategic. The free rider is characterized as someone who consciously recognizes the low cost–high gain opportunity that collective tasks afford – one can, at least in the short run, get something for nothing. This characterization reflects a strategic, intentional act of withholding effort. The person either decides not to work hard in order to take advantage of a competent coworker (free riding), or refuses to allow a poorly-performing coworker to free-ride and stops exerting maximal effort in order to avoid being taken for a 'sucker' (Kerr, 1983). In contrast, social loafing usually does not reflect such conscious, strategic concerns, as discussed earlier.

Therefore, a useful distinction, that is highlighted by the social loafing versus free riding debate, concerns the conditions under which social loafing is automatic and reflexive and the conditions under which it is strategic and thoughtful. We propose that, although social loafing often reflects an automatic response, several studies have demonstrated instances of strategic loafing (or a cognitively mediated decision either not to loaf or to compensate for others). A number of conditions may, in effect, 'jolt' a person out of the typical collective script, causing cognitive intervention and leading to either strategic loafing, an elimination of social loafing, or social compensation. Among the factors that might lead to cognitive intervention are making the task highly engaging, announcing that individual contributions will be evaluated, creating expectations regarding coworkers' performances, and making individuals' inputs to the collective product dispensable or redundant.

The potency of evaluation

Clearly, Harkins and Szymanski (1988, 1989; Szymanski & Harkins, 1987) have delineated quite nicely the extent to which evaluation potential plays an important role in social loafing. In their research as well as research by others, it has been shown that almost any form of evaluation potential can eliminate social loafing. The evaluation can come from the person who requests the work (usually the experimenter) (Williams, Harkins & Latané, 1981), an objective standard to which the participants themselves can compare their own productivity, group standards to which the individual can compare his or her group's success, and evaluation from one's coworkers (Williams, Nida, Baca & Latané, 1989). As stated earlier, the demonstration of how any form of evaluation can eliminate social loafing has led some to define social loafing as the lack of such evaluation (Harkins & Szymanski, 1989; Kerr, 1983). However, before we accept this premise, it would be wise to evaluate the boundary conditions that may limit this generalization. One way to do this is to examine the methodological similarities of all the studies thus far conducted, to see if they have tapped a large enough range of situational variations.

It is possible that the salience of the evaluation instructions overwhelms the effects of the individual/collective manipulation. Why? We agree with Harkins and Szymanski and others (Cottrell, 1972) that evaluation is a central concern of individuals, especially in Western cultures. Within experimental settings, participants are probably already concerned about the evaluation of their performance, whatever it may be. Add to that explicit instructions that indicate how and by whom they can be evaluated and it is almost a certainty that they will attend to and ruminate about their potential evaluation. Instructions concerning how the contributions are to be combined pale in comparison.

Secondly, at this point all social loafing experiments have measured individual versus collective effort over the period of an hour or less. Over time, its potency may well diminish. Other factors, such as how little one is able to control the success of the group's efforts, or how redundant one feels one's contributions are in collective efforts, may rise as time goes on. It is also possible that the singular importance of someone else's evaluation is less important as time and frequency of evaluations has risen, given that they are no longer strangers.

This leads us to our third point: most of the research on evaluation potential involves evaluation by strangers. In the typical laboratory social loafing study, an individual's performance on the task is not likely to change how favourably they are viewed by their friends or acquaintances. However, one's task performance might influence how well they are evaluated by strangers, who have no other information on which to base their impression. We can liken this concern with the impact of getting a D in a course during the first semester in college. That D carries enormous weight with respect to the initial grade-point average. With friends or acquaintances, the success one has on a single task is only one of perhaps thousands of pieces of information regarding that person's worth. Failing to exert maximum effort will not result in an overall negative evaluation, just as getting a D in a course has little effect on one's overall grade-point average at the end of the senior year. Therefore, the tendency for social loafing researchers to study strangers performing tasks within a single hour probably greatly exaggerates the impact of evaluation. In most everyday contexts in which people base their impressions of others on a wide range of information, evaluation for the performance of a single task is likely to have less influence on motivation.

Social comparison in groups

Another way to explain the motivation losses shown in social loafing studies is suggested by Goethals and Darley (1987). They propose that social comparison, while traditionally considered at the individual level, also operates at the level of the group. Not only can a positive identity be maintained by comparison with other individuals, but also by comparing ingroups with outgroups. Another theoretical perspective closely related to group social comparison theory is social identity theory (Tajfel & Turner, 1986). Social identity theory assumes that we derive a large part of our self-concept (and self-esteem) from identification with groups to which we belong. From either perspective, when we find out that a group to which we belong performs better than other groups on a task, we achieve an indirect method of self-validation. We often gain positive self-evaluation by increasing our identification with ingroups when they succeed, i.e. basking in reflected glory (Cialdini, Borden, Thorne, Walker, Freeman & Sloan, 1976), and we protect ourselves from reduced self-evaluation by distancing ourselves from ingroups when they fail, i.e. 'blasting' (Cialdini & Richardson, 1980).

Applied to social loafing, these perspectives suggest that people may loaf because the opportunity for self-validation is diffused when working on collective tasks. As group size increases, the opportunity for individuals to achieve self-validation from the group becomes increasingly indirect. When people work coactively and are individually evaluated, they have a great deal of control over their evaluation. However, when people work collectively, they have less control over the final group product as group size increases, resulting in an increased tendency to social loafing. On the other hand, it has been found that if a group standard for a task is made salient to people working collectively, they will not loaf (Harkins & Szymanski, 1989). We may also expect that providing a salient outgroup comparison reduces or eliminates social loafing (cf. James & Greenberg, 1989).

These viewpoints also explain why people who expect their coworkers to loaf may sometimes exit groups or engage in social compensation. Goethals and Darley (1987) speculate that when individuals are experiencing negative social identity as a result of being in a group, they will either leave the group or attempt to make the group better. Yamagishi (1988) found that Japanese working collectively tended to exit the group when they expected their coworkers to loaf. Presumably, exiting the group allowed participants to avoid a negative evaluation. As mentioned above, Williams and Karau (1991) found that people compensated on a meaningful task when they were low in trust or expected their coworkers to perform poorly, presumably in order to derive a positive social identity from the group's performance.

Finally, both of these theories predict that people should only socially loaf if they do not feel that the group is important to them or if they expect the group to succeed without their best effort. People are more likely to attach significance to their group membership when they are working with friends or respected others. This idea is supported by the meta-analytic finding that, across studies, social loafing is less likely to occur as group valence increases (Karau & Williams, 1991a).

Is social loafing culture-bound?

While the great majority of the research done on social loafing has been carried out in the United States, it may be that social loafing occurs because people have learned that it is adaptive in this culture. American society glorifies individual effort and achievement at the expense of the communal good. Competition seems to be a more dominant response in this culture than co-operation. To the extent that this is true, people may loaf because they will not get the credit they deserve when their individual input is not identifiable.

If this view of social loafing is accurate, we would not expect social loafing to occur within cultures which emphasize communal norms (e.g. Oriental society). In fact, cross-cultural research comparing collective task effort in the USA and Japan (Williams, Williams, Kawana & Latané, 1984) has shown that Japanese people do socially loaf, although to a lesser degree than Americans do. However, while Japanese society does emphasize communal norms more than US society, Japan is also the most 'Westernized' country in the Orient. However, studies from Taiwan and China also suggest that people socially loaf, although not to as great an extent (Gabrenya, Latané & Wang, 1983; Gabrenya, Wang & Latané, 1985). It may be that people from other Oriental cultures, as well as other cultures that emphasize communal norms (e.g. the kibbutzim movement in Israel), would not socially loaf and in fact may socially compensate. In support of this notion, the Karau and Williams (1991a) meta-analysis found that, although the loafing effect was robust across cultures, the magnitude of the effect was lower for participants in Eastern cultures than for participants in Western cultures.

In a series of cross-cultural developmental studies, Williams and Williams (1981) compared children and adults of varying ages in the United States and Japan. This project showed that young children in both cultures showed a slight tendency to loaf. As shown in Figure 8.2, as people get older in the United States, they tend to loaf more. Conversely, Japanese people decrease social loafing as they get older. These results suggest that while people show a slight tendency to loaf socially, cultural norms greatly determine subsequent collective behaviour. In an individualistic culture such as the United States, people learn that social loafing is adaptive. In the more communally oriented culture of Japan, people learn not to loaf socially.

The kibbutz movement in Israel is a prime example of a culture which emphasizes communal norms. The goal of socialization on the kibbutz, both inside and outside school, is to emphasize the group and de-emphasize the individual (Rabin & Beit-Hallahmi, 1982). Although no one has yet investigated social loafing or compensation among Israelis living on kibbutzim, results from other research on kibbutz-reared children raise some interesting questions.

On traditional kibbutzim, children are raised in age cohorts, living, eating and going to school with their age-mates. The concern is with the group, not the individual; even in the classroom individual achievement is unrecognized. Children do not receive individual grades. Learning in the kibbutz classroom is a collective task (e.g. individual inputs are not identifiable) in contrast with the coactive nature of traditionally educated children. Yet, kibbutz-reared children consistently perform as well as or better than the traditionally educated children (Rabin, 1965; Rabin & Beit-Hallahmi, 1982).

Kibbutzim in Israel also have been shown to yield greater crop outputs than individually owned farms (Criden & Gelb, 1976). So it seems that when collective norms are emphasized and group achievement is prized instead of individual achievement, social loafing is not necessarily inevitable. Indeed, we might speculate that in a communal culture we

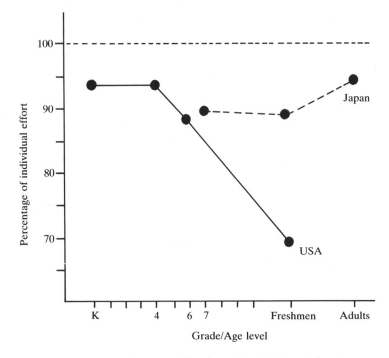

Note: Points indicate reduction in effort from individual levels for shouting in group sizes of two, across studies which contained such comparisons.

Figure 8.2 Social loafing as a function of grade/age level and USA versus Japan subjects. Taken from Williams and Williams (1981).

may find considerable motivation gains on collective tasks. Future research should examine this possibility.

Relationships and social loafing

If social loafing is in fact less likely to occur in cultures which emphasize communal norms, perhaps we would also expect less loafing in groups which emphasize communal norms. Clark (1984) has made a distinction between two types of relationships among groups of people. In exchange relationships, the type we have with strangers and acquaintances, we are concerned with everyone's individual inputs to a social situation; if one group member does a favour for another, the other is expected to reciprocate in kind. In relationships we have with close friends and loved ones, communal norms predominate. We are not concerned with each person's individual inputs and day-to-day reciprocity, perhaps figuring it will all even out in the long run.

To the extent that communal groups are more cohesive than exchange groups, perhaps less social loafing and more social compensation may occur in cohesive groups. Recent research supports the first proposition, but not the second (Karau & Williams, 1991b). The results of two experiments suggest that whereas members of non-cohesive groups socially loaf when working with high-ability coworkers and socially compensate when working with low-ability coworkers, people within cohesive groups showed no evidence of loafing and only a non-significant tendency to compensate. Across the long term, however, other factors may entice people in communal relationships to engage in social loafing. If other group members are unconcerned with keeping track of a person's individual inputs (rather than being unidentifiable), people may be able to reduce their efforts undetected. For example, in intimate dyads there are many obligatory day-to-day collective chores (e.g. housework, maintenance). Wegner's (1986) research on transactive memory suggests that when people in an intimate relationship become familiar with each other's knowledge domains, each tends to become an expert in certain fields. When exposed to tasks requiring different knowledge domains, whichever partner is expert in the field tends to take over (compensate). The less expert partner may use the transactive memory as an opportunity to loaf.

Extrapolating from Williams and Karau's (1991) findings, the more one person compensates, the more the other would be inclined to loaf. Likewise, the more one loafs, the more likely the other would feel obliged to compensate. However, if this continues to self-perpetuate the imbalance in the division of labour, we would expect that the compensator's resentment or the loafer's guilt would eventually cause a change in or dissolution of the relationship. Research derived from equity theory (Walster, Walster & Berscheid, 1978) has shown that within distressed couples, individuals do seem more concerned with their partner's inputs and outcomes than those in happier relationships. Inequitable distribution of rewards has also been shown to be related to distress in relationships. Perhaps we could think of these as relationships which have gone from being governed by communal norms to being governed by exchange norms.

Conclusion

Social loafing may have serious consequences for a variety of everyday collective settings. The effect was robust across both maximizing and optimizing tasks and across tasks demanding different types of effort.

Although the magnitude of the effect was reduced for field studies, for women and for subjects in Eastern cultures, the social loafing effect was still significant under all of these conditions. Even if we accept that social loafing is eliminated when participants' scores can be evaluated collectively or when they work collectively on highly meaningful tasks, it is still important to recognize that, in many real-world contexts, individual inputs cannot be reliably identified or evaluated and people are frequently asked to work on mundane or uninspiring tasks. It should also be noted that social loafing was eliminated when participants worked with close friends or team-mates, but mere acquaintance with one's coworkers was not sufficient to eliminate the effect.

It is also noteworthy that the tendency of social loafing researchers to focus on which factors contribute to motivation losses may have led them to disregard conditions under which motivation gains might emerge. Is there such a thing as synergy in collective groups whose individual outputs are pooled and unevaluable? Earlier, Jackson and Williams (1985) found that subjects working collectively were more successful than coactive workers on a complex task, although this was still because of social loafing (i.e., they succeeded because they were less anxious). Williams and Karau (1991) have recently found increased collective effort compared with coactive effort, but only by those within the group who thought others were not carrying their weight. So, for real groups, perhaps we can hope at best that only *some* of the coworkers will work harder, and not because of enhanced group spirit or camaraderie, but because they fear a low group output. Are there conditions in which *everyone*, or even the majority of group members, rises above their individual effort levels in a collective task? If more powerful manipulations of cohesiveness or task valence are used, there are conditions under which individuals work harder collectively. In addition to enhancing ingroup cohesiveness, it may be necessary to make outgroup differences or ingroup–outgroup competition salient before it is possible to obtain synergy.

It is perhaps ironic then that we can end our chapter as Latané *et al.* (1979) ended their first paper on social loafing: 'We think the cure [to social loafing] will come from finding ways of channeling social forces so that the group can serve as a means of intensifying individual responsibility rather than diffusing it' (page 832). Unfortunately, we are still in search of the cure.

9 Do group motives differ from individual motives? Considerations regarding process distinctiveness

Hugh Harrington and Norman Miller

Do distinctive emergent phenomena arise as a person moves from personal, to group, and to intergroup situations? Perhaps more important, do distinctly different psychological processes (e.g. motivations) operate in each arena? In considering these issues we first provide some framing by discussing briefly definition, explanation, situation and process. In the second section we discuss approaches to the issue of how to define situations as interpersonal, intragroup and intergroup, respectively. In the final section we address the problem of how to assess whether process distinctiveness distinguishes these three situations.

First, we dispel two myths about the individual and the collective, respectively, that may obscure the issues. The first myth is that of the isolated or 'pre-social' individual. There are few individuals without group memberships (Steiner, 1986). Virtually all behaviour occurs in a social context; and every individual is imbued with characteristics of their historical, societal and cultural heritage; even perceptions of physical reality are a product of this social context (Segall, Campbell & Herskovits, 1966). Some theorists, however, criticize an 'individualistic approach' by using the straw man argument that it denies a social reality (e.g. Tajfel, 1978b). If it is to be rejected, a better basis is needed. A second myth (cf. McPhail, 1991) is that various types of collectives are essentially identical – that a single set of social psychological principles will apply to all collectives: two individuals, an aggregate, a small *ad hoc* group, a crowd, an organized group, an interaction between two groups, a social class, a society, or an interaction between or among nations (e.g. Sherif, 1966). Differences among collectives, if made salient by a set of taxonomic criteria, may provide important theoretical clues that would be obscured when collectives are treated as homogeneous. As we will argue later, however, the science has not made good use of these differences in guiding theory and has not put sufficient empirical effort into examining whether different processes occur in various contexts.

Defining the situation

Asch (1952) provides a discussion (page 162) of the individual–group distinction that we use to frame our following discussion.

> This has perhaps been the fact most difficult to grasp about psychological interaction: that it is a process with an intrinsic social direction that has its locus in individuals. . . . We tend in theory to distort the character of a social act in one of two opposed ways: to consider it either as the sum of individual acts or as a new product that transcends individuals. It is precisely the achievement of psychological interaction to be neither of these.

Building on Asch, the area under discussion can be partitioned into three levels of analysis: (a) society (status, roles, values, norms); (b) psychological interaction (the situation in which people behave); and (c) intrapsychic processes. It is important to ask how society influences psychological interaction. Equally important, but a different question, is how social change occurs. Likewise, it is important to understand the intrapsychic processes that occur during psychological interaction. As indicated, however, the focus of this chapter is, in Asch's terms, the realm of psychological interaction, which can be further divided into interpersonal, group and intergroup situations. The key issue is whether the psychological and social psychological processes that occur within each of these three situations differ.

Levels of explanations

Nettler (1970) describes four types of explanation: definition, empathy, ideology and scientific regularity. He notes that social scientists aspire to the latter, but often succumb to the former modes of explanation. It is the purpose of theory to explain phenomena by describing the functional relations among variables. Such descriptions take the form of 'if . . . then' statements, namely laws (Hempel, 1952). Furthermore, theory requires the organization of a set of functional relations between independently defined variables. The first step, construct definition, should not be mistaken for explanation. Explanation by definition may allay curiosity but is, in fact, merely substituting terms.

Given the partition of intrapsychic events, interaction and society, at each higher level, the levels of potential *reductive explanation* increase. Processes at higher levels are thus constrained by laws at lower levels and explanation is not complete until such links are specified. At the same time, however, in contrast to the upward causation of reductionistic explanation, an opposite 'downward causation' operates at the level of biological evolution such that the prevalence, distribution or presence of species and their forms is explained by laws that govern the higher selection system (Campbell, 1974). All that is meant by *greater* explanation is knowing more laws (Bergmann, 1957; Simon, 1992). To the extent one knows more laws about X, it is better explained. Good health can be explained through laws relating a subjective state of well-being to biological and physiological events within the body, or to social psychological or sociological factors. Greater knowledge of lawful relations linking it to concepts at any level, increases our understanding of good health.

If an actor behaves in a particular way in the absence of other individuals, one might attempt to explain the behaviour in terms of social or situational variables, or intrapsychic events. The interaction between two individuals can be explained by the reciprocal pattern of interaction, by social or situational features, or in terms of the intrapsychic events within each person such as motivations. In a group setting, such as a jury, the discussion can be considered as group-level behaviour, as when it is summarized by the verdict. At the same time, the group discussion will contain interpersonal behaviours, as when one member argues with another; these, of course, can be further broken down into intrapsychic events. This applies to intergroup situations as well. The point is that analysis of process often occurs at the next level down, which, in turn, can be related to lower levels. Thus, there is greater 'reductionism' potential at some levels than at others. The test of a theory is how well it explains. Holding the generality of its laws constant, a better theory is one that contains more laws, irrespective of their kind and levels. An advantage of reductionistic explanation is that what is already known about the lower-level concepts invoked by it can be incorporated into the higher-level theorizing. Nevertheless, it is mistaken to think that explanation requires reductionistic laws or, conversely, that lower levels are less valuable. As Doise (1986) notes, the problem with explanations is often the failure to articulate different levels of explanation in order to provide a more complete explanation. However, that a distinction can be made between intergroup relations at the level of society and relations at the level of group members is not prima facie evidence for the view that interpersonal and intergroup interactions within a setting are controlled by different motivational, cognitive or affective intrapersonal processes.

An information-processing model

To integrate the array of relevant variables, we introduce an information-processing model of input–process–output (Figure 9.1). To summarize, in a given situation one can consider the *input*, subsequent *process* and the *output*. The input consists of both: (a) prior conditions that bring persons to the situation (i.e., create motivations to engage), as well as what persons bring to the situation, as a function of their individual differences and social representations, and (b) situational features, including those that are operationally defined (measured or manipulated), but also other variables that may be correlates of these. Process refers to what develops during the situation – events that occur over time or at a lower level of analysis. The output consists of (a) what outcomes occur in the setting (behaviour or attitudes towards individuals or groups) and (b) what effects are generalized to other times, persons or settings. The causal flow that is illustrated suggests that elements to the left can have direct and indirect effects on elements to the right.

Defining process

A process is any repeatable sequence by which inputs are transformed over time (and/or at a lower level of analysis) into predictable outputs. When considering psychological interaction, two types of process should be distinguished. Behavioural processes, the observable interactions among individuals, can be directly measured, tend to be extended in

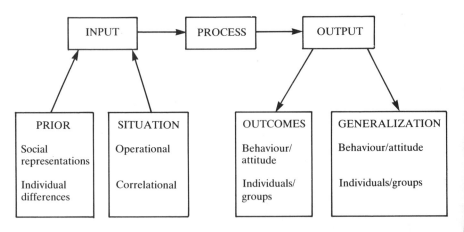

Figure 9.1 Information-processing model for organization of variables.

time, and can function as multiple and reciprocal frames of interaction (Warner, 1992). Conceptually, however, behavioural processes are often treated as dependent variables or output (e.g. number of co-operative choices, reward allocations). On the other hand, intrapsychic processes can be momentary and unobservable. Such internal processes can only be inferred, but can sometimes be linked to measurable psychophysiological events. It is intrapsychic events such as motivations that are at issue as mediating the behavioural patterns in various situations.

For example, Brewer and Miller (1984) proposed that, within intergroup situations, the relative salience of social categories will influence the 'depth of processing'. When category salience is high, processing of information about outgroup members will be shallow, existing stereotypes will exert strong influence, and resulting perceptions of outgroup members following interaction will be relatively undifferentiated. In contrast, when category salience is minimized, greater depth of processing is possible, thus allowing greater differentiation of the outgroup and personalization of its members. Central and peripheral processing (Petty & Cacioppo, 1986) may be distinct modes of dealing with information available in the environment. This does not necessarily imply, however, that distinctly different processes control situations that vary in category salience. If a defining feature of a situation (e.g. intergroup interaction) was shown empirically to be a necessary and sufficient cause of engaging one of these two modes of dealing with information (i.e., interpersonal situations engage central processing and intergroup situations engage peripheral processing), then there would be support for 'the fact that there is a discontinuity of social psychological *processes* between interpersonal and group behaviour' (Brown & Turner, 1981, page 65, italics in the original). In contrast, were there, as is seemingly likely, observed covariation between (a) those factors that determine which type of information-processing is most prominent, and (b) other situational features that covary with these three settings (viz., interpersonal, group and intergroup), this would support the process uniformity across levels of psychological interaction.

Emergent phenomena

If by 'emergent phenomena' one refers to distinctive processes (or more narrowly, motivations), this is treated in the third section. If one refers to behavioural outcomes (e.g. competitive, 'non-rational' or uniform responses), then these are treated as dependent variables, also in the third section. As such, this output cannot be a defining feature of a situation (input) without incurring problems of circularity. On the other hand, there may be phenomena that by definition occur only in one situation and not in others. We acknowledge that groups can have properties that are not present in or analogous to properties of an individual. For example, 'minority influence', which refers to situations in which there are numerically distinct subgroups, requires a proportional definition that could not apply to a dyadic situation (unless majority and minority status is conceptually isomorphic with unequal distribution of power between two individuals, or the definition is transmuted to include dyads in which the two persons are members of groups that are in a social majority–minority relationship). Likewise, others might propose that group polarization, defined as group consensus and induced as a result of group discussion, applies by definition only to group situations. As an analytical proposition this may be true. Empirically, however, one might want to compare group polarization to the effects of dyadic discussion to consensus, or even to increased individual thought about the issue, each of which also produces polarization by a combination of informational and/or normative influence. In the case of the individual, informational influence might be induced by cognitive elaboration (Tesser, 1978) and normative influence by projected consensus (Marks & Miller, 1987). Nonetheless, there may indeed be emergent phenomena in specific types of situations. If so, it does not follow that the process events associated with them must be distinctive or novel. For instance, differences between minority and majority influence may rest on principles contained in the elaboration likelihood model of persuasion (Petty & Cacioppo, 1986).

Definitions of interpersonal, group and intergroup situations

A host of constructs have been used by sociologists and psychologists to differentiate a society from an aggregate, a crowd from individuals, a crowd from a society, etc. Some of these constructs are listed in the first column of Table 9.1. Simmel (Nisbett & Perrin, 1977) used a classification scheme that involves increasing size and subsequent complexity; the four primary types of social union are: dyad, triad, group and organization. Asch (1952) also used four types – types based more on psychological significance to the persons; collection, class, group and organization. Approaches such as these tend to define entities in terms of the presence/absence of particular attributes. An alternative approach tends to describe dimensions on which characteristics vary. Roger Brown (1954) presented a broad taxonomy of collectives. His classification dimensions are listed in column 2 of Table 9.1. The primary dimensions, namely size, polarization of attention, importance of identification with the collective and nature of the interaction, are particularly relevant to the analysis of the three situations under discussion. The secondary characteristics are

Sources of taxonomies

Emphasis	Social[1]	Brown	Campbell	Experimental[2]
Social representations	Status Roles Norms Values Traditions Stereotypes			Situational status/roles
Group membership	Membership criteria Recognition of non-members/outgroup Recognition by others as a group Interaction with other groups		Boundaries Multiply-confirmed boundaries Permeability	Basis of membership Salience of membership Interaction with outgroup
Nature of setting and interaction		Size Congregation Identification Polarization Nature of interaction Degree of organization Duration/continuity Natural/unnatural Accidental/integral Leader/leaderless	Proximity Similarity	Number of ingroup/outgroup members
Interdependence			Internal diffusion Communication Common fate Co-ordinated action Covariation	Ingroup interaction Interdependence Nature of task Outcome

Notes
1. Traditional characteristics mentioned at the social level of group.
2. Additional characteristics relevant to experimental setting.

attributes of the collective. Campbell (1960) also proposed a number of dimensions along which collectives could be measured. He posed the problem as one of 'perceiving invisible entities such as social groups' (page 188). Following Gestalt principles for perceiving an entity, he argued that the diagnostic principles or basic epistemological criteria (see column 3 of Table 9.1) for knowing either an individual or a collective are the same, though the sharpness of individual and group boundaries may differ. As for the interdependence of these diagnostic principles, 'for human groups, face-to-face communication processes made possible by proximity generate similarity and feelings of belongingness which make coordinated action and hence common fate more likely' (page 197).

The minimal requirements for the presence of a group can vary. It may rest on a *nominal* definition based, for instance, on structural properties or features (e.g. assigning a common task). Alternatively, a *dispositional* definition may be invoked (e.g. a social category for which 'the arousal of its social-psychological significance for the individual' is part of the definitional criterion). This more typically is needed when motivational properties are viewed as a criterially important component.[1] Likewise, distinctions can be made between *aggregate* (average characteristics of members) and *structural* (relations among members) attributes of a group (Scott & Scott, 1981), as well as between *attributes* of a group and its members and *relationships* among self, other, ingroup and outgroup (Miller & Harrington, 1990a).

The crucial analytic problem is whether to define a context involving more than one person (i.e., psychological interaction) as an interpersonal, group or intergroup situation. What characteristics are necessary to define and distinguish each situation? Additionally, it is important to know which variables are relevant to conceptually independent of, and possibly correlative with those variables that are definitionally necessary (operational). We consider seven possible criteria: social representations, salience of group memberships, interdependence, size, interpretations of the situation, uniformity of response, and unidirectionality of influence.

Social representations

By 'social representations' we mean features derived from social structures beyond the interaction setting that can influence psychological interaction (cf. Farr & Moscovici, 1984). These include positional (status, role) and ideological (norms, values) characteristics (Doise, 1986), traditions and stereotypes (Hamilton, 1981). A social representation criterion allows one to define a situation as intergroup if the positional or ideological relationship among participants *differs* as a result of the social status or roles conferred by group membership. An interpersonal situation would be characterized by an *absence* of socially derived (positional or ideological) relationships between interactants. A group situation also may be characterized by differential status and roles, derived from society, the group structure or the immediate context. Based on this criterion, an interaction between a manager and an employee, though ordinarily interpersonal, also could be a group or an intergroup situation. If the actions of each were constrained by their respective roles in the immediate work group, then the situation is one of group interaction. If, however, each respectively represents the management and the labour groups within the company/country, then the situation could be defined as intergroup. Other criteria would determine whether they are interacting in their respective intragroup roles or as representatives of their larger and distinctive groups (e.g. explicit contractual agreement, nature of issue discussed, etc.). Further, if only one of the participants enters the interaction as a group representative, it may, under many circumstances (including the ordinary consequence of language usage), motivate the other also to interact as a representative, despite an absence of prior intent to do so.

The presence or absence of social representations, nonetheless, is not without problems. Everyone has many roles, group memberships and identifications that vary across situations and over time within a situation (Lewin, 1943). Consequently, it is conceivable that all psychological interactions are in some sense intergroup, if this is to mean that the interactants have relevant and differing social representations. That is, it is difficult to imagine instances when two (or more) individuals do not have some social role relationship that is relevant. Even marriage and friendships (viz., personal relationships) involve social roles with associated social norms and values. For example, a marital disagreement may provoke a motivation to justify one's position. If one invokes a previous contract between the two, then the situation would appear to be interpersonal (no social roles invoked). Shared norms (Weber, 1947) and differentiation of roles (Parsons, 1935) have been regarded as defining features of a group. Therefore, if mutually known norms or roles regarding 'married couples' are invoked, then the relationship is being cast in group terms. If contrasting social categories and consonant stereotypes are invoked ('husbands' and 'wives'), then the relationship takes on the appearance of an intergroup situation. This criterion makes it difficult to differentiate situations and may suffer from circular reasoning problems.

Salience of group memberships

To distinguish an interpersonal from both a group and an intergroup situation, one might require that no group membership be a salient feature of the situation. Attention to a single group membership appears necessary to distinguish an intragroup from both an interpersonal and intergroup situation. Attention to more than a single group would seem to be the *sine qua non* of an intergroup situation, if the participants in the situation belong to one but not the other group. In this perceptual or cognitive approach to the definitions of interpersonal, group and intergroup situations, either no, one or two (or more) groups are salient, respectively. We should note that more than two group memberships can reduce the overall salience of group differences if group boundaries are not convergent, whereas, if they are convergent (cf. Campbell, 1960), salience will be increased. For example, if a labour and a management group are negotiating a contract and there are also black and white (or male and female) members present in both groups, then the additional category of race (or gender) would diffuse the salience of the group categories. If, instead, the management group were all white (or male) and the labour group were predominantly black (or female) then these convergent categories would strengthen intergroup salience (Vanbeselaere, 1991). A school classroom or work department would be an interpersonal situation if there were no attention to any group membership. It would become a group situation if the focus of attention involved each person's membership in the group (class, department). It would become an intergroup situation if attention were directed at some subgroup (e.g. gender or racial membership) or a rival external group (another department or classroom). Such attentional variation could occur with respect to symbolic as well as physical presence of others.

Interdependence

Horwitz and Rabbie (1982) argue that common fate is the necessary feature of membership in order to distinguish a group *per se* from a category (e.g. 'redheads'). Belongingness to a group, therefore, implies sharing or merely believing that there is some common interest and, thus, a motivation to behave in the group interest. Extending this rationale, an intergroup situation is salient as such only if there is a common interest within each group and the common fate (interest) of each group is *not* the same. That is, there must be some real, symbolic or potential difference of interest associated with the two group memberships. A classroom or department in which individuals must independently compete for attention and other rewards would be an interpersonal situation. If a group interest is developed (common fate) during interaction, it becomes a group situation. If two or more (internal) factions or (external) interests develop, it becomes an intergroup situation.

Common fate, however, is not the only dimension available for defining positive interdependence. A more differentiated approach separates outcome interdependence into goal interdependence and reward interdependence. Furthermore, means interdependence, the process by which mutual goals or rewards are achieved, can be separated into resource, role and task interdependence (Johnson & Johnson, 1992). Whether inclusion by all components of positive interdependence in one's definition better separates group from individual situations, or whether the outcome components capture motivational distinctions between group and individual situations better than do the components of means interdependence, remains unclear.

Size

Although size has often been used as a definitional criterion (cf. Simmel, 1955; Insko, Schopler, Hoyle, Dardis & Graetz, 1990), size *per se* is not a useful criterion for distinguishing the three interaction situations. For instance, even though interpersonal or inter-individual behaviour some-times occurs within a dyad, it does not seem necessary that it be limited to two persons. (Parenthetically, it does seem to be bounded by the limits of the number with whom direct interaction is possible, as in Brown's (1954) room-size group.) Likewise, considerations other than numerosity suggest that a group could consist of two, as well as more, persons and that an intergroup situation can range from a dyad composed of members from two groups to multiple members of each group. That is, even though a dyad may be 'naturally' more interpersonal, it can become a group or intergroup situation, by the previous criteria, if each of the persons comprising it is seen by the other primarily as a group (same or different, respectively) representative. Moreover, the nature of inter-dependence further complicates the use of size as a criterion. Presumably, interpersonal situations can range from co-operative (positive) depend-ence, to independence, and to competitive (negative) dependence. If, however, two individuals form an alliance (common interest) are they not, by the interdependence criterion, now a group? Yet, if two individuals (but not two sets of coacting individuals) engage in competi-tion, it seemingly would remain interpersonal if there is no other person with whom to share elements of positive interdependence (e.g. a common fate).

Interpretations of the situation

Our preceding section on attention to group membership treated this criterion (salience) as an observable. However, others argue that the situation needs to be defined by the participants and that one must understand the meanings that social groups have to them (Mead, 1934; Condor & Brown, 1988). Allport (1954) thought of an intergroup situation as one in which the participants *perceive* the situation in terms of intergroup relations. Others have extended the 'definition of the situation' to define an intergroup situation as one in which each member is viewed as typical of their respective group and in which self- and other stereotyping occurs (Hewstone & Brown, 1986; Hogg & Abrams, 1988; Turner, Hogg, Oakes, Reicher & Wetherell, 1987). This reciprocal requirement for an intergroup situation – perception of self and others as group members and recognition by others that self is a group member – is a subjective process and in research is often determined after the fact. Instead, the significance of group memberships in a situation needs to be assessed independently of the consequences of such memberships. It would be circular to explain a behaviour pattern (e.g. competitive responses) by reference to a process (e.g. self-stereotyping) and then cite the behaviour as evidence for the process.

Uniformity of response

Sherif (1966) thought of an intergroup situation as one in which the participants *interact* in terms of group identification. Tajfel (1978b) extended this line of reasoning. In addition to the presence of at least two clearly identifiable categories, two other criteria are required, namely uniformity of attitude and behaviour within each group, and, within individuals, uniformity of attitude and behaviour towards others. Conversely, Tajfel (1978b) defined an interpersonal situation as one in which the interaction is determined by individual characteristics and personal relationships. A problem arises with these criteria, as with the use of interpretation of the situation as a criterion, if the assessment of these critical features is determined after the fact. Irrespective of whether the dependent variables are attitudes or behaviours towards individuals or groups, a *post hoc* assessment of presence of uniform responses within groups or individuals (output) cannot serve as a defining feature of the situation (input). Again, if these criteria are assessed *post hoc*, the argument becomes tautological.

Homogeneity of attitudes could be a consequence of group membership, as might intergroup antagonism. However, if homogeneous attitudes are said to mediate (as a process) a particular outcome (e.g. antagonistic behaviour), then they need to be shown to have causal and temporal precedence. One could, of course, test the causal role of uniformity of *attitude* on subsequent behaviour. From the standpoint of experimentation, one could gather the group together, require them to discuss an issue and reach consensus (uniformity) or simply to discuss it.

Attitudes can then be measured to assess whether uniformity of attitude leads to particular behaviours. Thus, it could be that uniformity (independent of extremity) of attitudes influences behaviours and, thereby, has process implications (e.g. informational or normative influence: Festinger, 1954). On the other hand, were uniformity of *behaviour* invoked to serve the same function as an antecedent condition (input), it would then be inappropriate to use it as evidence for the proposed process. That is, if uniformity is treated as a characteristic of behavioural outcomes, then it cannot serve a *post hoc* role as defining the situation. The same is true when group motivations are invoked as explanations of an outcome.[2]

Unidirectionality of influence

Additionally, some theorists (Brown & Turner, 1981) argue that the two separate domains, interpersonal and intergroup, can be distinguished by their unidirectional relationship. Specifically, in this view, intergroup relations can and do determine interpersonal relations; however, interpersonal relations between group members have 'no implications for intergroup attitudes' and provide 'no basis for generalizing' (page 49); they are also said to have 'little or no consequences for wider social change' because these interpersonal relations are 'mere epiphenomena' (page 63). The first two propositions, regarding the influence of interpersonal interactions on intergroup attitudes and the generalization of positive interpersonal interactions, ought to be determined by empirical test. Could it not be shown, for instance, that a severe interpersonal conflict within a group can reduce group morale, which in turn leads to a perception of the group as *weak*, and thereby invites aggression towards it by an outgroup? The latter proposition, however, appears to employ a shift in the level of analysis, in which the distinction between situation and society is mistakenly seen as isomorphic with the distinction between interpersonal and intergroup. Furthermore, one must acknowledge some relationship between the magnitude of a causal force and the magnitude of effect expected. Consequences in a situation involving a dozen or so participants, for example, would not be expected to change a society involving millions of people, whether it was seen by the participants as interpersonal or intergroup, unless those few participants wielded great social power. Extending this argument to a more reductionistic level of explanation, as argued, for instance, by jokes about menopause and marital relations, one would not say that, by definition, physiological changes within individuals cannot affect interpersonal behaviour. If confronted by instances in which they seemingly did not, one would, at least, take account of the magnitude of change in the independent (physiological) and dependent (interpersonal) variables of interest.

Generalization

The previous discussion is pertinent to the far right of Figure 9.1, namely the issue of generalization. Whether consequences within the situation generalize to other persons, places and times is important. However, it is not assumed in this analytical model that the processes by which inputs cause outputs are the same processes as those responsible for generalization from the situation. If we were to elaborate the model, we should insert another 'process' variable between the two outputs – 'outcome' and 'generalization'. The same could be said about the 'process' between the two inputs – 'prior' and 'situation' conditions. Despite its importance, the issue of generalization is distinct from the processes of interaction under discussion. Furthermore, the same process-assessment methods discussed in the next section would apply to the assessment of the generalization process. We have discussed some of the issues related to generalization elsewhere (Miller & Harrington, 1990b; Harrington & Miller, in press). Finally, we note that the generalizability of the situational outcomes, in fact, qualifies the nature of those outcomes and, as such, can play an important role in the analysis of outcome data (viz., which effects have the greatest generalization).

Summary

Not all situations can be fit neatly into the procrustean bed of the prototypes (interpersonal, group, intergroup), nor would everyone agree on necessary features and whether these are best conceived as attributes or dimensions. We find it difficult to select a single factor, or combination of factors, that can distinguish each situation. If criteria are viewed as dichotomous (present/absent), one must then make assertions about necessary and sufficient conditions. If, instead, criteria are continuous, then arbitrary points for dichotomization can yield problems of the sort discussed by Cook and Campbell (1979, pages 12–13). Furthermore, as these authors point out, the research paradigms employed to collect data rely on operational definitions of theoretical terms and no single measure/ operation 'can be "definitional" of a single theoretical variable' (page 14). Several criteria can be applied to the study of relevant research with relative objectivity (provided that such information is contained in the methods) – social representations of subjects, situational features that influence attention, both interaction and outcome interdependence, and size (absolute and relative). Within experimental settings, there are several, additionally relevant features (fourth column of Table 9.1): the basis of group membership, situational (versus social) status and roles, and the nature of the task and its outcome. In short, a review of the literature would best be served by initially coding experimental studies in terms of a broad array of objective measures that characterize the nature of the situation. Within this broader network, one can then compare the obtained pattern with theoretically deduced patterns (Popper, 1959).

Process distinctiveness

Given that various situations can be categorized or at least measured on a number of relevant dimensions, there must be valid methods to infer process events. How would one determine whether different psychological processes occur in interpersonal, group and intergroup situations? Process assessment requires, on the one hand, that one establish the relationships between: (a) the situation as operationalized and the outcome; (b) the situation and the process; and (c) the process and the outcome. On the other hand, it also requires that one, to some reasonable extent, rule out: (a) the influence of prior or concurrent conditions that are correlative to the situation as operationally defined; (b) concurrent conditions induced inadvertently by manipulations; and (c) alternative processes. Within the information-processing model of organizing variables, we can describe seven different methods that have been used to make inferences about process distinctiveness or uniformity (Figure 9.2). For simplification, 'situation' includes: (a) the defined (measured or manipulated) interpersonal, group and intergroup interaction settings; (b) other context features of the situation that are relevant but not necessary; and (c) other variables that might be affected by manipulations. Independent variables are additionally manipulated variables proposed to moderate or cause process events and outcome levels. Functional relationships can be based on correlations among measures (shown as curved, two-headed arrows) or be the result of experimentaly manipulated variables (shown as straight, single-direction arrows).

   In general, these process-assessment methods involve inferences based upon: (a) observed differences in outcome as a function of the observed situation; (b) direct manipulations of the situation and observed differences in outcome; (c) observed differences in outcome as a function of interactions between situations and other independent variables; (d) observed differences in process measurements as a function of the situation; (e) the effects of direct manipulations of the situation on a particular process and, subsequently, the effects of direct manipulations of the process on outcomes; (f) statistical mediational analysis involving effects of the situation on process and outcomes, and the covariation between the latter two; and (g) meta-analytic procedures to synthesize many of the foregoing procedures as they are represented in the literature. Each method has limitations, some more than others. In a synthesis of the research, all are valuable and contribute to the under-standing of the issue. The following sections discuss these methods in turn.

Observed outcome differences

The first three methods we review are based, primarily, on differences in outcomes and do not involve any process measures *per se*. Then, we review the three methods that do utilize process measures in their logic of inference. These are treated in the order of weakest to strongest conclusions that can be drawn.

Ecological validity

First, one could observe the array of behaviours committed by actors in different settings and ask whether the relative frequency of behaviours differs ('A' of Figure 9.2). Then, differences could be compared to systematically defined features of the context and explained in terms of a particular motivation, for example. Drawing from the strength of an ethnological perspective one would observe these behaviours in their natural settings. Most of these situations, however, are self-selected. Therefore, differences in behavioural patterns may not be construed as evidence of distinctive processes because differences in the motivation to engage in the situation (Asch, 1952) already bring with them distinctively focused sets of behavioural options. Motivation, in this sense, causes the situation to occur, as opposed to the conception that situational features cause a particular motivation to operate. At the risk of oversimplification, persons tend to meet as individuals to exchange personal information; as a group to solve common problems, make decisions affecting the group, confirm traditions or entertain members; and as two groups to win a competition, resolve a dispute or develop a compromise of interests. Different behavioural rates of response (e.g. competitiveness) in interper-sonal and intergroup settings are not, in themselves, evidence for process distinctiveness. The differences in output in natural settings (behavioural patterns) can be predicted by the differences in input (intentions, situational constraints, behavioural options) without providing support for process discontinuity. That people behave differently in these diffe-rent situations may be ecologically true. Note, however, that an external validity law, namely the influence of social or situational features on behaviour, does not demonstrate that process events are different.

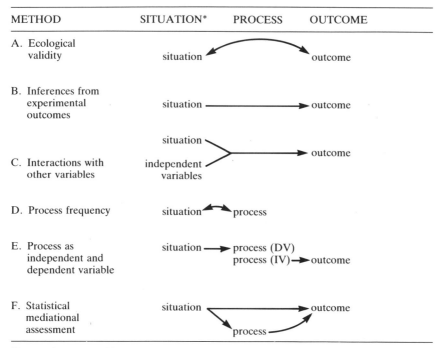

METHOD	SITUATION*	PROCESS	OUTCOME

A. Ecological validity — situation ⌢ outcome

B. Inferences from experimental outcomes — situation ⟶ outcome

C. Interactions with other variables — situation / independent variables ⟶ outcome

D. Process frequency — situation ⟷ process

E. Process as independent and dependent variable — situation ⟶ process (DV) / process (IV) ⟶ outcome

F. Statistical mediational assessment — situation ⟶ outcome / process

*Personal, group and intergroup.

Note: Straight arrows indicate an effect produced by experimental manipulation, and curved arrows indicate a correlational association.

Figure 9.2 Methods for making inferences about process events.

Inferences from experimental outcomes

It may also be true that behaviour patterns differ markedly when situations are experimentally manipulated and prior conditions controlled ('B' in Figure 9.2). If so, such discovered regularities would be environmental laws regarding social psychology. Again, however, differences in behaviour patterns do not constitute evidence of process distinctiveness. Consider the following hypothetical study. Individuals interact in dyads or as members of one or two groups. Greater competition is observed in the latter condition. One could propose that the two different rates of competitive response were mediated by different processes: degree of interpersonal attraction via perceived similarity of personal attributes in the former (cf. Byrne, 1971) and degree of intergroup conflict via categorization and comparison of group attributes in the latter (cf. Tajfel

& Turner, 1979). Process distinctiveness requires that manipulation of similarity of subjects' personal attributes would only affect the competitiveness of the dyad, whereas manipulation of their category salience would only affect the competitiveness in the intergroup situation. A single process and more parsimonious explanation can be constructed in terms of perceived threat and self-serving interest. Threat increases competitiveness (Deutsch & Krauss, 1960). Compared to the interpersonal condition, the intergroup condition may be adding several correlative features that are likely to increase perceived threat: polarization of opinion (Reid, 1983); common fate (Campbell, 1960); norms for group interest which are also self-serving (Horwitz & Rabbie, 1982); the perceived power of a group as greater than that of an individual and, hence, more threatening (Wilder, 1986); and the tendency to perceive individuals more favourably than groups (Sears, 1983). We suspect that if these latter features are well controlled, interpersonal and intergroup interactions may yield parallel outcomes, and thus not support the view that events (outcomes) at the two levels are discontinuous. Therefore, self-interest as a function of perceived threat may be the 'process event' underlying competitive behaviour (outcome) in both situations, albeit with unintended differences in the degree of threat (input).

Interactions with other variables

Another related method, following Kruglanski and Mackie (1990), assesses the effect of relevant independent variables on behaviour in different settings to determine whether they are similar or different ('C' of Figure 9.2). Process distinctiveness can be *inferred* if independent variables interact with context features. Because scaling differences between variables can affect the slope of a relationship, the case for distinctiveness is only strong when interaction is disordinal. Process uniformity can be inferred if there is a similar effect of these variables in different contexts, other things being controlled. For example, some have proposed that a different set of principles applies to intergroup behaviour than to interpersonal behaviour (Brown & Turner, 1981) – what affects intergroup behaviour are intergroup relations of social status, power and interdependence. If these same factors, namely status, power and interdependence, affect interpersonal relations in the same way, then this would support process uniformity. In contrast, if these variables produce opposite directions of effects in interpersonal and intergroup settings, there would be a strong case for process distinctiveness. Kruglanski and Mackie (1990) used this method to determine if majority and minority influence rely on the same or different processes and concluded that the evidence supports process uniformity.

This approach uses the criterion of *discriminative construct validity* (cf.

Baron, Kerr & Miller, 1992, pages 85–86). Carlson, Marcus-Newhall and Miller (1990) used this strategy in conjunction with meta-analytic procedures to assess the functional relation between indices of verbal and written aggression. Tedeschi and his colleagues had suggested that the two types of measures reflect distinct theoretical concepts rather than an underlying unitary one (Tedeschi, Smith & Brown, 1974; Tedeschi, 1983). In opposition to this view, measures of verbal and written aggression were affected similarly, apart from scaling differences, by anger, frustration, personal attack and directness of aggression, implying that the two types of measures assess the same underlying construct. Whereas the term 'construct validity' refers to the extent to which a concept enters lawful relationships with other concepts, this method invokes the notion of discriminative construct validity – the degree to which the functional relation between a pair of variables is moderated by whether they are examined in interpersonal, group and intergroup contexts.

A differential impact of independent variables in different settings would not be strong evidence, however, until other relevant variables that may systematically differ across situations are controlled. Independent variables (social representations, individual differences or manipulations) may also covary with situational features. This covariation is important to assess for each group of methodologies we address. With respect to methods that approach process distinctiveness via discriminative construct validity, other sources of situational influence that are correlated with the independent variable of interest must be systematically controlled.

Observed process differences

Process frequency

An alternative approach applies relevant measures to assess the psychological processes (e.g. categorization, comparison, expectations, motivations) that may occur in the different contexts ('D' of Figure 9.2). One could first consider whether different types of processes occur in one setting versus another, or rather whether the relative frequency of particular processes differs from one situation to another, i.e., the relatively dominant process varies across situations. The first, different contexts engaging a distinctly different set of processes, is consistent with discontinuity theories concerning the relation between interpersonal, group and intergroup events. Differences in frequency or dominance would provide mild evidence for a discontinuity if, after searching, these differences cannot be tied to other situational features. Alternatively, if frequency/dominance across situations varies continuously as a function of multiple features that covary with a specific defining feature of each situation, then this would suggest process uniformity. Whereas we noted the problem of drawing valid conclusions about process from outcome frequency in the previous group of methods, here we note the problem of drawing conclusions from process frequency.

Process as independent and dependent variables

A controlled approach to the functional relationships among input, process and output ('E' of Figure 9.2) is to: (a) determine the effect of various manipulations (independent variables) on process events (dependent variables); and (b) determine the effect of direct manipulations of process events (independent variables) on key outputs (dependent variables). This experimental approach has considerable utility; however, it does not establish the temporal ordering of the process variable. The situational manipulation could simultaneously vary both the independent variable of interest and the mediating process. For example, co-operation and competition, as defined by the structuring of outcomes, may elicit different motives. Instructions to co-operate may mean to subjects that they have to talk to each other, whereas instructions to compete may mean they have to work on the task (cf. Bettencourt, Brewer, Croak & Miller, 1992). Possessing those beliefs and behaving differently as a consequence is not evidence of process distinctiveness. Causal ordering could be demonstrated if process measures are taken over time as opposed to obtaining process measurements in conjunction with other dependent measures.

Statistical mediational assessment

Another method is to determine if process measures mediate the relationship between input and output within each situation ('F' of Figure 9.2). For example, in an intergroup setting one might propose that self-focus mediates the effect of relative numerosity of groups on bias – the tendency for the smaller group to display greater favouritism towards the ingroup and greater animosity towards the outgroup (e.g. Mullen, Brown & Smith, 1992). Judd and Kenny (1981) discuss the procedures for assessing mediation within a single experiment. In addition to showing that manipulation of the independent variable (relative numerosity) causes change in the dependent variable (magnitude of intergroup bias), one must show that: the mediator (self-focus) is affected by the independent variable; the mediator is correlated with the dependent variable; and when the correlation between the mediator and the dependent measure is controlled (as in analysis of covariance), the relation between the independent and dependent variables disappears. The basic finding relating relative group size to bias in intergroup settings is well established (Mullen *et al.*, 1992). The key issue is whether self-focus does indeed explain the relation not only in intergroup situations, but in other situations as well – group and interpersonal. A common process in each situation would provide evidence for continuity.

The advantages of demonstrating process mediation by means of the Judd and Kenny procedures are not without limitations. As indicated, that a given process can be shown to mediate the functional relationships among variables does not rule out other possible mediators. Furthermore, as previously noted, application of the Judd and Kenny procedures does not provide direct evidence of a causal connection between the mediator and the dependent measures (as in 'E' of Figure 9.2). The alleged mediator may even be structured into the dependent variable or be conceptually isomorphic with it. Continuing with a similar example, a researcher proposes that self-focus is the mediator of the functional relationship between situational manipulations and dependent variables. Further, assume that it is measured by a series of nine-point scales (how aware of yourself are you, how worried about how you are doing, to what degree were others watching you, etc.). Contrary to our researcher's view, however, responses on this scale may be more extreme with multiple members of two groups (3 + 3) than with individual members of two groups (1 + 1), not because of self-focus, but instead because of a more general arousal, which causes response amplification. The greater arousal provided by settings with more persons may produce response amplification on any scale. Consequently, on similar measurement scales, intergroup bias too will be exaggerated with multiple members. Thus, increased levels of self-focus and bias, in this example, are two measures of a common process – response amplification. A process is extended in time, even if momentarily. It must be shown to be: (a) independent from both the independent and dependent variables, whose functional relationship is mediated by this process; and (b) a consequence of the independent variable if it is to serve as a useful explanatory construct.

Meta-analytic synthesis

A final method (not shown), and an ambitious project, would be the attempt to synthesize the relevant research literature with meta-analytic procedures. Studies would be decomposed into their simple main effects and social, situational and manipulated features of each condition would be rated by independent judges on a variety of measures (cf. Carlson & Miller, 1987). The five key elements (situational features, social representations, manipulated variables, process measures and dependent variables) would each require a taxonomic structure along various dimensions that would allow one to combine or decompose categories.

Regression and causal modelling procedures can supplement the traditional magnitude-of-effect approach to test various theoretical predictions. Certainly different data sets (research literatures) would have to be included. For example, the effects of a single variable may have to be gathered from studies which use only individual interaction, others which use only two-groups interaction, and others which utilize both inter-individual and intergroup conditions. Notwithstanding the enormity of the task, it would be a valuable approach to cumulating the research and testing different theories. It is only across a representative body of studies that one can cast a 'nomological net' (Cronbach & Meehl, 1955) – a theoretical integration that predicts the multivariate pattern of relationships among these variables.

Before leaving this section on the potential value of meta-analytic techniques, it is worth noting that meta-analysis itself cannot provide any more certainty about causal relations. Meta-analytic comparisons between subsets of studies (or application of regression analysis when studies are ordered continuously) only provide associational (correlational) evidence. Further, it is limited by patterns of collecting and reporting information (mediator variables are less often reported than dependent variables and generalization measures are noticeably rare). Finally, meta-analysis will be affected by biases that may occur in publication procedures (Miller & Pollock, in press).

Summary

Among these various methods that constitute the basis for inferences about process events, the weakest is the first: observed differences in outcomes. Even outcome differences as a result of experimental manipulation are weak. Disordinal interactions with independent variables provide a somewhat stronger case; however, process measures are still lacking. Differences in the frequency of processes in different situations are stronger evidence than differences in outcomes alone; however, inferences based on frequency do not demonstrate that they mediate any functional relationship. Statistical mediational analysis can be a relatively strong procedure and is better than the preceding method. Even stronger is the direct manipulation and measurement of process events – separate experiments that, in addition to linking the key independent and dependent variables, also examine the measured process variable as a function of the independent variable and manipulate the process variable to assess its effect on the key dependent variable. Best for drawing conclusions about process distinctiveness is a combination of direct manipulation and measurement of process events, along with statistical mediational analysis within single experiments. Lest the reader assume we view the situation as one that is resolved by a set of three single experiments or a single mediational experiment, the final method argued is for the use of meta-analytic procedures to cumulate studies and provide integrated evidence from all of the preceding methods, albeit with the same reservations about the relative validity of inferences drawn from each of them.

Conclusions

In the first section we used the concept of *psychological interaction* to provide a framework for the question – how to assess process distinctiveness. We argued that: collectives vary across many dimensions, as do individuals; reductionism in explanation is relative to the level of analysis but not a criterion for the value of the explanation; and some phenomena will be emergent by definition (e.g. one cannot study majorities and minorities within a dyad if numerical status is conceptually distinct from other sources of status). In the second section we discussed a number of criteria that might be used to distinguish interpersonal, group and intergroup situations. Difficulties in neatly categorizing these situations were noted. The variables discussed in the section are, no doubt, relevant. It would be useful, if not necessary, that many of them be included in any cumulative review of research results. This would be particularly helpful when trying to compare research from different experimental paradigms (e.g. minimal group, social simulation, prisoner's dilemma, social dilemma). We must conclude that the proposition that interpersonal and intergroup relations are controlled by different processes cannot be true by definition (at least a non-tautological one). In the final section, we discussed various approaches to assessing process distinctiveness and the limitations that each has for valid inference. The view of process distinctiveness has yet to be convincingly demonstrated by empirical data. We contend that much of the data bearing on the issue is only partial and often based on inferences from outcomes. Furthermore, little of the vast data has been cumulatively integrated and a systematic integration would be of significant value to the social psychology of intergroup interaction. As a final note, the treatment of social problems, or recommendations for interventions, are likely to differ significantly as a result of assumptions about process events, causal precedence and generalization.

Notes

1. Dispositional concepts, such as *elasticity*, require an operational definition that, like a law, contains an *if . . . then* relationship (cf.

Hempel, 1952). That is, the existence of the property (e.g. a motivation) can best be defined as being present by performing an operation and then observing its consequence. Thus, if I stretch the rubber-band and then, on letting go, it returns to its initial length, it has the property of elasticity. Similarly, to study the effect of high versus low group motivation for social mobility on collective action (or whatever), would require a dispositional definition. If a researcher operationally defines high social mobility motivation as, for instance, low average income among group members (viz., a *nominal* operational definition) s/he may not adequately capture the meaning of the concept. In caste societies low income may not create a motivation for mobility. Thus, were s/he conducting the experiment in India, this manipulation of social mobility motivation would not be effective. Thus, presence of motivational states and other dispositional concepts seems to require a manipulation and subsequent observation of behaviour (viz., a manipulation check).

2. Parenthetically, the degree of uniformity of responses needs to be distinguished from the extremity of responses. On typical seven-point scales, for example, group means do not become extreme without a corresponding decline in variability, in which case uniformity becomes an artefact.

10 Towards a single-process uncertainty-reduction model of social motivation in groups

Michael Hogg and Dominic Abrams

The aim of this chapter is to present a model of social motivation in groups – a distinctly group-motivational model. We begin by identifying some general features of motivational concepts in psychology, and then review common social motivational constructs invoked by social psychology. We show that just as there is a dual-process dependency model of social influence in groups, social motivational concepts may also reflect a dual-process model of social motivation in which people are driven to seek social approval and positive evaluation or to seek valid knowledge about reality. We argue that this model of social motivation is reductionist because it is all about interpersonal dependence rather than group belongingness.

In contrast we propose a single-process subjective uncertainty-reduction model of group motivation. This model is based on, and is a development of, self-categorization theory and social identity theory. The basic social motivation is to reduce subjective uncertainty. This is satisfied by group identification through self-categorization. Affect is an associated aspect but is contingent on uncertainty-reduction. The explanation of group behaviour requires articulation of the uncertainty-reduction motive with more specific group-based motives that derive from intergroup relations. The mediating construct is social identity.

A short history of motivation

The word 'motivation' is difficult to define. It has a common semantic root with words such as 'motion' and 'move', and so refers, broadly, to changes in state or position over time. More specifically, it seems to refer to that which initiates, causes or induces movement, action or thought.

From a psychological point of view, then, motivation is the psychological 'cause' of thought and behaviour.

It is not surprising then that perhaps the first treatise on psychology, Thomas Hobbes's (1651) *Leviathan*, conceived of the brain as a closed container in which psychological energy moved from place to place to 'motivate', i.e. initiate and energize, various psychological and concomitant behavioural events. This model was directly based on William Harvey's 1628 treatise on the fluid dynamics of blood – blood moved around the body to nourish and energize its various parts.

Although somewhat more sophisticated, Freud's later theory of the human mind has clear links with Hobbes's earlier perspective – libidinal energy was aroused in order to motivate the psyche to perform various psychological functions (e.g. Freud, 1953–64). Once the action was performed the system would return to equilibrium, releasing the libidinal energy to be available to perform another function.

Similar sorts of motivational models of the human mind have pervaded social psychology (Peters, 1958): for example, drive theories, such as Zajonc's (1965) drive theory of social facilitation – increased psychological arousal, an innate response to social presence, energizes habitual (best learned) behaviour patterns (Geen & Gange, 1977). Another important, but slightly different, motivational perspective originates in the work of Kurt Lewin (1936, 1952). Lewin believed that individual needs and goals, ranging from basic physiological ones (e.g. hunger) to highly elaborate socially derived ones (e.g. social equality), create psychological tension in the relevant part of the 'life space' (the totality of the individual's life experiences). This 'tension' locomotes the individual, psychologically, to that part of the life space in order, through thought and/or action, to eliminate the tension.

This assumption of a basic human need to reduce psychological tension and to bring the mind back to equilibrium (i.e., a homeostatic mechanism) pervades much social psychology. It underpins a whole range of cognitive consistency theories that dominated social psychology from the 1940s through to the 1960s (Abelson, Aronson, McGuire, Newcomb, Rosenberg & Tannenbaum, 1968) – for example Osgood and Tannenbaum's (1955) cognitive congruency theory, Festinger's (1957) cognitive dissonance theory, and Heider's (1958) cognitive balance theory. (See discussions by Appley, 1991, and Billig, 1985.)

Some of these early motivational perspectives have had enormous impact on the social psychology of groups. For example, Freudian perspectives generated two seminal explanations of prejudice and discrimination (Dollard, Doob, Miller, Mowrer and Sears's, 1939, frustration–aggression hypothesis, and Adorno, Frenkel-Brunswik, Levinson and Sanford's, 1950, authoritarian personality), and Lewin's perspective cast a long shadow over work on small-group dynamics and the influence of group norms (e.g. Festinger, Schachter and Back's, 1950, work on cohesiveness and social standards).

In the 1970s these sorts of motivational perspectives lost popularity in social psychology. This coincided with an increasing emphasis on information-processing explanations of social behaviour. First there was attribution theory (e.g. Jones & Davis, 1965; Kelley, 1967 – see Hewstone, 1989), with its underlying assumption that people are naïve scientists (or even naïve statisticians) seeking to explain their world. Then there was social cognition (Fiske & Taylor, 1991; Landman & Manis, 1983; Markus & Zajonc, 1985), with its impressive array of cognitive processes and representations that automatically and 'mindlessly' give behaviour and thought the appearance of motivated action. People employ heuristics because, although they may not be optimal, they are quite adequate for most of us most of the time.

The shift from motives and motivational processes to cognitive processes and representations probably occurred for many reasons. One important factor was no doubt the computer revolution. Computers seemed to be able to do many things that people could do, and it seemed quite possible that all that was needed was *more* technology and very soon we would have robot-type computers that would be even more like humans. Since the 'psychology' of computers could be explained in terms of information processing and information storage, perhaps this was all that was needed to explain human thought and behaviour. No need for rather mysterious, and even rather old-fashioned, intervening constructs such as libido, balance, tension, dissonance, and so forth. All that might be required was an understanding of cognitive processes and cognitive representation. The old *deus ex machina* of motivation could be replaced by the new *deus ex machina* of cognition (cf. Markus & Zajonc, 1985).

Although this change in intellectual fashion (a preference perhaps for computer software metaphors rather than fluid dynamics metaphors for 'mind') may account, to some extent, for the demise of motivation it is unlikely to be the complete story. In some cases motivational and cognitive models seem simply to use different languages for basically the same thing – for example cognitive dissonance and self-perception theory explanations of attitude change (e.g. Fazio, Zanna & Cooper, 1977). In other cases, however, motivational explanations have been shown to be deficient – for example, psychodynamic explanations of prejudice and intergroup relations (see Billig, 1976), and balance explanations for social change (see Billig, 1985).

Whatever the reason, and in the light of concerns about whether social cognition in its current form may be rather restricted (e.g. Forgas, 1981; Moscovici, 1982; Wyer & Srull, 1984), we are left with the flotsam of previous motivational concepts from which to reconsider the role of motivation in the explanation of *group* behaviour.

Social motivations and group processes

Recent reviews and texts that deal with social motivation (i.e., social aspects of motivation) rarely directly confront group motivation *sui generis* (e.g. Brody, 1980; de Charms & Muir, 1978; Dienstbier, 1991; Geen, 1991; Pittman & Heller, 1987; Reykowski, 1982). However, some motivational constructs that might be relevant for an understanding of group behaviour do emerge.

Self-esteem and self-enhancement

Kreitler and Kreitler (1987) remark that practically all (i.e., 95 per cent) self-research deals with self-esteem (cf. Appley, 1991). Favourable self-evaluation is an important and enduring goal in human action (e.g. Greenwald & Pratkanis, 1984; McReynolds, 1987; Wylie, 1979). People appear to have a basic need to feel good about who they are – to have a sense of self-esteem, which is derived from self-enhancing comparisons with others. This is often reflected in attempts to present self in a relatively favourable light (e.g. Baumeister, 1982; Breckler & Greenwald, 1986, see Geen; 1991), in order to construct a favourable self-image (e.g. Schlenker, 1985). Failure to achieve or maintain self-esteem can have serious psychological consequences for self – e.g. depression (McReynolds, 1987) and lack of task motivation (Brehm & Self, 1989).

The self-esteem motive occupies a pivotal, though problematic, role in social identity theory where it is invoked largely to account for social change (see Abrams & Hogg, 1988; Hogg & Abrams, 1990). Where the self-concept is defined in group terms (i.e., social identity) the need for self-esteem can be pursued through particular types of inter- and intragroup group behaviours. (See Chapters 2 and 4, particularly, in this volume.) Because self-esteem is invoked to account for *change*, it is a motivational construct very much in the spirit of our discussion at the start of this chapter.

Self-knowledge

Cofer and Appley (1964, page 787) propose that there is a general motive to know the environment. It underlies social comparisons and in turn many 'secondary drives' such as needs for stimulation, affiliation and approval (Brody, 1980; DeCharms & Muir, 1978; McClelland, 1975; Reykowski, 1982). Others note that the pinnacle of the hierarchy of diverse human motivations may be self-actualization (Maslow, 1954; Rogers, 1951) or self-enlightenment. Maslow believes that a person hungers for 'a place in his group . . . [and] . . . a stable, firmly based, usually high evaluation' (1954, pages 89–90) of him or herself. Satisfaction of these motivations assures the integrity and coherence of self, and can enhance self-esteem (Hall, 1961; Rosenzweig, 1944).

Meaning

The possibility of a human desire to make one's experiences and one's self meaningful, what Bartlett (1932) referred to as a search after meaning, is accepted by many (e.g. Berkowitz, 1968; Katz, 1960; Reykowski, 1982). It is an important motivational assumption for much contemporary social psychology which explicitly or tacitly accepts that the ultimate human need is to construct meaning and order from the 'booming, buzzing confusion' of raw sensory experience. The human organism accomplishes this by means of an array of more or less fundamental and overlapping cognitive processes, such as causal attribution, categorization and judgemental heuristics.

There have been a number of attempts to analyze the search for meaning at the level of relatively conscious conceptual understanding. Cantril (1941) has tried to explain the emergence of all-consuming social ideologies during periods of social unrest in terms of their function in providing integrated self-contained explanatory frameworks. Tajfel (1981b) has proposed social justification and social causality as two related social functions of stereotypes that provide people, through their group membership, with a meaningful interpretation of their social world. Moscovici's (1981; Farr & Moscovici, 1984) notion of social representation is another concept addressing the same human need to render experience meaningful (also see Deconchy's, 1984, discussion of orthodox belief systems, and Larrain's, 1979, discussion of ideology).

Balance and consistency

The need for cognitive balance or consistency is an important intrinsic motivation which has homeostatic properties, such that, once satisfied by thought or action, the need temporarily abates (Appley, 1991; Deci & Ryan, 1985; Pittman & Heller, 1987; White, 1959). In social psychology the theme of self-consistency has a long history, where the need for balance or consistency between separate cognitions or separate aspects of self is considered a motivational force (e.g. Festinger, 1957; Heider, 1958). Although there is little unequivocal evidence to assess the *motivations* consequences of cognitive imbalance (Weiner, 1972), it does appear that consistency becomes increasingly important as the self becomes implicated (Aronson, 1969).

This latter point may be important for our discussion of group motivation. To the extent that a group member recognizes an inconsistency between self as defined in group terms and self as defined as a unique individual, there may under appropriate circumstances arise motivational pressure to reconcile the cognitive inconsistency by redefining self in terms of the group-defined self – behaviourally this might manifest itself as conformity or normative behaviour. It should, however, be noted that reduction of ingroup difference may be balanced by accentuation of intergroup difference – in which case, consistency alone is not sufficient to explain change. We need to be able to specify the parameters within which people seek consistency – in this case common group membership.

Power and control

In addition to cognitive balance or consistency, control and power are important motivational considerations. Mikula (1984) argues that people strive for control in order to achieve desired outcomes and avoid undesired outcomes. A similar analysis can be applied to power (see Ng's, 1980, discussion) – popularly believed to be a motive for much behaviour, particularly unacceptable behaviour. In speaking of power, a useful distinction is between 'power to' (the ability to produce intended effects) and 'power over' (the ability to cause others to produce *your* intended effects, or to set the agenda for others' intended effects).

Achievement of control and power may have consequences for self-evaluation. For example, Codol (1984) writes

The conception of oneself as the origin of certain effects, the feeling that one can influence things and people, the ability to guide or master, at least to some extent, the events in the surrounding world – all this is directly associated with a positive self-image. (page 330)

Self-efficacy

Gecas and Schwalbe (1983) believe that only through action can we know ourselves (cf. Marx, 1844/1963; Bem, 1972), and argue that people are motivated by a need to be efficacious in their actions (cf. Bandura, 1982; Deci, 1975; McClelland, 1975). The definition of what constitutes efficacious action is often socially constructed by the groups to which we belong, and in turn shaped by intergroup relations: 'social structural conditions enable and constrain efficacious action, influence the meanings we give to it, and are in turn reproduced by it' (Gecas & Schwalbe, 1983, page 87). For example, whether violence is perceived to be an efficacious form of intergroup behaviour will be determined by the legitimacy placed upon it by one's group.

Affiliation

Perhaps the motive that is most obviously relevant to social groups, is simply the motive for affiliation itself. This is a very powerful human motive for social contact that causes people to affiliate. It is assumed that affiliation occurs and persists because social contact is rewarding in some way or other. There is relatively good agreement in the literature that affiliation is not a unitary motive, but rather contains a number of sub-motives (e.g. Atkinson, 1966; Hill, 1987; Reykowski, 1982), of which four are particularly relevant (Hill, 1987): (1) affiliation provides enjoyable affective and cognitive stimulation; (2) affiliation provides the potential for positive self-regard through praise and attention from others; (3) affiliation provides, through social comparison, the opportunity for self-relevant knowledge that reduces subjective uncertainty; and (4) affiliation provides emotional support or sympathy.

The idea that people affiliate because it is rewarding in some way or other is enormously influential: for example Moreland and Levine's (1982; see also Chapter 7 in this volume) model of group socialization in which commitment depends on cost–benefit analyses by the individual and the group; Sherif's (1966) realistic-conflict theory in which the nature of intergroup relations depends on whether intergroup co-operation is necessary for the satisfaction of specific goals; and of course the traditional theory of group cohesiveness (e.g. Lott & Lott, 1965; cf. Hogg, 1992) in which the rewardingness of interpersonal relations influences group cohesiveness as interpersonal liking.

Affiliation is generally considered to be self-serving instrumental behaviour. However, in the conclusion to his review of social motivation, Reykowski (1982, page 149) suggests that another less 'selfish' motive may underlie affiliation. He argues that people have a basic need to be able to order and position people, including self, in a cognitive representation of a predictable network of social relations. Successfully 'fixing' someone in such a network imbues that person with a positive valence and thus, presumably, promotes affiliation.

A dual-process model of group motivation

We have given a very brief overview of some basic social motivational constructs that have relevance for group motivation. This revealed that there is significant interrelationship and overlap among these constructs.

For the remainder of this chapter we focus exclusively on group motivation.

First, we need to investigate whether there are some general principles governing group motivation. A useful place to start looking is literature on social influence in groups – conformity. The question of whether, and through what process, people accept or reject group influence invites the deeper question of what *motivates* acceptance of group influence. Without some form of influence, groups would very likely not exist psychologically at all, and so the motivations responsible for compliance and conformity in groups are presumably crucial, perhaps fundamental, group motivations.

The discussion of influence and motivation in groups of course raises the question of just what precisely is a social group, in psychological terms. On the basis of a definition of the social group we propose some suggestions about how one might go about constructing a general theory of group motivation.

Recent research into social influence processes in groups (conformity) highlights the existence of a two-process inter-individual dependence model (Abrams & Hogg, 1990b; Hogg & Abrams, 1988; Hogg & Turner, 1987b; Turner, 1985; 1991; Turner, Hogg, Oakes, Reicher & Wetherell, 1987; Turner & Oakes, 1989). Traditional theories of conformity contain a number of conceptual distinctions that can be simplified to a relatively straightforward distinction between two social influence processes: *normative* and *informational influence* (following Deutsch & Gerard's, 1955, terminology) – see Figure 10.1. Both processes address the dependence of one individual on another – dependence for social approval in the case of normative influence, and dependence for information about reality in the case of informational influence.

Normative influence (Deutsch & Gerard, 1955; Kelley, 1952) is based on *pressure to comply* (Abrams & Hogg, 1990b): it results from the individual's need for social approval and acceptance. It creates *public compliance* with, rather than *private acceptance* (Kiesler & Kiesler, 1969) or *internalization* (Kelman, 1958; 1961) of, the group's attitudes, opinions, beliefs or behaviours. The individual 'goes along with' the group for instrumental reasons such as attainment of group goals (called *group locomotion* by Festinger, 1950) or avoidance of punishment, censure or rejection for deviation, or in order to attract social approval and acceptance. There is no internal change. Normative influence arises where the group (or individual) is perceived to have *coercive power* (i.e., the power to criticize, derogate, threaten, punish or enforce laws and regulations for which there are penalties attached for non-compliance) or *reward power* (the power to reinforce compliance or administer affection, praise and material rewards) (French & Raven, 1959; Raven & Kruglanski, 1970).

Normative influence may also underpin the *referent power* (Raven &

Researchers	Two distinct terminologies	
Deutsch and Gerard (1955)	Normative influence	Informational influence
Kelley (1952)		
Kiesler and Kiesler (1969)	Public compliance	Private acceptance
Kelman (1958, 1961)	Compliance, identification	Internalization
Festinger (1950, 1954)	Group locomotion	Social reality testing, social comparisons
French and Raven (1959)	Coercive power, reward	Expert power,
Raven and Kruglanski (1970)	power, referent power	informational power
Jellison and Arkin (1977)	Cultural values	—
Sanders and Baron (1977)		
Burnstein and Vinokur (1977)	—	Persuasive arguments
Vinokur and Burnstein (1974)		
Moscovici (1976)	Majority influence	Minority influence
Mugny (1982)		
Abrams and Hogg (1990b).	Pressures to comply	Reasons to agree

Note: This figure taken from Hogg (1992, page 81) – by permission of Harvester Wheatsheaf.

Figure 10.1 Different terminologies to refer to two distinct processes of social influence.

Kruglanski, 1970) of a group: that is, its power to exact conformity on the basis of being a relevant reference group for the individual. Since reference groups are implicitly defined in terms of emotional attachment on the basis of liking and admiration (see Kelley, 1952), it is likely that pressures for uniformity in such groups are based on a desire for approval, acceptance, and so forth. This analysis is probably still true despite Kelman's (1958, 1961) use of the term *identification* to classify the conformity process underlying referent power. Kelman believes reference groups comprise significant reference others who are people to whom one is attracted, and with whom one therefore wishes to maintain a relationship. Conformity via referent power is thus a relationship-maintenance process.

Informational influence (Asch, 1952; Deutsch & Gerard, 1955; Kelley, 1952), in contrast, is based on subjectively valid *reasons to agree* (Abrams & Hogg, 1990b). It is 'true influence' in that it produces *private acceptance* or *internalization* of beliefs, attitudes and behaviours resulting from the individual's need to be correct. The power of informational influences resides in the perceived expertise or *expert power* (i.e., possession of knowledge that others repeatedly need to draw upon), or the *informational power* (possession of a specific piece of information that is needed) of others (French & Raven, 1959; Raven & Kruglanski, 1970). The precondition for effective informational influence is subjective uncertainty, or lack of confidence in the objective validity of one's beliefs, opinions, and so forth, which cannot be directly resolved by objective tests against physical reality. Under these conditions social comparisons (Festinger, 1954) or social reality tests (Festinger, 1950) are conducted.

This two-process model underlies explanations of other group influence phenomena. For example, group polarization (e.g. Isenberg, 1986; Myers & Lamm, 1976; Moscovici & Zavalloni, 1969; Wetherell, 1987) is traditionally explained in terms of two processes: *cultural values* (Jellison & Arkin, 1977; Sanders & Baron, 1977) and *persuasive arguments* (Burnstein & Vinokur, 1977; Vinokur & Burnstein, 1974). Cultural values relate to normative influence, and persuasive arguments to informational influence. Research into minority influence (e.g. Moscovici, 1976; Mugny, 1982; Paicheler, 1988; Perez & Mugny, 1990) also resurrects a two-process model. Majorities exact conformity through normative channels (they have power to administer rewards and punishments, impose sanctions, mobilize surveillance, etc.), while minorities do so by informational influence (they provide an alternative and more 'truthful' version of reality, one which appears more convincing and better able to resolve contradictions, etc.).

These two processes quite clearly reflect, or capture, two distinct types of social motivations. People become dependent on others because (1) they are motivated to seek emotional support and positive regard from others (normative influence is the associated influence process), and (2) they are motivated to reduce subjective uncertainty about themselves and the world around them (informational influence). The social motivations we discussed above generally fall into one or other of these two categories. Self-enhancement and self-esteem motives underpin, or are associated with, normative influence – so are those affiliative motives to do with social enjoyment, cognitive stimulation, social reinforcement and emotional support. In contrast, self-evaluation motives such as self-knowledge and meaning underpin, or are associated with, informational influence – so are motives to do with control over people and the environment, self-efficacy, and cognitive balance and consistency.

Thus, just as there are two distinct types of social influence process, there may be two distinct classes of social motivation which work in conjunction or differentially predominate in different circumstances to influence group processes. Furthermore, to the extent that motivations 'cause' behaviour, it is very likely that these motivations 'drive' the two separate influence processes, and that effective influence satisfies the underlying motivations.

The dual-process model of social influence has been criticized for overemphasizing interpersonal dependency and failing properly to recognize that influence in groups is a *group* process (Abrams & Hogg, 1990b; Hogg & Abrams, 1988; Hogg & Turner, 1987b; Turner, 1985; 1991; Turner *et al.*, 1987; Turner & Oakes, 1989). These issues can also be raised concerning the dual-process model of group motivation. Individuals are motivated to obtain and maintain positive self-evaluation – they are dependent on other individuals for positive regard, or simply relatively positive self-evaluation. Individuals are also motivated to reduce subjective uncertainty (to reduce entropy) – they are dependent on other individuals as a source of information about subjective reality. The problem with this model is that it is really only about individuals, and says little explicitly about groups – or rather, mistakenly treats the social group as an unproblematic social psychological construct.

The dual-process model is consistent with the traditional social psychological perspective on the social group in which a group is ultimately a face-to-face collection of individuals, and group processes are interpersonal processes among more than two people (e.g. Allport, 1924). This perspective has, however, been called into question on the grounds that it is reductionist and thus rather limited as a basis for theorizing about *groups* (e.g. Doise, 1978; 1986; Hogg, 1992; Hogg & Abrams, 1988; Moscovici, 1972; Taylor & Brown, 1979; Turner & Oakes, 1986). Perhaps separate constructs are necessary to explain group processes as distinct from interpersonal processes. If this is true, then at very least, either (1) the dual-process model of group motivation may be incorrect (entirely different motivations may operate in groups) or (2) the same motivations may operate but in an interrelated and articulated manner that is uniquely mediated by emergent properties of group belongingness, or (3) emergent motivations articulate, through group belongingness, with these fundamental motivations. To address these issues we need first to define the social group.

What is a group?

The question of how to define the social group is one of social psychology's greatest unresolved problematics. A full and proper discussion of this issue is, therefore, well beyond the scope of this chapter (e.g. Steiner, 1974; Turner, 1982; Turner & Oakes, 1986; see Chapter 9 in this volume). For our purposes we believe that an appropriate social psychological definition of the social group should: (1) account for groups of all sorts – large, small, enduring, short-lived, well structured, poorly structured, and so forth; (2) distinguish between groups, group processes and group relations on the one hand and individuals, interpersonal processes and interpersonal relations on the other; and (3) embrace a limited number of theoretical constructs that can be articulated in such a way as to avoid the pitfalls of reductionism (Doise, 1986; Lorenzi-Cioldi & Doise, 1990).

We feel that social identity theory satisfies these conditions. A group is a collection of individuals who classify, define and evaluate themselves in terms of a common social category membership (e.g. Hogg & Abrams, 1988; Turner, 1981; 1982; Tajfel & Turner, 1979). This self-definition is a social identity – it is quite distinct from personal identity which is grounded in idiosyncrasies of self and one's close interpersonal relationships. Social identity is cognitively represented as a component of the self-concept.

Equipped with this definition, the basic motivational questions to do with social groups now become: Why do people define themselves in terms of social identities, and why one social identity in preference to another? How do people identify with groups? What are the consequences of social identification?

Social identity, self-categorization and group motivation

Social identity theory analyzes intergroup relations and group behaviour in terms of two separate processes (see overview by Hogg & Abrams, 1988): (1) the cognitive process of categorization which assigns individuals to social categories and perceptually accentuates intracategory similarities and intercategory differences on dimensions believed to be associated with the categorization – this process is believed to satisfy a fundamental motive to simplify the subjective environment in ways which are meaningful in that particular context; (2) the 'motivational' process of self-enhancement or self-esteem (the self-esteem hypothesis) which causes individuals and groups to strive for relatively positive social identity. The particular strategies and tactics used depend on subjective representations of the nature of intergroup relations (see Chapters 2 and 3 in this volume). It was believed that the self-esteem motive was necessary in order (1) to account for why people associated some dimensions and not others with particular social categorizations, and (2) to account for the dynamics of social change.

While the categorization aspect of the theory is very well supported, the self-esteem aspect is associated with inconsistent and often contradictory findings (see Abrams & Hogg, 1988; Hogg & Abrams, 1990; also Chapter 4 in this volume). In fact, self-categorization theory (Turner, 1985; Turner et al., 1987), which is a recent theoretical development within the social identity framework (Hogg & McGarty, 1990), mainly focuses on categorization and has very little to say about self-esteem. For self-categorization theory, apparently motivated behaviour is accounted for in terms of the operation of the self-categorization process alone.

In order to function, people need to be confident and certain that their perceptions, attitudes and behaviours are valid and correct – that they have a valid understanding of their world and the significance and meaning of aspects of it. People need to be sure that they are correct, because subjective uncertainty is a poor basis for functional conduct. Correctness and validity are not intrinsic properties of stimuli but products of social agreement – not social agreement with just anyone, but agreement with those who are categorized as relevant and similar to self in that particular context for that particular judgement (Turner, 1991; also see Abrams & Hogg, 1990b; Hogg & Turner, 1987b; Turner, 1985; Turner *et al.*, 1987). So, for example, a piece of music is 'good' largely because others whom we categorize as similar to us agree that it is good. The motive here is not for social approval, but for subjectively correct perception.

The process is one in which people construct a cognitive representation of the defining and prescriptive attributes of the group from perceived intragroup similarities and intergroup differences. This is called a prototype and it acts as the group standard or norm. It is internalized by group members through the process of self-categorization, and thus, because it comes to govern self-perception, reduces subjective uncertainty. This is actually a group motivation because subjective certainty is grounded in perceived intra*group* consensus or agreement, not simply interpersonal agreement.

Social change is a product of changed intergroup relations that modify the group prototype. As one discovers that one is now out of step with the prototype, subjective uncertainty re-emerges and motivates subjective re-alignment with the prototype. Of course one could also redefine the 'others' as no longer similar to self, in which case one has defined oneself out of the group, and subjective uncertainty-reduction is sought in a different consensus defined by a different group membership.

Although self-esteem does not enter directly into this model, it is very likely that the reduction of subjective uncertainty, and the concomitant feelings of, for example, self-efficacy, power and control, and self-knowledge, are pleasing and thus elevate mood and improve feelings about self and relevant others. Enhanced self-esteem is thus a consequence of uncertainty-reduction – cf. Corollary 1 of the self-esteem hypothesis (Abrams & Hogg, 1988; Hogg & Abrams, 1990). Some support for this idea comes from a recent reformulation of group cohesiveness from a self-categorization perspective – the social attraction hypothesis (Hogg, 1987; 1992; 1993). Positive regard among group members seems to be based not on interpersonal similarity but on ingroup consensually defined prototypicality – people feel more positive about themselves and fellow group members when they are perceived to be more representative of the consensual ingroup prototype.

An uncertainty-reduction model of group motivation

Let us explore this uncertainty-reduction idea in more detail. We have seen that traditional ideas about group motivation may largely invoke two distinct motivations (self-enhancement and self-evaluation), and that these motivations are satisfied by interpersonal dependence for normative or informational purposes. We have also seen that this dual-process model may be deficient because it neglects to incorporate group belongingness.

As an alternative we propose a single-process uncertainty-reduction model of group motivation, that is based on social identity theory and self-categorization theory. People are motivated by a need to reduce subjective uncertainty. Uncertainty is reduced by agreement with others who are categorized as similar to self – in other words common social category members. On the basis of relevant similarities and differences among people we actively construct a social categorization that minimizes intracategory differences and maximizes intercategory differences around relevant contrasting ingroup and outgroup prototypes. Perceived agreement thus generates categories with which we identify, and prototypes which we internalize. Internalization of an ingroup- and thus self-defining prescriptive prototype, by definition reduces subjective uncertainty.

This mechanism accounts not only for personal change, but also for social change. The nature of the ingroup prototype depends on one's representation of the nature of intergroup relations in that specific context or historical epoch. As intergroup relations, or perceptions of intergroup relations, change, so do ingroup-defining properties. Self can gradually fall out of step with the group, and thus subjective uncertainty re-emerges. To reduce subjective uncertainty one can restructure the ingroup prototype in line with changing circumstances, or one can redefine erstwhile 'similar' others as no longer similar – one can effectively recategorize oneself as a member of a different group and seek uncertainty-reduction through internalization of that group's consensus, as embodied by its prototype (cf. Moreland et al.'s discussion of group socialization, Chapter 7 this volume).

Reduction of uncertainty is a pleasant state of affairs – we feel good when we are sure of the correctness of our attitudes and beliefs and uncomfortable and ill-at-ease when uncertain. So, although the basic motivation may appear rather rational, and the associated process rather cognitive, the entire mechanism is permeated by strong feelings. Subjective certainty thus imbues certainties with positive valence, and imbues those responsible for the consensus upon which the certainty rests with positive valence. Since self becomes part of the consensus, self also becomes imbued with positive valence. This constellation of effects may explain ethnocentrism (LeVine & Campbell, 1972; Sumner, 1906): we value and esteem our own group, its members and its beliefs and practices, above those of outgroups. It may thus account for positive social identity and group-based self-esteem. These strong feelings associated with uncertainty-reduction may, paradoxically, inhibit certain forms of social change by generating dislike for those who espouse an alternative reality (i.e., the outgroup) and those who seek to modify the existing ingroup reality (e.g. active ingroup minorities). Group membership-based liking for prototypical ingroup members ensures a relatively enduring prototypical consensus (Hogg, 1992; 1993).

Subjective certainty may be so cherished that an array of cognitive strategies is marshalled to inhibit subjective uncertainty. For example, groups generally isolate themselves from outgroups, in order not to confront different sources of consensual reality. When information is encountered that threatens subjective certainty, the information and/or its source may be discredited. In fact, active minorities often only achieve change by imposing a consensual message on majority-group members at the same time as they try to reassure the majority that they are in fact ingroup, not outgroup, members (e.g. Moscovici, 1976; Mugny, 1982; Perez & Mugny, 1990). The search for subjective certainty through group consensus can have undesirable consequences when a group develops its own consensus in isolation from wider social agreements – the phenomenon of groupthink (Janis, 1972; Janis & Mann, 1977) is a good example. At an apparently more individual level, because it reflects very wide social consensus, people may defend subjective reality by denial. For example, the pervasive belief in Western societies that each individual is an equally valued human being may help explain denial of personal disadvantage contingent on being a member of a quite obviously disadvantaged group (see Chapter 6, this volume).

In this model, subjective uncertainty-reduction is proposed as the single most basic motivational assumption underlying the explanation of group processes and intergroup relations. Self-esteem is a derivative, or higher-level, motivation. Although subjective uncertainty-reduction may motivate group behaviour, it is unlikely that we can make exact predictions from this motivation alone about the behaviour of specific social groups in specific socio-historical circumstances. However, the motivation does furnish general principles from which we can predict more specific motivations that may have a more direct impact on specific behaviours. For example, people may pursue positive social identity not because, or not only because, they seek positive self-esteem, but perhaps because positive social identity is often a reliable indicator of or cue to subjective certainty, and it is subjective certainty which is the underlying motivation.

The important caveat is that uncertainty-reduction is a fundamental motivational construct which is located at a very general level, and that predicting specific forms of group behaviour from it would be akin to trying to predict eating habits by simply knowing that there is a basic motivation to feed oneself. Furthermore, any explanatory attempt to jump directly from specific group actions to such a basic motivation is dangerously reductionist, and so inevitably leads to loss in explanatory power. In fact, one explanation for the problematic nature of self-esteem as a motivational construct in social identity theory may well be that too much was expected of it – it was a fundamental motivational assumption that was simply inappropriately fundamental to make more fine-grained and specific predictions (Abrams & Hogg, 1988; Hogg & Abrams, 1990).

In line with Doise's (1986; Lorenzi-Cioldi & Doise, 1990) idea of articulation of levels of analysis, we suggest that the basic uncertainty-reduction motive articulates with cognitively represented social beliefs about intergroup relations. The articulation is mediated by social identification – self-categorization as a group member, in order to explain both the general form and specific content of group behaviour. Group membership locates one in an intergroup dynamic that determines how one conceptualizes self; self-conception determines specific goals and motivations; and these in turn govern behaviour. Specific goals and motivations can be very superficial and context-specific (e.g. cheering as loud as possible when one's team scores at a rugby match), or they can be extremely fundamental organizing principles that appear to pervade almost all aspects of life (e.g. a socialist will develop strong egalitarian motives that pervade much behaviour, an anarchist will have different fundamental goals). It is important to recognize that the fundamentally *social* construction of self entails that motivations such as these are actually socially structured (they emerge from social history), not innately determined (emerging from genetic or biological imperatives).

Group motivation, or rather motivations, hinges on a fundamental need to reduce subjective uncertainty. This is satisfied by the cognitive process of categorization which produces the entire array of characteristic group behaviours. The strong feelings associated with group membership, particularly ethnocentrism and self-esteem, are intricately intertwined with uncertainty-reduction, but they may be conceptually secondary to uncertainty-reduction. Uncertainty-reduction may sometimes be a specific motivation for a particular piece of group behaviour, but in general it is likely to be a distal motive that is responsible for more specific goals and motives that have a proximal relationship to group conduct. The translation between uncertainty-reduction and specific motivations is via self-referent prototypical beliefs about one's social identity, one's group and the wider context of intergroup relations.

Conclusions and prospects

In this chapter we have tentatively suggested some principles for a single-process subjective uncertainty-reduction model of social motivation in groups. This model can be considered an extension and formalization of motivational implications of self-categorization theory. It also comprises a new emphasis in social identity theory.

The model stems from some concern about the motivational role of self-esteem, or self-enhancement, in social identity theory. In an earlier publication (Abrams & Hogg, 1988) we suggested that in addition to self-esteem, group behaviour might be motivated by a search for meaning and a coherent self-concept. Later (Hogg & Abrams, 1990), we simplified this to assign the search for meaning a more central motivational role that would probably operate through the self-categorization process. The present chapter goes a great deal further: (1) it identifies subjective uncertainty-reduction as the prime group motivation; (2) it places self-esteem in a secondary or derived motivational position; (3) it describes exactly how self-categorization is the process associated with the subjective uncertainty-reduction motivation; and (4) it explicitly calls for the articulation of uncertainty-reduction and higher-level socially derived motives in order to account for the contextualized behaviour of social group members.

Uncertainty-reduction is an individual motivation, but one that inevitably can only be realized by group belongingness. As such it is also truly a group motivation – since it is not associated with interpersonal relationships. However, since uncertainty-reduction is responsible for the construction of self, via group membership, it is inappropriate in most circumstances to attempt to make a predictive leap from uncertainty-reduction to specific group behaviours. Rather, specific group motivations are constructed by group members from beliefs about specific intergroup relations. Uncertainty-reduction and associated positive affect provide important parameters for the content of social identity.

This model makes some sense insofar as it is consistent with major assumptions in social cognition (Fiske & Taylor, 1991). It fits the general assumption that cognitive processes and representations are associated with a search for meaning and parsimony. It also fits some views about the self. For example, Markus and Nurius (1987) describe how people construct favourable and unfavourable possible selves and this motivates self-change towards the favourable self and away from the unfavourable self. Once translated to a group context, this is not dissimilar to the idea that people bring their self-concept in line with an ingroup prototype in order to reduce uncertainty.

Our model is a motivational one which requires a notion of group that is separate from interpersonal relationships, and it requires that fundamental psychological processes are articulated with social processes in order to explain group behaviour. It thus may minimize problems of reductionism on both counts. Finally, it has a degree of added elegance because it is a single-process model that explicitly locates affect and feelings within it. It is, however, at this stage only a preliminary model. It still needs further elaboration and specification, and research is yet to be undertaken to investigate its explanatory power and validity.

References

Abeles, R.P. (1976), 'Relative deprivation, rising expectations and black militancy', *Journal of Social Issues*, **32**, 119–37.

Abelson, R.P., Aronson, E., McGuire, W.J., Newcomb, T.M., Rosenberg, M.J. & Tannenbaum, P.H. (eds) (1968), *Theories of cognitive consistency: A sourcebook*, Chicago, IL: Rand-McNally.

Abrams, D. (1985), 'Focus of attention in minimal intergroup discrimination', *British Journal of Social Psychology*, **24**, 65–74.

Abrams, D. (1991), *Optimal distinctiveness: Young people in search of self*, unpublished manuscript, University of Kent.

Abrams, D. (1992), 'Processes of social identification', in G. Breakwell (ed.), *Social psychology of the self-concept*, London: Academic Press, pp. 57–99.

Abrams, D. & Emler, N. (1992), 'Self-denial as a paradox of political and regional identity: Findings from a study of 16- and 18-year olds', *European Journal of Social Psychology*, **22**, 279–95.

Abrams, D. & Hogg, M.A. (1988), 'Comments on the motivational status of self-esteem in social identity and intergroup discrimination', *European Journal of Social Psychology*, **18**, 317–34.

Abrams, D. & Hogg, M.A. (eds) (1990a), *Social identity theory: Constructive and critical advances*, London: Harvester Wheatsheaf.

Abrams, D. & Hogg, M.A. (1990b), 'Social identification, self-categorization and social influence', in W. Stroebe & M. Hewstone (eds), *European review of social psychology* (vol. 1), Chichester: Wiley, pp. 195–228.

Adorno, T.W., Frenkel-Brunswik, E., Levinson, D.J. & Sanford, R.N. (1950), *The authoritarian personality*, New York: Harper.

Ajzen, I. (1982), 'On behaving in accordance with one's attitudes', in M.P. Zanna, E.T. Higgins, & C.P. Herman (eds), *Consistency in social behavior: The Ontario symposium* (vol. 2), Hillsdale, NJ: Erlbaum, pp. 3–15.

Ajzen, I. (1988), *Attitudes, personality and behaviour*, Milton Keynes: Open University Press.

Alladina, S. (1985), 'Research methodology for language use surveys in Britain', in P.H. Nelde (ed.), *Methods in contact linguistics*, Bonn: Dummler, pp. 233–40.

Allard, R. & Landry, R. (1986), 'Subjective ethnolinguistic vitality viewed as a belief system', *Journal of Multilingual and Multicultural Development*, 7, 1–12.

Allard, R. & Landry, R. (in press), 'Subjective ethnolinguistic vitality: A comparison of two measures', *International Journal of the Sociology of Language*.

Alloy, L.B. & Abramson, L.Y. (1979), 'Judgement of contingency in depressed and nondepressed students: Sadder but wiser?', *Journal of Experimental Psychology: General*, 108, 441–85.

Allport, F.H. (1920), 'The influence of the group upon association and thought', *Journal of Experimental Psychology*, 3, 159–82.

Allport, F.H. (1924), *Social psychology*, New York: Houghton Mifflin.

Allport, G.W. (1937), *Personality: A psychological interpretation*, New York: Holt.

Allport, G.W. (1954/1979), *The nature of prejudice*, Reading, MA: Addison-Wesley.

Amir, Y. (1969), 'Contact hypothesis in ethnic relations', *Psychological Bulletin*, 71, 319–41.

Amir, Y. (1976), 'The role of intergroup contact in change of prejudice and ethnic relations', in P.A. Katz (ed.), *Towards the elimination of racism*, New York: Pergamon Press, pp. 73–123.

Anderson, C.A. (1983), 'Abstract and concrete data in the perseverance of social theories: When weak data lead to unshakeable beliefs', *Journal of Experimental Social Psychology*, 19, 93–108.

Anderson, C.A. & Sechler, E.S. (1986), 'Effects of explanation and counterexplanation on the development and use of social theories', *Journal of Personality and Social Psychology*, 50, 24–34.

Appley, M.H. (1991), 'Motivation, equilibration, and stress', in R.A. Dienstbier (ed.), *Perspectives on motivation: Nebraska symposium on motivation 1990* (vol. 38), Lincoln, NE: University of Nebraska Press, pp. 1–67.

Arkin, R.M. (1981), 'Self-presentational styles', in J.T. Tedeschi (ed.), *Impression management theory and social psychological research*, San Diego, CA: Academic Press, pp. 311–33.

Aronson, E. (1969), 'The theory of cognitive dissonance: A current perspective', in L. Berkowitz (ed.), *Advances in experimental social psychology* (vol. 4), New York: Academic Press, pp. 1–34.

Aronson, E., Brewer, M. & Carlsmith, J.M. (1985), 'Experimentation in social psychology', in G. Lindzey & E. Aronson (eds), *The handbook of social psychology*, New York: Random House, pp. 441–86.

Asch, S. (1952), *Social psychology*, Englewood Cliffs, NJ: Prentice Hall.

Ashmore, R.D. & DelBoca, F.K. (1981), 'Conceptual approaches to stereotypes and stereotyping', in D.L. Hamilton (ed.), *Cognitive processes in stereotyping and intergroup behavior*, Hillsdale, NJ: Erlbaum, pp. 1–35.

Atkinson, J.W. (1966), 'Motivational determinants of risk-taking behavior', in J.W. Atkinson & N.T. Feather (eds), *A theory of achievement motivation*, New York: Wiley, pp. 11–29.

Bandura, A. (1982), 'Self-efficacy mechanisms in human agency', *American Psychologist*, **37**, 122–47.

Bargh, J.A. (1984), 'Automatic and conscious processing of social information', in R.S. Wyer & T.K. Srull (eds), *Handbook of social cognition* (vol. 3), Hillsdale, NJ: Erlbaum, pp. 1–43.

Baron, R.S., Burgess, M.L., Kao, C.F. & Logan, H. (1990, May), *Fear and superficial social processing: Evidence of stereotyping and simplistic persuasion*, Paper presented at the Midwestern Psychological Association Convention, Chicago.

Baron, R.S., Kerr, N.C. & Miller, N. (1992), *Group process, group decision, and group action*, Pacific Grove, CA: Brooks Cole.

Bar-Tal, D. (1990), *Group beliefs: A conception for analyzing group structure, processes, and behavior*, New York: Springer-Verlag.

Bartlett, F.C. (1932), *Remembering*, Cambridge: Cambridge University Press.

Baumeister, R.F. (1982), 'A self-presentational view of social phenomena', *Psychological Bulletin*, **91**, 3–26.

Baumeister, R.F. (1986), *Public self and private self*, New York: Springer-Verlag.

Baumeister, R.F. & Tice, D.M. (1985), 'Self-esteem and responses to success and failure: Subsequent performance and intrinsic motivation', *Journal of Personality*, **53**, 451–67.

Baumeister, R.F., Tice, D.M. & Hutton, D.G. (1989), 'Self-presentational motivations and personality differences in self-esteem', *Journal of Personality*, **57**, 547–79.

Baumgardner, A.H. (1990), 'To know oneself is to like oneself: Self-certainty and self-affect', *Journal of Personality and Social Psychology*, **58**, 1062–72.

Becker, H.S. (1960), 'Notes on the concept of commitment', *American Journal of Sociology*, **66**, 32–40.

Bem, D.J. (1972), 'Self-perception theory', in L. Berkowitz (ed.), *Advances in experimental social psychology* (vol. 6), New York: Academic Press, pp. 1–62.

Bergmann, G. (1957), *Philosophy of science*, Madison, WI: University of Wisconsin Press.

Berkowitz, L. (1986), 'Social motivation', in G. Lindzey & E. Aronson (eds), *The handbook of social psychology*, Reading, MA: Addison-Wesley, pp. 50–135.

Berkowitz, L. & Macaulay, J.R. (1961), 'Some effects of differences in status level and status stability', *Human Relations*, **14**, 135–49.

Berlyne, D.E. (1971), *Aesthetics and psychobiology*, New York: Appleton-Century-Croft.

Bettencourt, B.A., Brewer, M.B., Croak, M.R. & Miller, N. (1992), 'Cooperation and the reduction of intergroup bias: The role of reward structure and social orientation', *Journal of Experimental Social Psychology*, **28**, 301–19.

Billig, M. (1976), *Social psychology and intergroup relations*, London: Academic Press.

Billig, M. (1985), 'Prejudice, categorization and particularization: From a perceptual to a rhetorical approach', *European Journal of Social Psychology*, **15**, 79–103.

Billig, M. (1987), *Arguing and thinking*, Cambridge: Cambridge University Press.

Birt, C.M. & Dion, K.L. (1987), 'Relative deprivation theory and responses to discrimination in a gay male and lesbian sample', *British Journal of Social Psychology*, **26**, 139–45.

Blaine, B. & Crocker, J. (in press), 'Self-esteem and self-serving biases in reactions to positive and negative events: An integrative review', in R.F. Baumeister (ed.), *Self-esteem: The puzzle of low self-regard*, New York: Plenum Press.

Blascovich, J. & Kelsey, R.M. (1990), 'Using electrodermal and cardiovascular measures of arousal in social psychological research', in C. Hendrick & M.S. Clark (eds), *Research methods in personality and social psychology*, Newbury Park, CA: Sage, pp. 45–73.

Blau, P.M. (1964), *Exchange and power in social life*, New York: Wiley.

Bless, H., Bohner, G., Schwarz, N. & Strack, F. (1990), 'Mood and persuasion: A cognitive response analysis', *Personality and Social Psychology Bulletin*, **16**, 331–45.

Bodenhausen, G.V. (in press), 'Emotions, arousal, and stereotype-based discrimination: A heuristic model of affect and stereotyping', in D. Mackie & D. Hamilton (eds), *Affect, cognition, and stereotyping: Interactive processes in group perception*, San Diego, CA: Academic Press.

Bodenhausen, G.V. & Kramer, G.P. (1990, June), *Affective states trigger stereotypic judgments*, paper presented at the annual convention of the American Psychological Society, Dallas.

Bourhis, R.Y. (1979), 'Language in ethnic interaction: A social psychological approach', in H. Giles & B. Saint-Jacques (eds), *Language and ethnic relations*, Oxford: Pergamon Press, pp. 117–42.

Bourhis, R.Y. (1982), 'Language policies and language attitudes: Le monde de la francophonie', in E.B. Ryan & H. Giles (eds), *Attitudes towards language variation*, London: Edward Arnold, pp. 34–62.

Bourhis, R.Y. (ed.), (1984), *Conflict and language planning in Québec*, Clevedon: Multilingual Matters.

Bourhis, R.Y. (1993), 'Power, gender and intergroup discrimination: Some minimal group studies', in M. Zanna & J. Olson (eds), *The psychology of prejudice: The 7th Ontario symposium on personality and social psychology*, Hillsdale, NJ: Erlbaum.

Bourhis, R.Y. (in press), 'Review of dimension et mesure de la vitalite linguistique' (vol. 1), *International Journal of the Sociology of Language*.

Bourhis, R.Y., Giles, H., Leyens, J.P. & Tajfel, H. (1979), 'Psycholinguistic distinctiveness: Language divergence in Belgium', in H. Giles & R. St Clair (eds), *Language and social psychology*, Oxford: Blackwell, pp. 158–85.

Bourhis, R.Y., Giles, H. & Rosenthal, D. (1981), 'Notes on the construction of a subjective vitality questionnaire for ethnolinguistic groups', *Journal of Multilingual and Multicultural Development*, **2**, 144–55.

Bourhis, R.Y. & Sachdev, I. (1984), 'Vitality perceptions and language attitudes: Some Canadian data', *Journal of Language and Social Psychology*, **3**, 97–126.

Bradley, G.W. (1978), 'Self-serving biases in the attribution process: A re-examination of the fact or fiction question', *Journal of Personality and Social Psychology*, **36**, 56–71.

Breckler, S.J. & Greenwald, A.G. (1986), 'Motivational facets of the self', in R.M. Sorrentino & E.T. Higgins (eds), *Handbook of motivation and cognition*, New York: Guildford, pp. 145–64.

Brehm, J.W. & Self, E.A. (1989), 'The intensity of motivation', *Annual Review of Psychology*, **40**, 109–31.

Brewer, M.B. (1979), 'In-group bias in the minimal intergroup situation: A cognitive-motivational analysis', *Psychological Bulletin*, **86**, 307–24.

Brewer, M.B. (1991), 'The social self: On being the same and different at the same time', *Personality and Social Psychology Bulletin*, **17**, 475–82.

Brewer, M.B. (1993), 'Social identity, distinctiveness, and in-group homogeneity', *Social Cognition*, **11**.

Brewer, M.B., Dull, V. & Lui, L. (1981), 'Perceptions of the elderly: Stereotypes as prototypes', *Journal of Personality and Social Psychology*, **41**, 656–70.

Brewer, M.B. & Kramer, R.M. (1986), 'Choice behaviour in social dilemmas: Effects of social identity, group size, and decision framing', *Journal of Personality and Social Psychology*, **50**, 543–9.

Brewer, M.B., Manzi, J. & Shaw, J. (1992), *Ingroup identification as a function of depersonalization, distinctiveness, and status*, unpublished manuscript, University of California, Los Angeles.

Brewer, M.B. & Miller, N. (1984), 'Beyond the contact hypothesis: Theoretical perspectives on desegregation', in N. Miller & M.B. Brewer (eds), *Groups in contact*, New York: Academic Press, pp. 281–302.

Brewer, M.B. & Schneider, S. (1990), 'Social identity and social dilemmas: A double-edged sword', in D. Abrams & M.A. Hogg (eds), *Social identity theory: Constructive and critical advances*, London: Harvester Wheatsheaf, and New York: Springer-Verlag, pp. 169–84.

Brinthaupt, T.M., Moreland, R.L. & Levine, J.M. (1991), 'Sources of optimism among prospective group members', *Personality and Social Psychology Bulletin*, **17**, 36–43.

Broadbent, D.E. (1971), *Decision and stress*, New York: Academic Press.

Brockner, J. (1983), 'Low self-esteem and behavioral plasticity: Some implications', in L. Wheeler & P. Shaver (eds), *Review of personality and social psychology*, (vol. 4), Beverly Hills, CA: Sage, pp. 237–71.

Brody, N. (1980), 'Social motivation', *Annual Review of Psychology*, **31**, 143–68.

Brown, B.B. & Lohr, M.J. (1987), 'Peer-group affiliation and adolescent self-esteem: An integration of ego-identity and symbolic-interaction theories', *Journal of Personality and Social Psychology*, **52**, 47–55.

Brown, J.D. (1986), 'Evaluations of self and others: Self-enhancement biases in social judgments', *Social Cognition*, **4**, 353–76.

Brown, J.D. (in press), 'Motivational conflict and the self: The double-bind of low self-esteem', in R.F. Baumeister (ed.), *Self-esteem: The puzzle of low self-regard*, New York: Plenum Press.

Brown, J.D., Collins, R.L. & Schmidt, G.W. (1988), 'Self-esteem and direct versus indirect forms of self-enhancement', *Journal of Personality and Social Psychology*, **55**, 445–53.

Brown, J.D., Novick, N., Lord, K. & Richards, J. (1992), 'When Gulliver travels: Social context, psychological closeness, and self-appraisals', *Journal of Personality and Social Psychology*, **62**, 717–27.

Brown, R. (1954), 'Mass phenomena', in G. Lindzey (ed.), *Handbook of social psychology* (vol. 2.), Cambridge, MA: Addison-Wesley, pp. 833–76.

Brown, R.J. (1978), 'Divided we fall: An analysis of relations between sections of a factory workforce', in H. Tajfel (ed.), *Differentiation between social groups*, London: Academic Press, pp. 395–429.

Brown, R.J. & Turner, J.C. (1981), 'Interpersonal and intergroup behaviour', in J.C. Turner & H. Giles (eds), *Intergroup behaviour*, Oxford: Blackwell, pp. 33–65.

Brown, R.J. & Wootton-Millward, L. (1993), 'Perceptions of group homogeneity during group formation: Further evidence for the ingroup homogeneity effect', *Social Cognition*, **11**.

Bruner, J. (1957), 'On perceptual readiness', *Psychological Review*, **64**, 123–51.

Burnstein, E. & Vinokur, A. (1977), 'Persuasive argumentation and social comparison as determinants of attitude polarization', *Journal of Experimental Social Psychology*, **13**, 315–32.

Byrne, D. (1971), *The attraction paradigm*, New York: Academic Press.

Byrne, D. & Wong, T.J. (1962), 'Racial prejudice, interpersonal attraction, and assumed dissimilarity of attitudes', *Journal of Abnormal and Social Psychology*, **65**, 246–53.

Cacioppo, J.T., Petty, R.E. & Tassinary, L.G. (1989), 'Social psychophysiology: A new look', in L. Berkowitz (ed.), *Advances in experimental social psychology* (vol. 22), San Diego, CA: Academic Press, pp. 39–91.

Caddick, B. (1982), 'Perceived illegitimacy and intergroup relations', in H. Tajfel (ed.), *Social identity and intergroup relations*, Cambridge: Cambridge University Press, pp. 137–54.

Campbell, D.T. (1960), 'Common fate, similarity and other indices of the status of aggregates of persons as social entities', in D. Winer (ed.), *Decisions, values and groups*, Oxford: Pergamon, pp. 185–201.

Campbell, D.T. (1974), '"Downward causation" in hierarchically organized biological systems', in F.J. Ayala & T. Dobzhansky (eds), *Studies in the philosophy of biology*, New York: McMillan Press, pp. 179–80.

Campbell, J.D. (1990), 'Self-esteem and the clarity of the self-concept', *Journal of Personality and Social Psychology*, **59**, 538–49.

Campbell, J.D. & Lavallee, D. (in press), 'Who am I? The role of self-concept confusion in understanding the behavior of low self-esteem people', in R. Baumeister (ed.), *Self-esteem: The puzzle of low self-regard*, New York: Plenum Press.

Cantril, H. (1941), *The psychology of social movements*, New York: Wiley.

Carlson, M., Marcus-Newhall, A. & Miller, N. (1990), 'Effects of situational aggression cues: A quantitative review', *Journal of Personality and Social Psychology*, **58**, 211–29.

Carlson, M. & Miller, N. (1987), 'Explanation of the relation between negative mood and helping', *Psychological Bulletin*, **102**, 91–108.

Charles, M.T. (1982), 'The Yellowstone Ranger: The social control and socialization of federal law enforcement officers', *Human Organization*, **41**, 216–26.

Cialdini, R.B., Borden, R.J., Thorne, A., Walker, M.R., Freeman, S. & Sloan, L.R. (1976), 'Basking in reflected glory: Three (football) field studies', *Journal of Personality and Social Psychology*, **34**, 366–75.

Cialdini, R.B. & Richardson, K.D. (1980), 'Two indirect tactics of image management: Basking and blasting', *Journal of Personality and Social Psychology*, **39**, 406–15.

Clark, M.S. (1982), 'A role for arousal in the link between feeling states, judgments, and behavior', in M.S. Clark & S.T. Fiske (eds), *Affect and cognition: The seventeenth annual Carnegie symposium on cognition*, Hillsdale, NJ: Erlbaum, pp. 263–89.

Clark, M.S. (1984), 'Record keeping in two types of relationships', *Journal of Personality and Social Psychology*, **47**, 549–57.

Clark, M.S. (1985), 'Implications of relationship type for understanding compatibility', in W. Ickes (ed.), *Compatible and incompatible relationships*,

New York: Springer-Verlag, pp. 119–40.

Clark, M.S., Milberg, S. & Erber, R. (1984), 'Effects of arousal on judgments of others' emotions', *Journal of Personality and Social Psychology*, **46**, 551–60.

Clayton, S. & Crosby, F. (1992), *Justice, gender, and affirmative action*, Ann Arbor: The University of Michigan Press.

Clement, R. (1980), 'Ethnicity, contact and communicative competence in a second language', in H. Giles, W.P. Robinson & P.M. Smith (eds), *Language: Social psychological perspectives*, Oxford: Pergamon, pp. 147–54.

Clement, R. (1986), 'Second language proficiency and acculturation: An investigation of the effects of language status and individual characteristics', *Journal of Language and Social Psychology*, **5**, 271–90.

Clement, R. & Krudenier, B. (1985), 'Aptitude, attitude and motivation in second language proficiency: A test of Clement's model', *Journal of Language and Social Psychology*, **4**, 21–37.

Clement, R. & Noels, K. (1991, August), *Ethnolinguistic vitality, language and identity*, paper presented at 4th International Conference on Language and Social Psychology, Santa Barbara, CA.

Coates, D. & Winston, T. (1983), 'Counteracting the deviance of depression: Peer support groups for victims', *Journal of Social Issues*, **39**, 169–94.

Codol, J.-P. (1984), 'Social differentiation and non-differentiation', in H. Tajfel (ed.), *The social dimension: European developments in social psychology* (vol. 1), Cambridge: Cambridge University Press, pp. 314–37.

Cofer, C.N. & Appley, M.H. (1964), *Motivation: Theory and research*, New York: Wiley.

Cohen, A.R. (1958), 'Upward communication in experimentally created hierarchies', *Human Relations*, **11**, 41–53.

Cohen, A. & Lowenberg, G. (1990), 'A re-examination of the side-bet theory as applied to organizational commitment: A meta-analysis', *Human Relations*, **43**, 1015–50.

Coleman, J.S. (1961), *The adolescent society*, New York: Free Press.

Commins, B. & Lockwood, J. (1979a), 'Social comparison and social inequality: An experimental investigation of intergroup behaviour', *British Journal of Social and Clinical Psychology*, **18**, 285–9.

Commins, B. & Lockwood, J. (1979b), 'The effects of status differences, favoured treatment and equity on intergroup comparisons', *European Journal of Social Psychology*, **9**, 281–9.

Condor, S. & Brown, R. (1988), 'Psychological processes in intergroup conflict', in W. Stroebe, A.W. Kruglanski, D. Bar-Tal & M. Hewstone (eds), *The social psychology of intergroup conflict*, Berlin: Springer-Verlag, pp. 3–26.

Cook, S.W. (1984), 'Cooperative interaction in multiethnic contexts', in N. Miller & M.B. Brewer (eds), *Groups in contact*, Orlando, FL: Academic Press, pp. 155–85.

Cook, T.D. & Campbell, D.T. (1979), *Quasi-experimentation: Design and analysis issues for field settings*, Chicago: Rand-McNally.

Coopersmith, S. (1967), *The antecedents of self-esteem*, San Francisco: Freeman.

Cordova, D.I. (1992), 'Cognitive limitations and affirmative action: The effects of aggregate versus sequential data in the perception of discrimination', *Social Justice Research*, **5**, 101–16.

Cottrell, N. (1972), 'Social facilitation', in C. McClintock (ed.), *Experimental social psychology*, New York: Holt, Rinehart & Winston, pp. 185–236.

Criden, Y. & Gelb, S. (1976), *The kibbutz experience*, New York: Schocken Books.

Crocker, J. & Blaine, B. (1992), *Self-esteem and self-serving biases: The role of self-concept positivity, certainty and importance*, unpublished manuscript, State University of New York, Buffalo.

Crocker, J. & Luhtanen, R. (1990), 'Collective self-esteem and ingroup bias', *Journal of Personality and Social Psychology*, **58**, 60–7.

Crocker, J. & Major, B. (1989), 'Social stigma and self-esteem: The self-protective properties of stigma', *Psychological Review*, **96**, 608–30.

Crocker, J. & Schwartz, I. (1985), 'Prejudice and ingroup favouritism in a minimal intergroup situation: Effects of self-esteem', *Personality and Social Psychology Bulletin*, **11**, 379–86.

Crocker, J., Thompson, L., McGraw, K. & Ingerman, C. (1987), 'Downward comparison, prejudice, and evaluations of others: Effects of self-esteem and threat', *Journal of Personality and Social Psychology*, **52**, 907–16.

Cronbach, L.J. & Meehl, P.E. (1955), 'Construct validity in psychological tests', *Psychological Bulletin*, **52**, 281–302.

Crosby, F.J. (1982), *Relative deprivation and working women*, New York: Oxford University Press.

Crosby, F.J. (1984), 'The denial of personal discrimination', *American Behavioral Scientist*, **27**, 371–86.

Crosby, F.J. (1991), *Juggling: The unexpected advantages of balancing a career and home for women and their families*, New York: The Free Press.

Crosby, F.J., Burris, L., Censor, C. & MacKethan, E.R. (1986), 'Two rotten apples spoil the whole justice barrel', in H.W. Bierhoff, R. Cohen & J. Greenberg (eds), *Justice in social relations*, New York: Plenum, pp. 267–81.

Crosby, F.J., Clayton, S., Hemker, K. & Alksnis, O. (1986), 'Cognitive biases in the perception of discrimination', *Sex Roles*, **14**, 637–46.

Crosby, F.J., Pufall, A., Snyder, R.C., O'Connell, M. & Whalen, P. (1989), 'The denial of personal disadvantage among you, me, and all the other ostriches', in M. Crawford & M. Gentry (eds), *Gender and thought*, New York: Springer-Verlag, pp. 79–99.

Crosby, F. & Stewart, A. (1991, June), *Women overcoming the denial of discrimination*, paper given at the International Conference of Law and Society, Amsterdam, Holland.

Currie, M. & Hogg, M.A. (in press), 'Subjective ethnolinguistic vitality and social adaptation among Vietnamese refugees in Australia', *International Journal of the Sociology of Language*.

Cusick, P.A. (1973), *Inside high school*, New York: Holt, Rinehart & Winston.

Dabbs, J.M. & Ruback, R.B. (1987), 'Dimensions of group process: Amount and structure of vocal interaction', in L. Berkowitz (ed.), *Advances in experimental social psychology* (vol. 20), San Diego, CA: Academic Press, pp. 123–69.

Dalessio, A. & Imada, A.S. (1984), 'Relationships between interview selection decisions and perceptions of applicant similarity to an ideal employee and self: A field study', *Human Relations*, **37**, 67–80.

Darke, S. (1988), 'Anxiety and working memory capacity', *Cognition and Emotion*, **2**, 145–54.

de Charms, R. & Muir, M.S. (1978), 'Motivation: Social approaches', *Annual Review of Psychology*, **29**, 91–113.

Deci, E.L. (1975), *Intrinsic motivation*, New York: Plenum.

Deci, E.L. & Ryan, R.M. (1985), *Intrinsic motivation and self-determination in human behavior*, New York: Plenum.

Deconchy, J.-P. (1984), 'Rationality and social control in orthodox systems', in H. Tajfel (ed.), *The social dimension: European developments in social psychology* (vol. 2), Cambridge: Cambridge University Press, and Paris: Editions de la Maison des Sciences de l'Homme, pp. 425–45.

Deutsch, M. & Gerard, H.B. (1955), 'A study of normative and informational influences upon individual judgement', *Journal of Abnormal and Social Psychology*, **51**, 629–36.

Deutsch, M. & Krauss, R.M. (1960), 'The effect of threat on interpersonal bargaining', *Journal of Abnormal and Social Psychology*, **61**, 181–9.

Devine, P.G. (1989), 'Stereotypes and prejudice: Their automatic and controlled components', *Journal of Personality and Social Psychology*, **56**, 5–18.

Dienstbier, R.A. (ed.) (1991), *Perspectives on motivation: Nebraska symposium on motivation 1990* (vol. 38), Lincoln, NE: University of Nebraska Press.

Doise, W. (1978), *Groups and individuals: Explanations in social psychology*, Cambridge: Cambridge University Press.

Doise, W. (1986), *Levels of explanation in social psychology*, Cambridge: Cambridge University Press.

Doise, W. (1988), 'Individual and social identities in intergroup relations', *European Journal of Social Psychology*, **18**, 99–112.

Dollard, J., Doob, L.W., Miller, N.E., Mowrer, O.H. & Sears, R.R. (1939), *Frustration and aggression*, New Haven, CT: Yale University Press.

Easterbrook, J.A. (1959), 'The effect of emotion on cue utilization and the organization of behavior', *Psychological Review*, **66**, 183–201.

Edwards, J. (1985), *Language, society and identity*, Oxford: Blackwell.

Ehrlich, H.J. (1973), *The social psychology of prejudice*, New York: Wiley.

Ellemers, N., Doosje, B., van Knippenberg, A. & Wilke, H. (1992), 'Status protection in high status minority groups', *European Journal of Social Psychology*, **22**, 123–40.

Ellemers, N., van Knippenberg, A., de Vries, N. & Wilke, H. (1988), 'Social identification and permeability of group boundaries', *European Journal of Social Psychology*, **18**, 497–513.

Ellemers, N., van Knippenberg, A. & Wilke, H. (1990), 'The influence of permeability of group boundaries and stability of group status on strategies of individual mobility and social change', *British Journal of Social Psychology*, **29**, 233–46.

Ellemers, N., Wilke, H. & van Knippenberg, A. (1993), 'Effects of the legitimacy of low group or individual status on individual and collective identity enhancement strategies', *Journal of Personality and Social Psychology*, **64**.

Ellis, H.C. & Ashbrook, P.W. (1988), 'Resource allocation model of the effects of depresssed mood states on memory', in K. Fiedler & J. Forgas (eds), *Affect, cognition, and social behavior*, Toronto: Hogrefe, pp. 25–43.

Espinoza, J.A. & Garza, R.T. (1985), 'Social group salience and interethnic cooperation', *Journal of Experimental Social Psychology*, **21**, 380–92.

Farr, R.M. & Moscovici, S. (eds) (1984), *Social representations*, Cambridge: Cambridge University Press.

Fazio, R.H., Zanna, M.P. & Cooper, J. (1977), 'Dissonance and self-perception: An integrative view of each theory's proper domain of application', *Journal of Experimental Social Psychology*, **13**, 464–79.

Festinger, L. (1950), 'Informal social communication', *Psychological Review*, **57**, 271–82.

Festinger, L. (1954), 'A theory of social comparison processes', *Human Relations*, **7**, 117–40.

Festinger, L. (1957), *A theory of cognitive dissonance*, Stanford, CA: Stanford University Press.

Festinger, L., Schachter, S. & Back, K. (1950), *Social pressures in informal groups*. New York: Harper & Row.

Finchilescu, G. (1986), 'Effect of incompatibility between internal and external group membership criteria on intergroup behaviour', *European Journal of Social Psychology*, **16**, 83–7.

Fishbein, M. (1967), 'Attitudes and the prediction of behavior', in M. Fishbein (ed.), *Readings in attitude theory and measurement*, New York: Wiley, pp. 477–92.

Fiske, S.T. & Neuberg, S.L. (1990), 'A continuum of impression formation from category-based to individuating processes: Influences of information and motivation on attention and interpretation', in M.P. Zanna (ed.), *Advances in experimental social psychology* (vol. 23), Orlando, FL: Academic Press, pp. 1–74.

Fiske, S.T. & Taylor, S.E. (1991), *Social cognition* (2nd ed.), New York: McGraw-Hill.

Ford, D.L. (1988), 'Minority and non-minority MBA progress in business', in D.E. Thompson & N. DiTomaso (eds), *Ensuring minority success in corporate management*, New York: Plenum, pp. 57–69.

Forgas, J.P. (ed.) (1981), *Social cognition: Perspectives on everyday understanding*, London: Academic Press.

Forgas, J.P. (1989), 'Mood effects on decision making strategies', *Australian Journal of Psychology*, **41**, 197–214.

Frable, D., Blackstone, T. & Scherbaum, C. (1990), 'Marginal and mindful: Deviants in social interaction', *Journal of Personality and Social Psychology*, **59**, 140–9.

French, J.R.P. & Raven, B.H. (1959), 'The bases of social power', in D. Cartwright (ed.), *Studies in social power*, Ann Arbor, MI: University of Michigan Press, pp. 118–49.

Freud, S. (1953–64), *Standard edition of the complete psychological works* (ed. J. Strachey). London: Hogarth Press.

Friend, R. & Gilbert, J. (1973), 'Threat and fear of negative evaluation as determinants of locus of social comparison, *Journal of Personality*, **41**, 328–40.

Fromkin, H.L. (1970), 'Effects of experimentally aroused feelings of undistinctiveness upon valuation of scarce and novel experiences', *Journal of Personality and Social Psychology*, **16**, 521–9.

Fromkin, H.L. (1972), 'Feelings of interpersonal undistinctiveness: An unpleasant affective state', *Journal of Experimental Research in Personality*, **6**, 178–82.

Gabrenya, W.K., Latané, B. & Wang, Y.E. (1983), 'Social loafing in cross-cultural perspective: Chinese in Taiwan', *Journal of Cross-Cultural Psychology*, **14**, 368–84.

Gabrenya, W.K., Wang, T.E. & Latané, B. (1985), 'Social loafing on an optimizing task: Cross-cultural differences among Chinese and Americans', *Journal of Cross-Cultural Psychology*, **16**, 223–42.

Gao, G., Schmidt, K.L. & Gudykunst, W.B. (1990, June), *Strength of ethnic identity and perceptions of ethnolinguistic vitality*, paper presented at the 40th International Communication Association Convention, Dublin.

Garrett, P., Giles, H. & Coupland, N. (1989), 'The contexts of language learning: Extending the intergroup model of second language acquisition', in S. Ting Toomey & F. Korzenny (eds), *Language, communication and culture*, Newbury Park, CA: Sage, pp. 201–21.

Gecas, V. & Schwalbe, M.L. (1983), 'Beyond the looking-glass self: Social structure and efficacy-based self-esteem', *Social Psychology Quarterly*, **46**, 77–88.

Geen, R.G. (1991), 'Social motivation', *Annual Review of Psychology*, **42**, 377–99.

Geen, R.G. & Gange, J.J. (1977), 'Drive theory of social facilitation: Twelve years of theory and research', *Psychological Bulletin*, **84**, 1267–88.

Genesee, F. & Bourhis, R.Y. (1982), 'The social psychological significance of code-switching in cross-cultural communication', *Journal of Language and Social Psychology*, **1**, 1–28.

Genesee, F. & Bourhis, R.Y. (1988), 'Evaluative reactions to language choice strategies: The role of sociostructural factors', *Language and Communication*, **8**, 229–50.

Gergen, K.J., Greenberg, M.S. & Willis, R.H. (eds) (1980), *Social exchange: Advances in theory and research*, New York: Plenum Press.

Gibbons, F.X. (1985), 'Social stigma perception: Social comparison among mentally retarded persons', *American Journal of Mental Deficiency*, **90**, 98–106.

Gibbons, F.X., Gerrard, M., Lando, H. & McGovern, P. (1991), 'Social comparison and smoking cessation: The role of the "typical smoker"', *Journal of Experimental Social Psychology*, **27**, 239–58.

Gibbons, F.X. & McCoy, B. (1991), 'Self-esteem, similarity, and reactions to active vs. passive downward comparison', *Journal of Personality and Social Psychology*, **60**, 414–24.

Gilbert, D.T. & Hixon, J.G. (1991), 'The trouble of thinking: Activation and application of stereotypic beliefs', *Journal of Personality and Social Psychology*, **60**, 509–17.

Giles, H. (1978), 'Linguistic differentiation between ethnic groups', in H. Tajfel (ed.), *Differentiation between social groups*, London: Academic Press, pp. 361–93.

Giles, H., Bourhis, R.Y. & Taylor, D.M. (1977), 'Towards a theory of language in ethnic group relations', in H. Giles (ed.), *Language, ethnicity, and inter-group relations*, London: Academic Press, pp. 307–48.

Giles, H. & Byrne, J. (1982), 'The intergroup model of second language acquisition', *Journal of Multilingual and Multicultural Development*, **3**, 17–40.

Giles, H. & Johnson, P. (1981), 'The role of language in ethnic group relations', in J.C. Turner & H. Giles (eds), *Intergroup behaviour*, Oxford: Blackwell, pp. 199–243.

Giles, H. & Johnson, P. (1987), 'Ethnolinguistic identity theory: A social psychological approach to language maintenance', *International Journal of the Sociology of Language*, **68**, 256–69.

Giles, H., Leets, L. & Coupland, N. (1990), 'Minority language group status; A theoretical conspexus', *Journal of Multilingual and Multicultural Development*, **11**, 37–56.

Giles, H., Mulac, A., Bradac, J.J. & Johnson, P. (1987), 'Speech accommodation theory: The first decade and beyond', in M.L. McLaughlin (ed.), *Communication Yearbook 10*, Beverly Hills, CA: Sage, pp. 13–48.

Giles, H. & Powesland, P. (1975), *Speech style and social evaluation*, London: Academic Press.

Giles, H. & Robinson, W.P. (eds) (1990), *The handbook of language and social psychology*, Chichester & New York: Wiley.

Giles, H., Rosenthal, D. & Young, L. (1985), 'Perceived ethnolinguistic vitality: the Anglo- and Greek-Australian setting', *Journal of Multilingual and Multicultural Development*, 3, 253–69.

Giles, H., Scherer, K. & Taylor, D. (1979), 'Speech markers in social interaction', in K. Scherer & H. Giles (eds), *Social markers in speech*, Cambridge: Cambridge University Press, pp. 343–81.

Giles, H., Smith, P., Ford, B., Condor, S. & Thakerar, J. (1980), 'Speech style and the fluctuating salience of sex', *Language Sciences*, 2, 260–82.

Goethals, G. & Darley, J. (1987), 'Social comparison theory: Self-evaluation and group life', in B. Mullen & G. Goethals (eds), *Theories of group behavior*, New York: Springer-Verlag, pp. 21–47.

Goffman, E. (1967), *Interaction ritual*, Garden City, NY: Doubleday Anchor.

Gotlib, I.H., McLachlan, A.L. & Katz, A.N. (1988), 'Biases in visual attention in depressed and nondepressed individuals', *Cognition and Emotion*, 2, 185–200.

Greenwald, A.G. & Pratkanis, A.R. (1984), 'The self', in R.S. Wyer, Jr & T.K. Srull (eds), *Handbook of social cognition* (vol. 3), Hillsdale, NJ: Erlbaum, pp. 129–78.

Guimond, S. & Dube, L. (1983), 'Relative deprivation theory and the Quebec nationalist movement: On the cognitive-emotion distinction and the personal-group deprivation issue', *Journal of Personality and Social Psychology*, 44, 526–35.

Gumperz, J.J. & Hymes, D. (eds) (1972), *Directions in sociolinguistics*, New York: Holt, Rinehart & Winston.

Gur, R.C., Gur, R.E., Skolnick, B.E., Resnick, S.M., Silver, F.I., Chawluk, J., Muenz, L., Obrist, W.D. & Reivich, M. (1988), 'Effects of task difficulty on regional cerebral blood flow: Relationships with anxiety and performance', *Psychophysiology*, 24, 392–9.

Gurin, P. (1987), 'The political implications of women's status', in F.J. Crosby (ed.), *Spouse, parent, worker: On gender and multiple roles*, New Haven, CT: Yale University Press, pp. 165–96.

Gurin, P., Miller, A. & Gurin, G. (1980), 'Stratum identification and consciousness', *Social Psychology Quarterly*, 43, 30–47.

Gurwitz, S. & Dodge, K. (1977), 'Effects of confirmations and discon-firmations on stereotype-based attributions', *Journal of Personality and Social Psychology*, 35, 495–500.

Hafer, C. & Olson, J. (1989), 'Beliefs in a just world and reactions to personal deprivation', *Journal of Personality*, 57, 799–823.

Hafer, C. & Olson, J. (1993), 'Discontent, beliefs in a just world, and assertive actions by working women', *Personality and Social Psychology Bulletin*, **19**, 30–8.

Hall, J.F. (1961), *Psychology of motivation*, Philadelphia, PA: Lippincott.

Hamers, J.H. & Blanc, M.H. (1989), *Bilinguality and bilingualism*. Cambridge: Cambridge University Press.

Hamilton, D.L. (1979), 'A cognitive-attributional analysis of stereotyping', in L. Berkowitz (ed.), *Advances in experimental social psychology* (vol. 12), New York: Academic Press, pp. 53–84.

Hamilton, D.L. (ed.) (1981), *Cognitive processes in stereotyping and intergroup behavior*, Hillsdale, NJ: Erlbaum.

Hamilton, D.L. & Rose, T.L. (1980), 'Illusory correlation and the maintenance of stereotypic beliefs', *Journal of Personality and Social Psychology*, **39**, 832–45.

Hamilton, D.L. & Trolier, T.K. (1986), 'Stereotypes and stereotyping: An overview of the cognitive approach', in J.F. Dovidio & S.L. Gaertner (eds), *Prejudice, discrimination and racism*, New York: Academic Press, pp. 127–63.

Harkins, S.G. (1987), 'Social loafing and social facilitation', *Journal of Experimental Social Psychology*, **23**, 1–18.

Harkins, S.G., Latané, B. & Williams, K.D. (1980), 'Social loafing: Allocating effort or taking it easy?', *Journal of Experimental Social Psychology*, **16**, 457–65.

Harkins, S.G. & Petty, R.E. (1981), 'The multiple source effect in persuasion: The effects of distraction', *Personality and Social Psychology Bulletin*, **7**, 627–35.

Harkins, S.G. & Petty, R.E. (1982), 'Effects of task difficulty and task uniqueness of social loafing', *Journal of Personality and Social Psychology*, **43**, 1214–29.

Harkins, S.G. & Szymanski, K. (1988), 'Social loafing and self evaluation with an objective standard', *Journal of Experimental Social Psychology*, **24**, 354–65.

Harkins, S.G. & Szymanski, K. (1989), 'Social loafing and group evaluation', *Journal of Personality and Social Psychology*, **56**, 934–41.

Harrington, H.J. & Miller, N. (in press), 'Research and theory in intergroup relations: Issues of consensus and controversy', in J. Lynch, M. Modgil & S. Modgil (eds), *Cultural diversity in the schools*, London: Falmer Press.

Harter, S. (1986), 'Processes underlying the construction, maintenance, and enhancement of the self-concept in children', in J. Suls & A. Greenwald (eds), *Psychological perspectives on the self* (vol. 3), Hillsdale, NJ: Erlbaum, pp. 137–81.

Harwood, J., Giles, H. & Bourhis, R.Y. (in press), 'The genesis of vitality theory: Historical patterns and discoursal dimensions', *International Journal of the Sociology of Language*.

Hasher, L. & Zacks, R.T. (1979), 'Automatic and effortful processes in memory', *Journal of Experimental Psychology: General*, **108**, 356–88.

Hastie, R. (1981), 'Schematic principles in human memory', in E.T. Higgins, C.P. Herman & M.P. Zanna (eds), *Social cognition: The Ontario symposium on personality and social psychology* (vol. 1), Hillsdale, NJ: Erlbaum, pp. 39–88.

Heider, F. (1958), *The psychology of interpersonal relations*, New York: Wiley.

Hempel, C. (1952), *Fundamentals of concept formation in empirical science*, Chicago, IL: University of Chicago Press.

Hewstone, M. (1989), *Causal attribution: From cognitive processes to collective beliefs*, Oxford: Blackwell.

Hewstone, M. (1990), 'The ultimate attribution error? A review of the literature on intergroup causal attributions', *European Journal of Social Psychology*, **20**, 311–35.

Hewstone, M. & Brown, R. (1986), 'Contact is not enough: An intergroup perspective', in M. Hewstone & R. Brown (eds), *Contact and conflict in intergroup encounters*, Oxford: Blackwell, pp. 1–44.

Hewstone, M., Johnston, L. & Aird, P. (1992), 'Cognitive models of stereotype change (2): Perceptions of homogeneous and heterogeneous groups', *European Journal of Social Psychology*, **22**, 235–49.

Higgins, E.T., Kuiper, N.A. & Olson, J.M. (1981), 'Social cognition: A need to get personal', in E.T. Higgins, C.P. Herman & M.P. Zanna (eds), *Social cognition: The Ontario symposium on personality and social psychology* (vol. 1), Hillsdale, NJ: Erlbaum, pp. 395–420.

Hill, C.A. (1987), 'Affiliation motivation: People who need people . . . but in different ways', *Journal of Personality and Social Psychology*, **52**, 1008–18.

Hinkle, S. & Brown, R.J. (1990), 'Intergroup comparisons and social identity: Some links and lacunae', in D. Abrams and M.A. Hogg (eds), *Social identity theory: Constructive and critical advances*, London: Harvester Wheatsheaf, pp. 48–70.

Hinkle, S., Taylor, D., Fox-Cardamone, L. & Cook, K. (1989), 'Intragroup identification and intergroup differentiation: A multi-component approach', *British Journal of Social Psychology*, **28**, 305–17.

Hoelter, J. (1983), 'The effects of role evaluation and commitment on identity salience', *Social Psychology Quarterly*, **46**, 140–7.

Hogg, M.A. (1987), 'Social identity and group cohesiveness', in J.C. Turner, M.A. Hogg, P.J. Oakes, S.D. Reicher & M.S. Wetherell, *Rediscovering the social group: A self-categorization theory*, Oxford & New York: Blackwell, pp. 89–116.

Hogg, M.A. (1992), *The social psychology of group cohesiveness: From attraction to social identity*, London: Harvester Wheatsheaf, and New York: New York University Press.

Hogg, M.A. (1993), 'Group cohesiveness: A critical review and some new directions', in W. Stroebe & M. Hewstone (eds), *European review of social psychology* (vol. 4), Chichester: Wiley.

Hogg, M.A. & Abrams, D. (1988), *Social identifications: A social psychology of intergroup relations and group process*, London & New York: Routledge.

Hogg, M.A. & Abrams, D. (1990), 'Social motivation, self-esteem and social identity', in D. Abrams & M.A. Hogg (eds), *Social identity theory: Constructive and critical advances*, London: Harvester Wheatsheaf, and New York: Springer-Verlag, pp. 28–47.

Hogg, M.A., D'Agata, P. & Abrams, D. (1989), 'Ethnolinguistic betrayal and speaker evaluations among Italian Australians', *Genetic, Social and General Psychology Monographs*, **115**, 153–81.

Hogg, M.A. & Hardie, E.A. (1991), 'Social attraction, personal attraction, and self-categorization: A field study', *Personality and Social Psychology Bulletin*, **17**, 175–80.

Hogg, M.A. & McGarty, C. (1990), 'Self-categorization and social identity', in D. Abrams & M.A. Hogg (eds), *Social identity theory: Constructive and critical advances*, London: Harvester Wheatsheaf, and New York: Springer-Verlag, pp. 10–27.

Hogg, M.A. & Sunderland, J. (1991), 'Self-esteem and intergroup discrimination in the minimal group paradigm', *British Journal of Social Psychology*, **30**, 51–62.

Hogg, M.A. & Turner, J.C. (1985a), 'Interpersonal attraction, social identification and psychological group formation', *European Journal of Social Psychology*, **15**, 51–66.

Hogg, M.A. & Turner, J.C. (1985b), 'When liking begets solidarity: An experiment on the role of interpersonal attraction in psychological group formation', *British Journal of Social Psychology*, **24**, 267–81.

Hogg, M.A. & Turner, J.C. (1987a), 'Intergroup behaviour, self-stereotyping and the salience of social categories', *British Journal of Social Psychology*, **26**, 325–40.

Hogg, M.A. & Turner, J.C. (1987b), 'Social identity and conformity: A theory of referent informational influence', in W. Doise & S. Moscovici (eds), *Current issues in European social psychology* (vol. 2), Cambridge: Cambridge University Press, pp. 139–82.

Homans, G.C. (1961), *Social behavior: Its elementary forms*, New York: Harcourt, Brace & World.

Horwitz, M. & Rabbie, J.M. (1982), 'Individuality and membership in the intergroup system', in H. Tajfel (ed.), *Social identity and intergroup relations*, Cambridge: Cambridge University Press, pp. 241–74.

Husband, C. & Saifullah Khan, V. (1982), 'The viability of ethnolinguistic vitality: Some creative doubts', *Journal of Multilingual and Multicultural Development*, **3**, 139–205.

Ingham, A.G., Levinger, G., Graves, J. & Peckham, V. (1974), 'The Ringelmann effect: Studies of group size and group performance', *Journal of Experimental Social Psychology*, **10**, 371–84.

Insko, C., Schopler, J., Hoyle, R., Dardis, G. & Graetz, K. (1990), 'Individual-group discontinuity as a function of fear and greed', *Journal of Personality and Social Psychology*, **58**, 68–79.

Isen, A.M. (1987), 'Positive affect, cognitive processes, and social behavior', in L. Berkowitz (ed.), *Advances in experimental social psychology* (vol. 20), Orlando, FL: Academic Press, pp. 203–53.

Isen, A.M. & Levin, P.F. (1972), 'The effect of feeling good on helping: Cookies and kindness', *Journal of Personality and Social Psychology*, **21**, 384–8.

Isenberg, D.J. (1986), 'Group polarization: A critical review and meta-analysis', *Journal of Personality and Social Psychology*, **50**, 1141–51.

Jackson, J.M. & Williams, K.D. (1985), 'Social loafing on difficult tasks: Working collectively can improve performance', *Journal of Personality and Social Psychology*, **49**, 937–42.

Jackson, J.M. & Williams, K.D. (1986), *Social loafing: A review and theoretical analysis*, unpublished manuscript, University of Toledo.

James, K. & Greenberg, J. (1989), 'Ingroup salience, intergroup comparison, and individual performance and self-esteem', *Personality and Social Psychology Bulletin*, **15**, 604–16.

Janis, I.L. (1972), *Victims of groupthink: A psychological study of foreign policy decisions and fiascoes*, Boston, MA: Houghton Mifflin.

Janis, I.L. & Mann, L. (1977), *Decision making*, New York: The Free Press.

Jellison, J. & Arkin, R. (1977), 'Social comparison of abilities: A self-presentation approach to decision making in groups', in J.M. Suls & R.L. Miller (eds), *Social comparison processes: Theoretical and empirical perspectives*, Washington, DC: Hemisphere, pp. 235–57.

Johnson, D.W. & Johnson, R.T. (1992), 'Positive interdependence: Key to effective cooperation', in R. Hertz-Lazarowitz & N. Miller (eds), *Interaction in cooperative groups: The theoretical anatomy of group learning*, New York: Cambridge University Press, pp. 174–99.

Johnson, P., Giles, H. & Bourhis, R.Y. (1983), 'The viability of ethnolinguistic vitality: A reply', *Journal of Multilingual and Multicultural Development*, **4**, 255–69.

Johnston, L. & Hewstone, M. (1992), 'Cognitive models of stereotype change: (3) Subtyping and the perceived typicality of disconfirming group members', *Journal of Experimental Social Psychology*, in press.

Jones, E.E. & Davis, K.E. (1965), 'From acts to dispositions: The attribution process in person perception', *Advances in Experimental Social Psychology*, **2**, 219–66.

Judd, C.M. & Kenny, D.A. (1981), *Estimating the effects of social interventions*, Cambridge: Cambridge University Press.

Kahneman, D. (1973), *Attention and effort*, Englewood Cliffs, NJ: Prentice Hall.

Kahneman, D. & Tversky, A. (1973), 'On the psychology of prediction', *Psychological Review*, **80**, 237–51.

Kanter, R.M. (1972), *Commitment and community: Communes and utopias in sociological perspective*, Cambridge, MA: Harvard University Press.

Karau, S.J. & Williams, K.D. (1991a), *Social loafing: A meta-analytical review and theoretical integration*, unpublished manuscript, University of Toledo.

Karau, S.J. & Williams, K.D. (1991b), *The effects of group cohesiveness on social loafing and social compensation*, unpublished manuscript, University of Toledo.

Katz, D. (1960), 'The functional approach to the study of attitudes', *Public Opinion Quarterly*, **24**, 163–204.

Kelley, H.H. (1952), 'Two functions of reference groups', in G.E. Swanson, T.M. Newcomb & E.L. Hartley (eds), *Readings in social psychology* (2nd ed.), New York: Holt, Rinehart & Winston, pp. 410–14.

Kelley, H.H. (1967), 'Attribution theory in social psychology', in D. Levine (ed.), *Nebraska symposium on motivation* (vol. 15), Lincoln, NE: University of Nebraska Press, pp. 192–240.

Kelman, H.C. (1958), 'Compliance, identification and internalization: Three processes of opinion change', *Journal of Conflict Resolution*, **2**, 51–60.

Kelman, H.C. (1961), 'Processes of opinion change', *Public Opinion Quarterly*, **25**, 57–78.

Kerr, N.L. (1983), 'Motivation losses in small groups: A social dilemma analysis', *Journal of Personality and Social Psychology*, **45**, 819–28.

Kerr, N.L. & Bruun, S.E. (1981), 'Ringelmann revisited: Alternative explanations to the social loafing effect', *Personality and Social Psychology Bulletin*, **7**, 224–31.

Kerr, N.L. & Bruun, S.E. (1983), 'The dispensability of member effort and group motivation losses: Free-rider effects', *Journal of Personality and Social Psychology*, **44**, 78–94.

Kiesler, C.A. & Kiesler, S.B. (1969), *Conformity*, Reading, MA: Addison-Wesley.

Kim, H.S. & Baron, R.S. (1988), 'Exercise and illusory correlation: Does arousal heighten stereotypic processing?', *Journal of Experimental Social Psychology*, **24**, 366–80.

Kraemer, R. & Olshtain, E. (1989), 'Perceived ethnolinguistic vitality and language attitudes: The Israeli setting', *Journal of Multilingual and Multicultural Development*, **10**, 255–69.

Kraemer, R., Olshtain, E. & Badier, S. (in press), 'Ethnolinguistic vitality, attitudes and networks of linguistic contact: The case of the Israel Arab minority', *International Journal of the Sociology of Language*.

Kramarae, C. (1981), *Women and men speaking*, Rowley, MA: Newbury House.

Kravitz, D.A. & Martin, B. (1986), 'Ringelmann rediscovered: The original article', *Journal of Personality and Social Psychology*, 50, 936–41.

Kreitler, H. & Kreitler, S. (1976), *Cognitive orientation and behaviour*, New York: Springer.

Kreitler, S. & Kreitler, H. (1987), 'The psychosemantic aspects of the self', in T. Honess & K. Yardley (eds), *Self and identity: Perspectives across the lifespan*, London: Routledge, pp. 338–58.

Krueger, J. & Rothbart, M. (1990), 'Contrast and accentuation effects in category learning', *Journal of Personality and Social Psychology*, 59, 651–63.

Kruglanski, A.W. & Mackie, D.M. (1990), 'Majority and minority influence: A judgemental process analysis', in W. Stroebe & M. Hewstone (eds), *European review of social psychology* (vol 1), Chichester: Wiley, pp. 229–61.

Kunda, Z. (1987), 'Motivated inference: Self-serving generation and evaluation of causal theories', *Journal of Personality and Social Psychology*, 53, 636–47.

Labrie, N. & Clement, R. (1986), 'Ethnolinguistic vitality, self-confidence and second language proficiency: An investigation', *Journal of Multilingual and Multicultural Development*, 7, 269–82.

Landman, J. & Manis, M. (1983), 'Social cognition: Some historical and theoretical perspectives', *Advances in Experimental Social Psychology*, 16, 49–123.

Landry, R. & Allard, R. (1984), 'Bilinguisme additif, bilinguisme soustractif et identité ethnolinguistique', *Recherches Sociologiques*, 15, 337–58.

Landry, R. & Allard, R. (1987), 'Etude du developpement bilingue chez les Acadiens des provinces Maritimes', in R. Theberge & J. Lafontant (eds), *Demain, la francophonie en milieu minoritaire*, Winnipeg: Centre de recherches du College de Saint-Boniface, pp. 112–28.

Landry, R. & Allard, R. (1990), 'Contact des langues et developpement bilingue: Un modele macroscopique', *Revue Canadienne des Langues Vivantes/Canadian Modern Language Review*, 46, 527–53.

Landry, R. & Allard, R. (1991, May), *Subjective ethnolinguistic vitality and subtractive identity in Canada*, paper presented at 40th International Communication Association Convention, Chicago.

Landry, R. & Allard, R. (eds) (in press, a), 'Ethnolinguistic vitality', *International Journal of the Sociology of Language*.

Landry, R. & Allard, R. (in press, b), 'Ethnolinguistic vitality: A viable construct?', *International Journal of the Sociology of Language*.

Landry, R. & Allard, R. (in press, c), 'Diglossia, ethnolinguistic vitality and language behaviour', *International Journal of the Sociology of Language*.

Landry, R. & Allard, R. (in press, d), 'The Acadians of New Brunswick:

Demolinguistic realities and the vitality of the French language', *International Journal of the Sociology of Language*.

Larrain, J. (1979), *The concept of ideology*, London: Hutchinson.

Latané, B. (1981), 'The psychology of social impact', *American Psychologist*, **36**, 343–56.

Latané, B., Williams, K.D. & Harkins, S. (1979), 'Many hands make light the work: The causes and consequences of social loafing', *Journal of Personality and Social Psychology*, **37**, 822–32.

Lau, R.R. (1989), 'Individual and contextual influences on group identification', *Social Psychology Quarterly*, **52**, 220–31.

Le Bon, G. (1896), *The crowd: A study of the popular mind*, London: T. Fisher Unwin.

Lemaine, G. (1974), 'Social differentiation and social originality', *European Journal of Social Psychology*, **4**, 17–52.

Lerner, M.J. (1980), *The belief in a just world*, New York: Plenum.

Lerner, M.J. & Miller, D.T. (1978), 'Just world research and the attribution process: Looking back and ahead', *Psychological Bulletin*, 1030–51.

Lerner, M.J., Miller, D.T. & Holmes, J.G. (1976), 'Deserving and the emergence of forms and justice', in L. Berkowitz (ed.), *Advances in experimental social psychology*, New York: Academic Press, pp. 133–62.

LeVine, R.A. & Campbell, D.T. (1972), *Ethnocentrism: Theories of conflict, ethnic attitudes and group behavior*, New York: Wiley.

Levinger, G.E. (1980), 'Toward the analysis of close relationships,' *Journal of Experimental Social Psychology*, **16**, 510–44.

Lewin, K. (1936), *Principles of topological psychology*, New York: McGraw-Hill.

Lewin, K. (1943), 'Defining the "field at a given time"', *Psychological Review*, **50**, 292–310.

Lewin, K. (1952), *Field theory in social science*, London: Tavistock.

Locksley, A., Ortiz, V. & Hepburn, C. (1980), 'Social categorization and discriminatory behavior: Extinguishing the minimal intergroup discrimination effect', *Journal of Personality and Social Psychology*, **39**, 773–83.

Lord, C. & Saenz, D. (1985), 'Memory deficits and memory surfeits: Differential cognitive consequences of tokenism for tokens and observers', *Journal of Personality and Social Psychology*, **49**, 918–26.

Lorenzi-Cioldi, F. & Doise, W. (1990), 'Levels of analysis and social identity', in D. Abrams & M.A. Hogg (eds), *Social identity theory: Constructive and critical advances*, London: Harvester Wheatsheaf, and New York: Springer-Verlag, pp. 71–88.

Lott, A.J. & Lott, B.E. (1965), 'Group cohesiveness as interpersonal attraction', *Psychological Bulletin*, **64**, 259–309.

Luhtanen, R., Blaine, B. & Crocker, J. (1991, April), *Personal and collective self-esteem and depression in African-American and White students*, paper presented at the annual meeting of the Eastern Psychological Association, New York.

Luhtanen, R. & Crocker, J. (1991), 'Self-esteem and intergroup comparisons: Toward a theory of collective self-esteem', in J. Suls & T.A. Wills (eds), *Social comparison: Contemporary theory and research*, Hillsdale, NJ: Erlbaum, pp. 211–34.

Luhtanen, R. & Crocker, J. (1992), 'A collective self-esteem scale: Self-evaluation of one's social identity', *Personality and Social Psychology Bulletin*, **18**, 302–18.

Maass, A. & Schaller, M. (1991), 'Intergroup biases and the cognitive dynamics of stereotype function', *European Review of Social Psychology*, **2**, 189–209.

McCauley, C. & Stitt, C.L. (1978), 'An individual and quantitative measure of stereotypes', *Journal of Personality and Social Psychology*, **36**, 929–40.

McClelland, D.C. (1975), *Power: The inner experience*, New York: Irvington.

McClintock, C.G., Kramer, R.M. & Keil, L.J. (1984), 'Equity and social exchange in human relationships', in L. Berkowitz (ed.), *Advances in experimental social psychology* (vol. 17), Orlando, FL: Academic Press, pp. 183–228.

McDougall, W. (1933), *The energies of men: A study of the fundamentals of dynamic psychology*, New York: Scribner's.

McGuire, W.J., McGuire, C.V., Child, P. & Fujioka, T. (1978), 'Salience of ethnicity in the spontaneous self-concept as a function of one's ethnic distinctiveness in the social environment', *Journal of Personality and Social Psychology*, **36**, 511–20.

McGuire, W.J., McGuire, C.V. & Winton, W. (1979), 'Effects of household sex composition on the salience of one's gender in the spontaneous self-concept', *Journal of Experimental Social Psychology*, **15**, 77–90.

McGuire, W.J. & Padawer-Singer, A. (1976), 'Trait salience in the spontaneous self-concept', *Journal of Personality and Social Psychology*, **33**, 743–54.

Mackie, D.M. (1986), 'Social identification effects in group polarization', *Journal of Personality and Social Psychology*, **50**, 720–28.

Mackie, D.M., Hamilton, D.L., Schroth, H.A., Carlisle, C.J., Gersho, B.F., Meneses, L.M., Nedler, B.F. & Reichel, L.D. (1989), 'The effects of induced mood on expectancy-based illusory correlations', *Journal of Experimental Social Psychology*, **25**, 524–44.

McPhail, C. (1991), *The myth of the madding crowd*, Hawthorne, NY: Walter de Gruyter.

McReynolds, P. (1987), 'Self-theory, anxiety and intrapsychic conflicts', in N. Cheshire & H. Thomae (eds), *Self, symptoms and psychotherapy*, New York: Wiley, pp. 197–223.

Major, B., Testa, M. & Bylsma, W.H. (1991), 'Responses to upward and downward social comparisons: The impact of esteem-relevance and perceived control', in J. Suls & T.A. Wills (eds), *Social comparison: Contemporary theory and research*, Hillsdale, NJ: Erlbaum, 237–60.

Mann, J.W. (1961), 'Group relations in hierarchies', *The Journal of Social Psychology*, **54**, 283–314.

Marks, G. & Miller, N. (1987), 'Ten years of research on the "false consensus effect": An empirical and theoretical review', *Psychological Bulletin*, **102**, 72–90.

Markus, H. & Nurius, P. (1986), 'Possible selves', *American Psychologist*, **41**, 954–69.

Markus, H. & Nurius, P. (1987), 'Possible selves: The interface between motivation and the self-concept', in K. Yardley & T. Honess (eds), *Self and identity: Psychosocial perspectives*, New York: Wiley, pp. 157–72.

Markus, H. & Zajonc, R.B. (1985), 'The cognitive perspective in social psychology', in G. Lindzey & E. Aronson (eds), *The handbook of social psychology* (3rd ed., vol. 1), Reading, MA: Addison-Wesley, pp. 137–229.

Marques, J. (1990), 'The black-sheep effect: Outgroup homogeneity in social comparison settings', in D. Abrams & M.A. Hogg (eds), *Social identity theory: Constructive and critical advances*, London: Harvester Wheatsheaf, and New York: Springer-Verlag, pp. 131–51.

Marsh, H.W. (1986), 'Global self-esteem: Its relation to specific facets of self-concept and their importance', *Journal of Personality and Social Psychology*, **51**, 1224–36.

Martin, J. & Murray, A. (1983), *Theories of equity: Psychological and sociological perspectives*, New York: Praeger.

Marx, K. (1844/1963). *Early writings* (ed. and trans. T.B. Bottomore), New York: McGraw-Hill.

Maslow, A.H. (1954), *Motivation and personality*, New York: Harper.

Mathieu, J.E. & Zajac, D.M. (1990), 'A review and meta-analysis of the antecedents, correlates, and consequences of organizational commitment', *Psychological Bulletin*, **108**, 171–94.

Mead, G.H. (1934), *Mind, self, and society*, Chicago, IL: University of Chicago Press.

Merton, R. & Rossi, A.S. (1957), 'Contributions to the theory of reference group behavior', in R. Merton (ed.), *Social theory and social structure*, New York: Free Press, pp. 279–333.

Messick, D.M. & Mackie, D. (1989), 'Intergroup relations', *Annual Review of Psychology*, **40**, 45–81.

Meyer, J.P. & Allen, N.J. (1984), 'Testing the "Side-Bet Theory" of organizational commitment: Some methodological considerations', *Journal of Applied Psychology*, **69**, 372–8.

Mikula, G. (1984), 'Personal relationships: Remarks on the current state of research', *European Journal of Social Psychology*, **14**, 339–52.

Miller, N. & Brewer, M.B. (eds) (1984), *Groups in contact*. Orlando, FL: Academic Press.

Miller, N. & Harrington, H.J. (1990a), 'A model of social category salience for intergroup relations: Empirical tests of relevant variables', in P.J. Drenth, J.A. Sergeant & R.J. Takens (eds), *European perspectives in psychology*, Chichester: Wiley, pp. 205–20.

Miller, N. & Harrington, H.J. (1990b), 'A situational identity perspective on cultural diversity and teamwork in the classroom', in S. Sharan (ed.), *Cooperative learning*, New York: Praeger Press, pp. 39–76.

Miller, N. & Pollock, V.E. (in press), 'Meta-analysis and some science-compromising problems in social psychology', in W.R. Shadish (ed.), *The social psychology of science*, Oxford: Oxford University Press.

Moreland, R.L. & Levine, J.M. (1982), 'Socialization in small groups: Temporal changes in individual-group relations', in L. Berkowitz (ed.), *Advances in experimental social psychology* (vol. 15), New York: Academic Press, pp. 137–92.

Moreland, R.L. & Levine, J.M. (1984), 'Role transitions in small groups', in V.L. Allen & E. van de Vliert (eds), *Role transitions: Explorations and explanations*, New York: Plenum Press, pp. 181–95.

Moreland, R.L. & Levine, J.M. (1989), 'Newcomers and oldtimers in small groups', in P.B. Paulus (ed.), *Psychology of group influence* (2nd ed), Hillsdale, NJ: Erlbaum, pp. 143–86.

Moreland, R.L. & Levine, J.M. (1992), 'The composition of small groups', in E. Lawler, B. Markovsky, C. Ridgeway & H. Walker (eds), *Advances in group processes* (vol. 9), Greenwich, CT: JAI Press, pp. 237–80.

Moscovici, S. (1972), 'Society and theory in social psychology', in J. Israel & H. Tajfel (eds), *The context of social psychology: A critical assessment*, New York: Academic Press, pp. 17–68.

Moscovici, S. (1976), *Social influence and social change*, London: Academic Press.

Moscovici, S. (1981), 'On social representations', in J. Forgas (ed.), *Social cognition: Perspectives on everyday understanding*, London: Academic Press, pp. 181–209.

Moscovici, S. (1982), 'The coming era of representations', in J.-P. Codol & J.P. Leyens (eds), *Cognitive analysis of social behaviour*, The Hague: Martinus Nijhoff, pp. 115–50.

Moscovici, S. & Zavalloni, M. (1969), 'The group as a polarizer of attitudes', *Journal of Personality and Social Psychology*, **12**, 125–35.

Mugny, G. (1982), *The power of minorities*, London: Academic Press.

Mullen, B., Brown, R. & Smith, C. (1992), 'Ingroup bias as a function of salience, relevance, and status: An integration', *European Journal of Social Psychology*, **22**, 103–22.

Mullen, B. & Goethals, G.R. (eds) (1987), *Theories of group behavior*, New York: Springer-Verlag.

Mullen, B. & Hu, L. (1989), 'Perceptions of ingroup and outgroup variability: A meta-analytic integration', *Basic and Applied Social Psychology*, **10**, 233–52.

Myers, D.G. & Lamm, H. (1976), 'The group polarization phenomenon', *Psychological Bulletin*, **83**, 602–27.

Nagata, D.K. (1987, August), *Long-term effects of the Japanese-American internment on the children of internees*, paper presented at the meeting of the Asian American Psychological Association, New York.

Nagata, D.K. (1988, August), 'The long-term effects of victimization: Present day effects of Japanese-American internment', in D.K. Nagata (Chair), *Various forms of victimization during World War II*, symposium conducted at the meeting of the American Psychological Association, Atlanta, GA.

Nagata, D.K. (1990), 'The Japanese-American internment: Exploring the transgenerational consequences of traumatic stress', *Journal of Traumatic Stress*, **3**, 47–69.

Nagata, D.K. (1992), *Legacy of silence: Effects of the Japanese-American internment*, New York: Plenum.

Nagata, D.K. & Crosby, F.J. (1991), 'Comparisons, justice and the internment of Japanese-Americans,' in J. Suls & T. Wills (eds), *Social comparison: Contemporary theory and research*, Hillsdale, NJ: Erlbaum, pp. 347–68.

Nettler, G. (1970), *Explanations*, New York: McGraw-Hill.

Ng, S.H. (1980), *The social psychology of power*, London: Academic Press.

Ng, S.H. (1985), 'Bias in reward allocation resulting from personal status, group status, and allocation procedure', *Australian Journal of Psychology*, **37**, 297–307.

Ng, S.H. & Cram, F. (1988), 'Intergroup bias by defensive and offensive groups in majority and minority conditions', *Journal of Personality and Social Psychology*, **55**, 749–57.

Ng, S.H. & Wilson, S. (1989), 'Self-categorization theory and belief polarization among Christian believers and atheists', *British Journal of Social Psychology*, **28**, 47–56.

Nicholas, J. (1988), 'British language diversity surveys (1977–87): A critical examination', *Language and Education*, **2**, 15–33.

Niedenthal, P.M., Cantor, N. & Kihlstrom, J.F. (1985), 'Prototype-matching: A strategy for social decision-making', *Journal of Personality and Social Psychology*, **48**, 575–84.

Nisbett, R. & Perrin, R.G. (1977), *The social bond* (2nd ed.), New York: Alfred Knopf.

Nisbett, R. & Ross, L. (1980), *Human inference: Strategies and shortcomings of social judgment*, Englewood Cliffs, NJ: Prentice Hall.

Oakes, P.J. & Turner, J.C. (1990), 'Is limited information-processing capacity the cause of social stereotyping?', in W. Stroebe & M.

Hewstone (eds), *The European review of social psychology* (vol. 1), Chichester: Wiley, pp. 111–35.

Orne, M.T. (1962), 'On the social psychology of the psychological experiment: With particular reference to demand characteristics and their implications', *American Psychologist*, **17**, 776–83.

Osgood, C.E. & Tannenbaum, P.H. (1955), 'The principle of congruity in the prediction of attitude change', *Psychological Review*, **62**, 42–55.

Ostrom, T., Pryor, J. & Simpson, D. (1981), 'The organisation of social information', in E.T. Higgins, C.P. Herman & M.P. Zanna (eds), *Social cognition: The Ontario symposium on personality and social psychology* (vol. 1), Hillsdale, NJ: Erlbaum, pp. 3–38.

Paicheler, G. (1988), *The psychology of social influence*, Cambridge: Cambridge University Press.

Park, B. & Judd, C.M. (1990), 'Measures and models of perceived group variability', *Journal of Personality and Social Psychology*, **59**, 173–91.

Parsons, T. (1935), *The structure of social action*, New York: McGraw-Hill.

Pelham, B.W. & Swann, W.B., Jr (1989), 'From self-conceptions to self-worth: On the sources and structure of global self-esteem', *Journal of Personality and Social Psychology*, **57**, 672–80.

Perez, J.A. & Mugny, G. (1990), 'Minority influence, manifest discrimination and latent influence', in D. Abrams & M.A. Hogg (eds), *Social identity theory: Constructive and critical advances*, London: Harvester Wheatsheaf, and New York: Springer-Verlag, pp. 152–68.

Perloff, L.S. (1983), 'Perceptions of vulnerability to victimization', *Journal of Social Issues*, **39**, 41–61.

Peters, R.S. (1958), *The concept of motivation*, London: Routledge & Kegan Paul.

Pettigrew, T.F. (1986), 'The intergroup contact hypothesis reconsidered', in M. Hewstone & R. Brown (eds), *Contact and conflict in intergroup encounters*, Oxford: Blackwell, pp. 169–95.

Petty, R.E. & Cacioppo, J.T. (1986), 'The elaboration likelihood model of persuasion', in L. Berkowitz (ed.), *Advances in experimental social psychology* (vol. 19), Orlando, FL: Academic Press, pp. 124–205.

Petty, R.E., Harkins, S.G., Williams, K.D. & Latané, B. (1977), 'The effects of group size on cognitive effort and evaluation', *Personality and Social Psychology Bulletin*, **3**, 579–82.

Piaget, J. (1952), *The origins of intelligence in children*, New York: International Universities Press.

Pierson, H.D., Giles, H. & Young, L. (1987), 'Intergroup vitality perceptions during a period of political uncertainty: The case of Hong Kong', *Journal of Multilingual and Multicultural Development*, **8**, 451–60.

Pittman, T.S. & Heller, J.F. (1987), 'Social motivation', *Annual Review of Psychology*, **38**, 461–89.

Popper, K.R. (1959), *The logic of scientific discovery*, New York: Basic Books.

Quattrone, G.A. & Jones, E.E. (1980), 'The perception of variability within groups and outgroups: Implications for the law of small numbers', *Journal of Personality and Social Psychology*, **38**, 141–52.

Rabin, A.I. (1965), *Growing up in the kibbutz*, New York: Springer.

Rabin, A.I. & Beit-Hallahmi, B. (1982), *Twenty years later: Kibbutz children grow up*, New York: Springer.

Raven, B.H. & Kruglanski, A. (1970), 'Conflict and power', in P. Swingle (ed.), *The structure of conflict*, New York: Academic Press, pp. 69–109.

Reichers, A.E. (1985), 'A review and reconceptualization of organizational commitment', *Academy of Management Review*, **10**, 465–76.

Reid, F.J.M. (1983), 'Polarizing effects of intergroup comparisons', *European Journal of Social Psychology*, **13**, 103–6.

Reykowski, J. (1982), 'Social motivation', *Annual Review of Psychology*, **33**, 123–54.

Rogers, C.R. (1951), *Client-centered therapy*, Boston: Houghton Mifflin.

Rokeach, M. (1960), *The open and closed mind*, New York: Basic Books.

Ros, M., Huici, C. & Cano, J.I. (in press), 'Ethnolinguistic vitality and social identity: Their impact on ingroup bias and social attribution', *International Journal of the Sociology of Language*.

Rosenberg, S. (1965), *Society and the adolescent self-image*, Princeton: Princeton University Press.

Rosenblatt, A., Greenberg, J., Solomon, S., Pyszczynski, T. & Lyon, D. (1989), 'Evidence for terror management theory: I. The effects of mortality salience on reactions to those who violate or uphold cultural values', *Journal of Personality and Social Psychology*, **57**, 681–90.

Rosenzweig, S. (1944), 'Frustration theory', in J.M. Hunt (ed.), *Personality and the behavior disorders* (vol. 1), New York: Ronald Press, pp. 379–88.

Ross, G.F. (1975), *An experimental investigation of open and closed groups*, unpublished manuscript, University of Bristol.

Rothbart, M. (1981), 'Memory processes and social beliefs', in D. Hamilton (ed.), *Cognitive processes in stereotyping and intergroup behavior*, Hillsdale, NJ: Erlbaum, pp. 145–82.

Rothbart, M. & John, O.P. (1985), 'Social categorization and behavioral episodes: A cognitive analysis of the effects of intergroup contact', *Journal of Social Issues*, **41**, 81–104.

Rowe, P.M. (1984), 'Decision processes in personnel selection', *Canadian Journal of Behavioral Science*, **4**, 326–37.

Rubin, Z. & Peplau, L.A. (1975), 'Who believes in a just world?', *Journal of Social Issues*, **31**, 65–89.

Rusbult, C.E. (1980), 'Commitment and satisfaction in romantic associations: A test of the investment model', *Journal of Experimental Social Psychology*, **16**, 172–86.

Rusbult, C.E. (1983), 'A longitudinal test of the investment model: The development (and deterioration) of satisfaction and commitment in heterosexual involvements', *Journal of Personality and Social Psychology*, **45**, 101–17.

Rusbult, C.E., Johnson, D.J. & Morrow, G.D. (1986), 'Predicting satisfaction and commitment in adult romantic involvements: An assessment of the generalizability of the investment model', *Social Psychology Quarterly*, **49**, 81–9.

Ryan, E.B., Giles, H. & Sebastian, R.J. (1982), 'An integrative perspective for the study of attitudes towards language variation', in E.B. Ryan & H. Giles (eds), *Attitudes towards language variation: Social and applied contexts*, London: Edward Arnold, pp. 1–19.

Sachdev, I. (1991, May), *The ethnolinguistic vitality of minorities in London (U.K.)*, paper delivered at the 40th Annual International Communication Association Convention, Chicago.

Sachdev, I. & Bourhis, R.Y. (1984), 'Minimal majorities and minorities', *European Journal of Social Psychology*, **14**, 35–52.

Sachdev, I. & Bourhis, R.Y. (1985), 'Social categorization and power differentials in group relations', *European Journal of Social Psychology*, **15**, 415–34.

Sachdev, I. & Bourhis, R.Y. (1987), 'Status differentials and intergroup behaviour', *European Journal of Social Psychology*, **17**, 277–93.

Sachdev, I. & Bourhis, R.Y. (1990a), 'Language and social identification', in D. Abrams & M.A. Hogg (eds), *Social identity theory: Constructive and critical advances*, London: Harvester Wheatsheaf, and New York: Springer-Verlag, pp. 101–24.

Sachdev, I. & Bourhis, R.Y. (1990b), 'Bi-multilinguality', in H. Giles & W.P. Robinson (eds), *The handbook of language and social psychology*, Chichester & New York: Wiley, pp. 293–308.

Sachdev, I. & Bourhis, R.Y. (1991), 'Power and status differentials in minority and majority group relations', *European Journal of Social Psychology*, **21**, 1–24.

Sachdev, I., Bourhis, R.Y., D'Eye, J. & Phang, S.W. (1990), 'Cantonese-Chinese vitality in London (U.K.)', *Journal of Asian Pacific Communication*, **1**, 209–27.

Sachdev, I., Bourhis, R.Y., Phang, S.W. & D'Eye, J. (1987), 'Language attitudes and vitality perceptions: Intergenerational effects amongst Chinese Canadian communities', *Journal of Language and Social Psychology*, **6**, 287–307.

Sanders, G.S. & Baron, R.S. (1977), 'Is social comparison irrelevant for producing choice shifts', *Journal of Experimental Social Psychology*, **13**, 303–14.

Schachter, S. (1959), *The psychology of affiliation*, Palo Alto, CA: Stanford University Press.

Schlenker, B.R. (1980), *Impression management: The self-concept, social identity, and interpersonal relations*, Monterey, CA: Brooks-Cole.

Schlenker, B.R. (ed.) (1985), *The self and social life*, New York: McGraw-Hill.

Scott, W.A. & Scott, R. (1981), 'Intercorrelations among structural properties of primary groups', *Journal of Personality and Social Psychology*, **41**, 279–92.

Sears, D.O. (1983), 'The person-positivity bias', *Journal of Personality and Social Psychology*, **44**, 233–50.

Segall, M.H., Campbell, D.T. & Herskovits, M.J. (1966), *The influence of culture on visual perception*, Indianapolis, IN: Bobbs-Merrill.

Sherif, M. (1966), *Group conflict and cooperation: Their social psychology*, London: Routledge & Kegan Paul.

Shrauger, J.S. (1972), 'Self-esteem and reactions to being observed by others', *Journal of Personality and Social Psychology*, **23**, 192–200.

Shrauger, J.S. (1975), 'Responses to evaluation as a function of initial self-perceptions', *Psychological Bulletin*, **82**, 581–96.

Simmel, G. (1955), *Conflict and the web of group-affiliations*, New York: Free Press.

Simon, B. & Brown, R. (1987), 'Perceived intergroup homogeneity in minority-majority contexts', *Journal of Personality and Social Psychology*, **53**, 703–11.

Simon, B. & Pettigrew, T.F. (1990), 'Social identity and perceived group homogeneity: Evidence for the ingroup homogeneity effect', *European Journal of Social Psychology*, **20**, 269–86.

Simon, H.A. (1992), 'What is an explanation of behavior?' *Psychological Science*, **3**, 150–61.

Sinclair, R.C. (1988), 'Mood, categorization breadth, and performance appraisal: The effects of order of information acquisition and affective state on halo, accuracy, information retrieval, and evaluations', *Organizational Behavior and Human Decision Processes*, **42**, 22–46.

Smith, R. & Insko, C. (1987), 'Social comparison choice during ability evaluation', *Personality and Social Psychology Bulletin*, **13**, 111–22.

Snyder, C.R. & Fromkin, H.L. (1980), *Uniqueness: the human pursuit of difference*, New York: Plenum Press.

Snyder, C.R., Lassegard, M. & Ford, C.E. (1986), 'Distancing after group success and failure: Basking in reflected glory and cutting off reflected failure', *Journal of Personality and Social Psychology*, **51**, 382–8.

Snyder, M. (in press, 'A functional analysis of prejudice', in M.P. Zanna, P. Herman (eds), *The Ontario symposium: The psychology of prejudice*, Hillsdale, NJ: Erlbaum.

Snyder, M. & Ickes, W. (1985), 'Personality and social behavior', in G. Lindzey & E. Aronson (eds), *Handbook of social psychology* (3rd ed., vol. 2), New York: Random House, pp. 883–947.

Solomon, R. (1980), 'The opponent process theory of acquired motivation', *American Psychologist*, **35**, 691–712.

Spears, R. & Manstead, A. (1989), 'The social context of stereotyping and differentiation', *European Journal of Social Psychology*, **19**, 101–21.

Sprecher, S. (1988), 'Investment model, equity, and social support determinants of relationship commitment', *Social Psychology Quarterly*, **51**, 318–28.

Steele, C.M. (1992), 'Race and the schooling of black Americans', *The Atlantic Monthly*, April, 68–78.

Steiner, I.D. (1972), *Group process and productivity*, New York: Academic Press.

Steiner, I.D. (1974), 'Whatever happened to the group in social psychology', *Journal of Experimental Social Psychology*, **10**, 94–108.

Steiner, I.D. (1986), 'Paradigms and groups', in L. Berkowitz (ed.), *Advances in experimental social psychology* (vol. 19), Orlando, FL: Academic Press, pp. 251–92.

Stephan, W.G. (1985), 'Intergroup relations', in G. Lindzey & E. Aronson (eds), *Handbook of social psychology* (3rd ed., vol. 2), New York: Random House, pp. 599–658.

Stephan, W.G. & Stephan, C.W. (1985), 'Intergroup anxiety', *Journal of Social Issues*, **41**, 157–75.

Stryker, S. (1968), 'Identity salience and role performance: The relevance of symbolic interaction theory for family research', *Journal of Marriage and the Family*, **30**, 558–64.

Stryker, S. (1987), 'Identity theory: Developments and extensions', in K. Yardley & T. Honess (eds), *Self and identity: Psychosocial perspectives*, New York: Wiley, pp. 89–103.

Stryker, S. & Serpe, R.T. (1982), 'Commitment, identity, salience, and role behavior: Theory and research example', in W. Ickes & E.S. Knowles (eds), *Personality, roles, and social behavior*, New York: Springer-Verlag, pp. 199–218.

Sumner, W.G. (1906), *Folkways*, Boston, MA: Ginn.

Swann, W.B. (1987), 'Identity negotiation: Where two roads meet', *Journal of Personality and Social Psychology*, **53**, 1038–51.

Szymanksi, K. & Harkins, S.G. (1987), 'Social loafing and self-evaluation with a social standard', *Journal of Personality and Social Psychology*, **53**, 891–7.

Tajfel, H. (1972a), 'Social categorization, English manuscript of "La catégorisation sociale', in S. Moscovici (ed.), *Introduction à la psychologie sociale* (vol. 1), Paris: Larousse, pp. 272–302.

Tajfel, H. (1972b), 'Experiments in a vacuum', in J. Israel & H. Tajfel (eds), *The context of social psychology: A critical assessment*, London: Academic Press, pp. 69–119.

Tajfel, H. (1974a), *Intergroup behaviour, social comparison and social change*, unpublished Katz-Newcomb lectures, University of Michigan.

Tajfel, H. (1974b), 'Social identity and intergroup behaviour', *Social Science Information*, **13**, 65–93.

Tajfel, H. (1975), 'The exit of social mobility and the voice of social change', *Social Science Information*, **14**, 101–18.

Tajfel, H. (1978a), 'The psychological structure of intergroup relations', in H. Tajfel (ed.), *Differentiation between social groups: Studies in the social psychology of intergroup relations*, London: Academic Press.

Tajfel, H. (ed.) (1978b), *Differentiation between social groups: Studies in the social psychology of intergroup relations*, London: Academic Press.

Tajfel, H. (1981a), *Human groups and social categories: Studies in social psychology*, Cambridge: Cambridge University Press.

Tajfel, H. (1981b), 'Social stereotypes and social groups', in J.C. Turner & H. Giles (eds), *Intergroup behaviour*, Oxford: Blackwell, pp. 144–67.

Tajfel, H. (1982a), 'Social psychology of intergroup relations', *Annual Review of Psychology*, **33**, 1–59.

Tajfel, H. (ed.) (1982b), *Social identity and intergroup relations*, Cambridge: Cambridge University Press.

Tajfel, H. & Turner, J.C. (1979), 'An integrative theory of intergroup conflict', in W.G. Austin & S. Worchel (eds), *The social psychology of intergroup relations*, Monterey, CA: Brooks/Cole, pp. 33–47.

Tajfel, H. & Turner, J.C. (1986), 'The social identity theory of intergroup behaviour', in S.G. Worchel & W. Austin (eds), *Psychology of intergroup relations* (2nd ed.), Chicago: Nelson-Hall, pp. 7–24.

Taylor, D.M. & Brown, R.J. (1979), 'Towards a more social social psychology', *British Journal of Social and Clinical Psychology*, **18**, 173–9.

Taylor, D.M. & McKirnan, D.J. (1984), 'A five-stage model of intergroup relations', *British Journal of Social Psychology*, **23**, 291–300.

Taylor, D.M., Moghaddam, F.M., Gamble, I. & Zellerer, E. (1987), 'Disadvantaged group responses to perceived inequality: From passive acceptance to collective action', *Journal of Social Psychology*, **127**, 259–72.

Taylor, D.M., Wright, S., Moghaddam, F. & Lalonde, R. (1990), 'The personal/group discrimination discrepancy: Perceiving my group, but not myself, to be a target for discrimination', *Personality and Social Psychology Bulletin*, **16**, 254–62.

Taylor, S.E. & Brown, J.D. (1988), 'Illusion and well-being: A social psychological perspective on mental health', *Psychological Bulletin*, **103**, 193–210.

Tedeschi, J.T. (1983), 'Social influence theory and aggression', in R.T. Geen & E.I. Donnerstein (eds), *Aggression: Theoretical and empirical reviews*, Orlando, FL: Academic Press, pp. 135–62.

Tedeschi, J.T., Smith, R.B. & Brown, R.C. (1974), 'A reinterpretation of research on aggression', *Psychological Bulletin*, **81**, 544–62.

Tesser, A. (1978), 'Self-generated attitude change', in L. Berkowitz (ed.), *Advances in experimental social psychology* (vol. 11), New York: Academic Press, pp. 181–227.

Tesser, A. (1988), 'Toward a self-evaluation maintenance model of social behavior', in L. Berkowitz (ed.), *Advances in experimental social psychology* (vol. 21), San Diego, CA: Academic Press, pp. 181–227.

Tetlock, P.E. & Levi, A. (1982), 'Attribution bias: On the inconclusiveness of the cognition-motivation debate', *Journal of Experimental Social Psychology*, **18**, 68–88.

Thakerar, J., Giles, H. & Cheshire, J. (1982), 'Psychological and linguistic parameters of speech accommodation theory', in C. Fraser & K. Scherer (eds), *Advances in the social psychology of language*, Cambridge: Cambridge University Press, pp. 205–55.

Thibaut, J.W. & Kelley, H.H. (1959), *The social psychology of groups*, New York: Wiley.

Tice, D.M. (1991), 'Esteem protection or enhancement? Self-handicapping motives differ by trait self-esteem', *Journal of Personality and Social Psychology*, **60**, 711–25.

Tickle-Degnen, L. & Rosenthal, R. (1987), 'Group rapport and nonverbal behavior', in C. Hendrick (ed.), *Review of personality and social psychology* (vol. 9), Newbury Park, CA: Sage, pp. 113–36.

Tougas, F. & Veilleux, F. (1988), 'The influence of identification, collective relative deprivation, and procedure of implementation on women's response to affirmative action: A causal modeling approach', *Canadian Journal of Behavioural Science*, **20**, 15–27.

Tougas, F. & Veilleux, F. (1989), 'Who likes affirmative action: Attitudinal processes among men and women', in F.A. Blanchard & F.J. Crosby (eds), *Affirmative action in perspective*, New York: Springer-Verlag, pp. 111–24.

Triandis, H.C. (1989), 'The self and social behavior in different cultural contexts', *Psychological Review*, **96**, 506–20.

Triplett, N. (1898), 'The dynamogenic factors in pacemaking and competition', *American Journal of Psychology*, **9**, 507–33.

Turner, J.C. (1975), 'Social comparison and social identity: Some prospects for intergroup behaviour', *European Journal of Social Psychology*, **5**, 5–34.

Turner, J.C. (1981), 'The experimental social psychology of intergroup behaviour', in J.C. Turner & H. Giles (eds), *Intergroup behaviour*, Oxford: Blackwell, pp. 66–101.

Turner, J.C. (1982), 'Towards a cognitive redefinition of the social group', in H. Tajfel (ed.), *Social identity and intergroup relations*, Cambridge: Cambridge University Press, pp. 15–40.

Turner, J.C. (1984), 'Social identification and psychological group formation', in H. Tajfel (ed.), *The social dimension* (vol. 2), Cambridge: Cambridge University Press, pp. 518–38.

Turner, J.C. (1985), 'Social categorization and the self-concept: A social cognitive theory of group behavior', in E.J. Lawler (ed.), *Advances in group processes: Theory and research* (vol. 2), Greenwich, CT: JAI Press, pp. 77–122.

Turner, J.C. (1987), 'A self-categorization theory', in J.C. Turner, M.A. Hogg, P.J. Oakes, S.D. Reicher, & M.S. Wetherell, *Rediscovering the social group: A self-categorization theory*, Oxford & New York: Blackwell, pp. 42–67.

Turner, J.C. (1991), *Social influence*, Milton Keynes: Open University Press.

Turner, J.C. & Brown, R. (1978), 'Social status, cognitive alternatives and intergroup relations', in H. Tajfel (ed.), *Differentiation between social groups: Studies in the social psychology of intergroup relations*, London: Academic Press, pp. 201–34.

Turner, J.C., Hogg, M.A., Oakes, P.J., Reicher, S.D. & Wetherell, M.S. (1987), *Rediscovering the social group: A self-categorization theory*, Oxford & New York: Blackwell.

Turner, J.C., Hogg, M.A., Turner, J.P. & Smith, P.M. (1984), 'Failure and defeat as determinants of group cohesiveness', *British Journal of Social Psychology*, **23**, 97–111.

Turner, J.C. & Oakes, P.J. (1986), 'The significance of the social identity concept for social psychology with reference to individualism, interactionism and social influence', *British Journal of Social Psychology*, **25**, 237–52.

Turner, J.C. & Oakes, P.J. (1989), 'Self-categorization theory and social influence', in P.B. Paulus (ed.), *Psychology of group influence* (2nd ed.), Hillsdale, NJ: Erlbaum, pp. 233–75.

Turner, J.C., Wetherell, M.S. & Hogg, M.A. (1989), 'Referent informational influence and group polarization', *British Journal of Social Psychology*, **28**, 135–47.

Tversky, A. & Kahneman, D. (1974), 'Judgment under uncertainty: Heuristics and biases', *Science*, **185**, 124–31.

Twiss, C., Tabb, S. & Crosby, F.J. (1989), 'Affirmative action and aggregate data: The importance of patterns in the perception of discrimination', in F.A. Blanchard & F.J. Crosby (eds), *Affirmative action in perspective*, New York: Springer-Verlag, pp. 159–67.

Vanbeselaere, N. (1991), 'The different effects of simple and crossed categorization: A result of the category differentiation process or of differential category salience?', in W. Stroebe & M. Hewstone (eds), *European review of social psychology* (vol. 2), Chichester: Wiley, pp. 247–78.

van Knippenberg, A.F.M. (1978), 'Status differences, comparative relevance and intergroup differentiation', in H. Tajfel (ed.), *Differentiation between social groups: Studies in the social psychology of intergroup relations*, London: Academic Press, pp. 171–99.

van Knippenberg, A.F.M. (1984), 'Intergroup differences in group perceptions', in H. Tajfel (ed.), *The social dimension: European developments in social psychology* (vol. 2), Cambridge: Cambridge University Press, pp. 560–78.

van Knippenberg, A.F.M. (1989), 'Strategies of identity management', in J.P. van Oudenhoven & T.M. Willemsen (eds), *Ethnic minorities: Social psychological perspectives*, Berwyn, PA: Swets North America, pp. 59–76.

Vinokur, A. & Burnstein, E. (1974), 'The effects of partially shared persuasive arguments on group-induced shifts: A problem-solving approach', *Journal of Personality and Social Psychology*, **29**, 305–15.

Wagner, U., Lampen, L. & Syllwasschy, J. (1986), 'Ingroup inferiority, social identity, and outgroup devaluation in a modified minimal group study', *British Journal of Social Psychology*, **25**, 15–23.

Walker, I. & Mann, L. (1987), 'Unemployment, relative deprivation, and social protest', *Personality and Social Psychology Bulletin*, **13**, 275–83.

Walker, I. & Pettigrew, T.F. (1984), 'Relative deprivation theory: An overview and conceptual critique', *British Journal of Social Psychology*, **23**, 301–10.

Walster, E., Walster, G.W. & Berscheid, E. (1978), *Equity: Theory and research*, Boston: Allyn & Bacon.

Wanous, J.P. (1980), *Organizational entry: Recruitment, selection, and socialization of newcomers*, Reading, MA: Addison-Wesley.

Warner, R.M. (1992), 'Sequential analysis of social interaction: Assessing internal versus social determinants of behavior', *Journal of Personality and Social Psychology*, **63**, 51–60.

Weber, M. (1947), *The theory of social and economic organization*, New York: Oxford University Press.

Weber, R. & Crocker, J. (1983), 'Cognitive processes in the revision of stereotypic beliefs', *Journal of Personality and Social Psychology*, **45**, 961–77.

Wegner, D.M. (1986), 'Transactive memory: A contemporary analysis of the group mind', in B. Mullen & G.R. Goethals (eds), *Theories of group behavior*, New York: Springer-Verlag, pp. 185–208.

Weiner, B. (1972), *Theories of motivation: From mechanism to cognition*, Chicago: Markham.

Weinstein, N.D. (1980), 'Unrealistic optimism about future life events', *Journal of Personality and Social Psychology*, **39**, 806–20.

Weinstein, N.D. (1984), 'Why it won't happen to me: Perceptions of risk factors and susceptibility', *Health Psychology*, **3**, 431–57.

Wells, H.G. (1905), *A modern utopia*, London: Chapman & Hall.

Wells, L.E. & Stryker, S. (1988), 'Stability and change in self over the life course', in P.B. Baites, D.L. Featherman & R.L. Lerner (eds), *Life-span development*, Hillsdale, NJ: Erlbaum, pp. 191–229.

Wetherell, M.S. (1987), 'Social identity and group polarization', in J.C. Turner, M.A. Hogg, P.J. Oakes, S.D. Reicher & M.S. Wetherell, *Rediscovering the social group: A self-categorization theory*, Oxford & New York: Blackwell, pp. 142–70.

White, R.W. (1959), 'Motivation reconsidered: The concept of competence', *Psychological Review*, **66**, 297–333.

Wilder, D.A. (1977), 'Perception of groups, size of opposition, and social influence', *Journal of Experimental Social Psychology*, **13**, 253–68.

Wilder, D.A. (1978), 'Homogeneity of jurors: The majority's influence depends upon their perceived independence', *Law and Human Behavior*, **2**, 363–76.

Wilder, D.A. (1984), 'Intergroup contact: The typical member and the exception to the rule', *Journal of Experimental Social Psychology*, **20**, 177–94.

Wilder, D.A. (1986), 'Social categorization: Implications for creation and reduction of intergroup bias', in L. Berkowitz (ed.), *Advances in experimental social psychology* (vol. 19), San Diego, CA: Academic Press, pp. 291–355.

Wilder, D.A. (1990), 'Some determinants of the persuasive power of in-groups and out-groups: Organization of information and attribution of independence', *Journal of Personality and Social Psychology*, **59**, 1202–13.

Wilder, D.A. (in press), 'Arousal and intergroup bias: Facilitative effects of arousal on stereotyping', in D. Mackie & D. Hamilton (eds), *Affect, cognition, and stereotyping: Interaction processes in group perception*, San Diego, CA: Academic Press.

Wilder, D.A., Cooper, W.E. & Thompson, J.E. (1981, August), *Effects of anxiety on perceptions of differences among group members*, paper presented at the American Psychological Association Convention, New York.

Wilder, D.A. & Faith, M. (1992), *Enhancing the impact of counterstereotypic information: Dispositional attribution for deviance*, unpublished manuscript, Rutgers University.

Wilder, D.A. & Shapiro, P. (1989a), 'Role of competition-induced anxiety in limiting the beneficial impact of positive behavior by an out-group member', *Journal of Personality and Social Psychology*, **56**, 60–9.

Wilder, D.A. & Shapiro, P. (1989b), 'Effects of anxiety on impression formation in a group context: An anxiety-assimilation hypothesis', *Journal of Experimental Social Psychology*, **25**, 481–99.

Wilder, D.A. & Shapiro, P. (1992), *The role of in-group salience in determining the impact of counterstereotypic information*, unpublished manuscript, Rutgers University.

Williams, G. (1992), *Sociolinguistics: A sociological critique*, London: Routledge.

Williams, K.D. (1977), *The loss of control as a determinant of social loafing*, unpublished master's thesis, Columbus, OH.

Williams, K.D., Harkins, S.G. & Latané, B. (1981), 'Identifiability as a deterrent to social loafing: Two cheering experiments', *Journal of Personality and Social Psychology*, **40**, 303–11.

Williams, K.D. & Karau, S.J. (1991), 'Social loafing and social compensation: The effects of expectations of coworker performance', *Journal of Personality and Social Psychology*, **61**, 570–81.

Williams, K.D., Nida, S.A., Baca, L.D. & Latané, B. (1989), 'Social loafing and swimming: Effects of identifiability on individual and relay performance of intercollegiate swimmers', *Basic and Applied Social Psychology*, **10**, 73–81.

Williams, K.D. & Williams, K.B. (1981, August), *The development of social loafing in America*, paper presented at the Asian Conference of the International Association for Cross-Cultural Psychology, Taipei, Taiwan.

Williams, K.D., Williams, K.B., Kawana, Y. & Latané, B. (1984, May), *Collective effort in small groups in the United States and Japan*, paper presented at the annual meeting of the Midwestern Psychological Association, Chicago.

Wills, T.A. (1981), 'Downward comparison principles in social psychology', *Psychological Bulletin*, **90**, 245–71.

Wills, T.A. (1991), 'Similarity and self-esteem in downward comparison', in J. Suls & T.A. Wills, (eds), *Social comparison: Contemporary theory and research*, Hillsdale, NJ: Erlbaum, pp. 51–74.

Wilson, S. & Benner, L. (1971), 'The effects of self-esteem and situation on comparison choices during ability evaluation', *Sociometry*, **34**, 381–97.

Winter, D.G. (1973), *The power motive*, New York: The Free Press.

Wood, J.V. (1989), 'Theory and research concerning social comparisons of personal attributes', *Psychological Bulletin*, **106**, 231–48.

Wood, J.V. & Taylor, K.L. (1991), 'Serving self-relevant goals through social comparison', in J. Suls & T.A. Wills (eds), *Social comparison: Contemporary theory and research*, Hillsdale, NJ: Erlbaum, pp. 23–49.

Wright, S.C., Taylor, D.M. & Moghaddam, F.M. (1990), 'Responding to membership in a disadvantaged group: From acceptance to collective protest', *Journal of Personality and Social Psychology*, **58**, 994–1003.

Wyer, R. & Srull, T. (eds) (1984), *Handbook of social cognition*, Hillsdale, NJ: Erlbaum.

Wylie, R.C. (1979), *The self concept: Theory and research on selected topics* (vol. 2), Lincoln, NE: University of Nebraska Press.

Yamagishi, T. (1988), 'Exit from the group as an individualistic solution to the free rider problem in the United States and Japan', *Journal of Experimental Social Psychology*, **24**, 530–42.

Yerkes, R.M. & Dodson, J.D. (1980), 'The relation of strength of stimulus to rapidity of habit formation', *Journal of Comparative Neurology and Psychology*, **18**, 459–82.

Young, L., Bell, N. & Giles, H. (1988), 'Perceived vitality and context: A national majority in a minority setting', *Journal of Multilingual and Multicultural Development*, **9**, 285–9.

Ytsma, J., Viladot, M.A. & Giles, H. (in press), 'Ethnolinguistic vitality and ethnic identity: Some Catalan and Frisian data', *International Journal of the Sociology of Language*.

Zajonc, R.B. (1965), 'Social facilitation', *Science*, **149**, 269–74.

Zajonc, R.B. (1980a), 'Feeling and thinking: Preferences need no inferences', *American Psychologist*, **35**, 151–75.

Zajonc, R.B. (1980b), 'Compresence', in P.B. Paulus (ed.), *Psychology of group influence*, Hillsdale, NJ: Erlbaum, pp. 35–60.

Zanna, M., Crosby, F. & Lowenstein, G. (1987), 'Male reference groups and discontent among female professionals', in B. Gutek & L. Larwood (eds), *Pathways to women's career development*, Beverly Hills, CA: Sage, pp. 28–41.

Zuckerman, M. (1979), 'Attribution of success and failure revisited, or: The motivational bias is alive and well in attribution theory', *Journal of Personality*, **47**, 245–87.

Author index

Subject index